CONCEPTS IN COMMUNICATION

Teacher's Guide for

LANGUAGE – BENEATH THE SURFACE

This Teacher's Guide is designed for use with
Language – Beneath the Surface, the language portion
of *Structure and Plan. Language – Beneath the Surface*
is also available in a paperback edition.

CONCEPTS IN COMMUNICATION

Albert R. Kitzhaber, *General Editor*

Annabel Kitzhaber
Clarence Sloat
with **Jean Tate**

Teacher's Guide for

LANGUAGE— BENEATH THE SURFACE

HOLT, RINEHART AND WINSTON, INC.
New York • Toronto • London • Sydney

Contents

v

Teacher's Guide for

LANGUAGE—BENEATH
THE SURFACE

Concepts in Communication:

The Language Curriculum

In the language program in *Concepts in Communication,* we attempt to present the study of language in a framework which the student can understand in much the same way he understands his study of history, mathematics, or science. The basis for this kind of language study is, as with most other disciplines, an observable body of facts which the student can discuss and from which he can draw inferences and reach conclusions.

A study of language may include many topics. In the six books in this series, we deal not only with grammar but also with language history (how English has evolved through the years from its remote beginnings in Indo-European); with varieties (dialects) of English; with semantics and the sounds of English; with style and dictionaries; and with writing systems and usage. Each book includes syntactic as well as nonsyntactic chapters.

The grammar developed in the series is *transformational grammar.* Briefly, it begins with a description of the parts and relationships found in the basic sentence structure which are described by means of a set of *phrase structure* rules; the grammar then shows how these basic sentence structures can be changed (transformed) into the various kinds of sentences found in the language. We have chosen to use this system because we feel that it presents, clearly and concisely, an accurate description of the English language which is based on observable facts and which can readily be understood by students.

1

No previous experience with transformational grammar is assumed for either teacher or students. It is likely, however, that teachers with some general knowledge of the underlying theory of transformational grammar will be more comfortable with the material. For this reason we are including a "Teacher's Introduction to Grammar Study" (pp. 3–51). It not only presents the grammar dealt with in this volume, but also the grammar introduced in the other books in the series. The teacher will then have some notion of how the material in this book fits into the general scheme of the series and also how to provide answers to questions that may arise about material not found in the student text itself. It should provide a useful reference for the teacher.

Each concept is carefully developed in the student texts so that teachers should be able to use the books with no other preparation than reading the text and the material in this Teacher's Guide. For each chapter in the student text the Teacher's Guide includes a statement of objectives, a synopsis of the chapter, and suggestions for teaching it. Also included is a complete key to each exercise, including a statement of the purpose of the exercise and a discussion of any possible problems and any background information that is necessary.

We urge you to study and familiarize yourself with the "Teacher's Introduction to Grammar Study" and to use it as a reference whenever necessary. In the key to the exercises you will frequently be referred to appropriate pages in the "Introduction" for necessary background information. We also urge you to work through the student text yourself ahead of time, referring to the key as you go.

What the Series Contains

In *Blueprint for Language,* the seventh-grade text, we concentrate on describing the parts of sentences by means of phrase structure rules. Nouns and noun phrases, verbs and verb phrases, determiners, pronouns, adjectives, adverbs are among the parts that are identified. The book also examines some of the features of nouns, and includes a chapter on dialects or varieties of English.

Inside Language, the eighth-grade text, reviews basic phrase structure rules and presents the transformations which change basic sentences into questions, negatives, and passives. Features of nouns are reviewed and expanded, and features of verbs are introduced. Chapters are included on human versus animal communication and on the development of writing systems.

The ninth-grade course, *Language—Beneath the Surface,* presents the concept of combining basic sentence structures to form compound sentences and sentences with compound parts as well as sentences which include such noun modifiers as adjectives, appositives and relative clauses.

Language—Putting It All Together, the tenth-grade text, begins with a thorough review of previous years' work and introduces restrictive and nonrestrictive clauses, participial modifiers, and adverbial clauses. This year also begins the sequence of study of language history, tracing the development of English from its beginnings in Anglo-Saxon England.

In the eleventh-grade book, *Language—Parts Within Parts,* the work on transformations is concluded with investigation of noun clauses, verb complements, and imperatives. This book also includes a section on the features that distinguish the various sounds we use in speaking English, two chapters on the structure of words (morphology), a chapter on the placement of stress in words, and a chapter on the place of English in the Indo-European language family.

By the twelfth-grade program, *Perspectives on Language,* students have completed their formal study of grammar and are ready to deal with such topics as the history of language description, universals found in all languages, style, and grammar versus usage. Students also examine the Germanic background of English and discuss some changes in English syntax from Shakespeare's time to our own. The book also includes a set of readings illustrating various attitudes that exist concerning English usage.

TEACHER'S INTRODUCTION TO GRAMMAR STUDY

The term *grammar* means different things to different people. For some it refers to the system of putting words and groups of words together to form sentences in a particular language. Every language has such a system. A *grammar* is also a description of the system, or a book in which the description is found.

For others *grammar* has something to do with a notion of the "correct" way to use language. This meaning is found in statements like "He's a polite boy, but his grammar is atrocious." When people say someone's grammar is atrocious, they mean that he may say things like "he don't" instead of "he doesn't," or "had went" instead of "had gone," or may use some other form that the speaker does not approve of. *Grammar* used in this way refers to a variety of language which the speaker feels is the preferred one. In this sense a better term than *grammar* would be *usage.*

Usage is important but it shouldn't be confused with grammar. Among users of any language there is some variety within the system. Some speakers of English, for example, normally say "he don't" while others say "he doesn't". Both are choices within the system of English. When we refer to such choices in this book, we will use the term *usage;* when we use the term *grammar* we will mean either the system of putting together parts to form sentences of English or a description of that system.

What Does Grammar Describe?

When he learns his native language, a child acquires a working knowledge of the system of that language that enables him to produce and understand sentences. The system can be said to consist of a set of parts and a set of internalized rules that speakers of the language follow in putting these parts together. The parts that the rules govern are the words and parts of words that make up the vocabulary of the language. The rules are said to be internalized because human beings acquire them without realizing they are doing so and use them without thinking about it.

Although a great deal about how children learn a language is still unknown, it is at least clear that they do not memorize and store up thousands of individual utterances in the hope of finding some use for them in later conversation. Rather, by trial and error, the child arrives at certain broad generalizations about the system of his language. That he is making these generalizations can be observed when the child produces such forms as *mans* for *men.* By adding the z sound to *man* the child reveals that he has arrived at an important generalization about the formation of the plural of English nouns, which in this exceptional case doesn't apply. Similarly, forms like *goed* (for *went*) and *comed* (for *came*) show that the child who produces them has made a generalization about the formation of the past tense of regular verbs. What the child is generalizing about are the rules according to which his language operates. These are not usage rules but grammatical rules. Of course, the child is no more conscious that he is generalizing rules for his language than he is conscious of the complex transaction of nerves and muscles he initiates when he pops another jelly bean into his mouth. He can do it, and he doesn't have to introspect about it.

Linguistic Competence

The set of internalized rules a native speaker follows in producing and understanding sentences is called his **linguistic competence.** Such a set of rules enables a native speaker, for example, to arrange the parts of sentences in the right order, make plurals of singular nouns, change present tense forms to past, and produce statements and their related questions. Linguistic competence also enables a native speaker to pronounce sentences and to understand them.

Linguistic competence—the internalized rules—should not be confused with **linguistic performance,** which is the actual use a speaker makes of his knowledge in the utterances he makes and the way he interprets what he hears. The difference between competence and performance can be illustrated by comparing them to mathematical competence and mathematical performance. We can assume that an average high school graduate has mathematical competence in long division. He knows how to do it. It is theoretically possible, because he knows the rules for performing long division, that he could perform an endless series of problems in long division without error, but of course it does not usually work out that way. People make mistakes in figuring, and they make mistakes in forming sentences, mistakes which are not at all related to competence but rather caused by such things as lapses of memory, fatigue, nervousness, or haste. Competence, then, is one thing and performance is another.

The rules of language are not rules externally imposed by some super-authority or by the authors of grammar textbooks, though many people have mistakenly assumed that they are. These rules exist below the level of consciousness in the human mind. This internalized system is the grammar of the language. Every human language has a grammar in this sense, even languages of the most primitive people. And speakers of the same language share essentially the same set of internalized rules. A description of these rules is called a grammar. It is concerned with describing competence, not performance.

How Does a Grammar Describe Linguistic Competence?

For centuries, civilized men have tried to discover what the rules of languages are and to describe them. In other words, they have tried to become conscious of what men know unconsciously when they know a language. Since it is often difficult to bring to the level of consciousness what it is that we know unconsciously, there have been many different descriptions, that is, many grammars. The various ways of describing the internalized grammar have differed, depending on the assumptions about language that have been made, the purposes of the description, the data available to the people making the description, and the techniques that have been

5

used. Traditional grammar represents one way of describing language, structural grammar another. Transformational grammar represents still another.

The grammar developed in this book is a form of transformational grammar. Transformational grammar uses some of the techniques of structural grammar, but it also has many ties with traditional grammar, so that if this is your first experience with it, you will find much that is familiar. But transformational grammar differs from earlier attempts to describe language—in its basic assumptions, its techniques, and its goals.

What Are the Goals of Transformational Grammar?

The ultimate goal of transformational grammar is to make explicit all of the rules that are used implicitly in the production and interpretation of the sentences of a language. It tries not only to identify the various kinds of parts that go to make up a sentence and to describe the rules according to which they are put together, but it is also particularly interested in explaining certain characteristics of human language. Among the most important of these is the ability human beings have to create an infinite number of sentences, and to produce them at will, to recognize, and to be able to interpret, sentences that they have never heard or produced before. Transformational grammar asks what kind of rules enable human beings to do these things, and how they acquire these rules so early in life that, no matter what their intelligence, normal children of six can produce sentences that involve all the syntactic structures of their language.

No speaker will ever produce an infinite number of sentences, but he has the knowledge of how to do so, just as he has the knowledge of how to add one number onto another forever once he understands the number system. This ability to use a limited number of parts in an infinite number of combinations is known as **recursiveness.** In language, though an infinite number of sentences is theoretically possible, obviously no speaker knows an infinite number of rules for making sentences. It follows that it must be possible to learn how to produce an infinite number of sentences by learning a limited number of rules. Transformational grammar tries to find out what these rules are.

The grammar also hopes to explain the ability humans have to recognize when sentences are synonymous or closely related. For example, any speaker of English knows that *The burglar broke the lock* and *The lock was broken by the burglar* are synonymous. We

6

know that *The mouse has escaped* is closely related to *Has the mouse escaped?* though they are different sentences. What kind of rules enable us to know these things?

Another characteristic of human language is related to the ability to recognize ambiguity in a sentence. *Ringing bells annoyed the children* can mean either *Bells that were ringing annoyed the children* or *It annoyed the children to ring bells.* How are we able to understand two meanings in the same sentence?

Finally, transformational grammar tries to explain how it is possible for human beings to understand much that isn't actually represented at all in the sentences that they hear and speak. For instance, how do we all know that the subject of *Close the door* is *you?* How do we know, when we interpret *Joshua was hard to help,* that *Joshua* is related to *help* as an object, but that in *Joshua was happy to help, Joshua* has a subject relationship to *help?* Yet the two sentences appear to have the same structure.

What Are the Basic Assumptions of Transformational Grammar?

In attempting to describe language and to explain these characteristics which seem to be typical of all languages, transformational grammar makes some fundamental assumptions about language.

1. The first basic assumption is that we often understand more than actually appears in a sentence. The easiest way to explain this characteristic is to assume that sentences have two kinds of structure, a *deep structure* and a *surface structure,* and therefore can be described at two levels. The deep structure of a sentence represents all of what the sentence means. We might think of it as the basic underlying structure. It includes all the parts and all the relationships between the parts that are involved in our interpretation of a sentence. The surface structure of a sentence is that structure which is actually pronounced. In the sentence *Close the door,* for example, the deep structure includes *you.* The surface structure, however, includes only the verb and the object of the verb. Our understanding of the deep structure of the sentence *The man I saw on the ferry was going to Alaska* includes *the man was on the ferry, the man was going to Alaska,* and *I saw the man.* In the surface structure, *I saw* and *on the ferry* are both reductions of sentences which we actually understand and which we therefore know exist in the deep structure.

2. A second assumption of transformational grammar is related to the first. It is that at the level of deep structure, sentences are simple basic structures which can be described by a very small

7

number of rules, and that all the actual sentences of the language are derived from such simple basic structures. The easiest way to explain what these basic sentence structures are is to compare them to what traditional grammar calls simple, active, affirmative sentences without any noun modifiers or compound parts. In this series we refer to such sentences as **basic sentences.** *George climbed in the window* is such a sentence. But *George and Bill climbed in the small window* is not a basic sentence, both because it has a compound subject and because *window* is modified by *small.* In other words, we understand three basic sentences in the deep structure: *George climbed in the window, Bill climbed in the window,* and *the window was small.* To take another example, *Are you going?* is not a basic sentence because it is a question rather than an affirmative statement.

Basic sentence structures exist, either singly or in various combinations, in the deep structure of all sentences. To account for the actual sentences of the language, then, we need to do two things: describe the simple basic sentences that exist in the deep structure and then show how they are related to the surface structure.

3. A third assumption of transformational grammar is that the internalized rules which human beings use in producing and understanding sentences are very general rules, few in number but with very wide application. The rules which we use to describe the grammar of the language—that is, to make explicit what we already know implicitly—must also be very general rules. Such a description can show that, in spite of their apparent complexity and variety, the sentences of a language can be accounted for by a limited number of general rules which any normal human being can acquire at a very early age.

Constructing a Model

Obviously, there is no way of saying exactly what the rules that make up a speaker's competence are like or how they are applied. But it is possible to work out a set of rules—in words or in symbols—which, if applied, will yield essentially the same results as the internalized set of rules. This set of rules may be thought of as a grammatical model in the same sense that a rectangle in geometry is a model of a field, or a diagram of an atom is a model of an atom. The diagram of the atom is not the same thing as an atom and may not really look like an atom, but it helps us to understand what an atom is like and how it works. The grammatical model of the internalized rules of language is not the same thing as the rules in a speaker's mind, but it provides a convenient way to study unconscious and otherwise indescribable language rules. It is in effect a description of a native speaker's competence—what he knows that enables him to use his language.

Describing the Structure of Sentences

In constructing a set of rules to describe how sentences are produced, three related but different kinds of rules are involved. The rules that govern how we interpret sentences are called **semantic rules.** Since what is understood in a sentence is found in the deep structure, semantic rules are said to operate at the level of deep structure. What we pronounce when we pronounce sentences is the surface structure. Rules that govern the pronunciation of sentences, called **phonological rules,** obviously then operate at the surface level.

Both the way we interpret a sentence and the way we pronounce it depend on the structure of the sentence, that is, on how the parts have been put together and how they relate to each other. For example, though the following two sentences include the same words, they are pronounced differently and have different meanings because of the way the parts are put together: *The man caught the bear / The bear caught the man.* Rules that govern how parts are put together in the structure of a sentence are called **syntactic rules.** These rules are concerned both with the basic structure of sentences found in the deep structure and with how it becomes surface structure. We will be most concerned in *Concepts in Communication* with syntactic rules since they are central to both pronunciation and meaning.

Phrase Structure Rules

To account for both the deep and surface structure of sentences, transformational grammar begins by describing the deep structure and then shows how this deep structure is related to the surface structure. An important fact about basic sentence structure is that it consists of parts, which consist of other parts, which consist of still other parts. On the surface, sentences look as if they were simply words strung together one after the other, but we know— perhaps unconsciously—that some words are more closely related than others; that is, words are combined into units. For instance, in the sentence *My sister caught the hamster* we recognize that *my*

9

is more closely related to *sister* than to any other word in the sentence. *My sister* forms a unit, or part, of the sentence. Similarly, *the* is more closely related to *hamster* than to the other words. So we know that *the hamster* forms a unit. We also know that *caught the hamster* forms a still larger unit. The sentence then might be said to have the following structure:

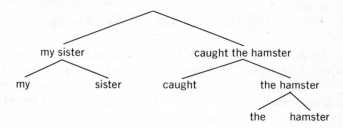

So, in reality, sentences consist of units of various kinds which may be part of larger units and which in turn may themselves consist of lesser or subordinate units. To describe this kind of structure, transformational grammar makes use of a set of rules called **phrase structure rules** which identify the various kinds of units or constituents that can occur in sentences and show how those constituents are related to each other.

In writing phrase structure rules, we use symbols to stand for the various constituents, **N** for **noun,** **V** for **verb,** and so on. We use symbols also to show how the various constituents are related to each other. Symbols are used because they provide an economical way to talk and write about the various parts. They provide a visible and concrete way to illustrate the relationships among the parts. How the symbols are used will become clear as the various rules are discussed in the following material.

The Sentence

In describing basic sentence structure we start with the largest constituent, **sentence,** which we will symbolize as *S,* and break it down into its various parts. The most general statement that can be made about any basic sentence is that it consists of two main parts. These two parts have been called various things at different times in history (subject/predicate; noun/verb, and so on). We will call them **noun phrase** and **verb phrase.** Each of these parts can be broken down into subordinate parts, but for now we will consider them only as separate units which have a coordinate relationship in forming a sentence.

They may each consist of only one word, as in *Jack laughed,* or they may each be long and complex, as in *The long thin cloud of smoke, frightening in its appearance, streamed off endlessly toward the horizon.* But whatever the noun phrase and the verb phrase consist of, the important thing to realize is that they stick together as units. In most cases, speakers of a language intuitively recognize that there are two distinct parts and are able to indicate where one ends and the other begins.

There is evidence in sentences themselves to verify our intuitive feeling that these two parts of a sentence are distinct units. It lies in the fact that we can find them occurring at various places in sentences, always sticking together as a unit. For example, when we change the sentence *The flashy car has attracted a crowd* into the form of a question, *has* simply moves in front of *the flashy car,* leaving the noun phrase intact: *Has the flashy car attracted a crowd?* We can find *the flashy car* in various other positions also: *I saw the flashy car; We rode in the flashy car,* and so on. This explains why in *The flashy car attracted a crowd* we intuitively feel the sentence breaks right after *car.*

Normally the noun phrase occurs first in a sentence and the verb phrase second. That a sentence consists of a noun phrase and a verb phrase, then, is a rule of language. If we use *S* as a symbol for a basic sentence structure, *NP* for noun phrase, and *VP* for verb phrase, this rule can be expressed symbolically as:

$$S \rightarrow NP + VP$$

The arrow is a symbol used to mean "consists of." It is used whenever we want to show how one part consists of, or can be broken down into, other subordinate parts, which is one of the possible ways parts are related in the structure of sentences.

The information given in the phrase structure rule $S \rightarrow NP + VP$ can also be illustrated on a branching or tree diagram. The rule, in effect, tells us how to construct such a diagram. We make the parts found to the right of the arrow branch off from the part found to the left of the arrow, like this:

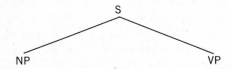

Note: There are certain other optional parts that can be included as constituents of *S* coordinate with the *NP* and *VP.* These will be discussed on pp. 33–41 when questions, negatives, and imperatives are described.

11

The Noun Phrase

There are various kinds of noun phrases. One kind consists of a **noun** and of a group of parts which precede it (**the determiner phrase**). The term *determiner phrase* has been chosen deliberately, as it is more inclusive than just *determiner,* and has several parts. *Determiners* can be defined as parts that normally occur before nouns in a noun phrase and do not occur elsewhere. Eventually we will see that the determiner phrase includes not only such determiners as *the, a/an, some, a few of, some of the, these, three of those,* and so on, but also adjectives and other noun modifiers occurring either before or after the noun.

Speakers of English undoubtedly have some intuition about the two parts of a noun phrase. They can recognize that the noun is somehow different from what comes before it. Traditionally a *noun* has been defined as "the name of a person, place, or thing" or as a "naming word." While these definitions are not wrong, they do not cover all instances and they do not explain why we recognize nouns as being different from other parts of the sentence. Actually, again there is evidence right in the sentence itself that nouns are distinct from the parts that precede them in the noun phrase. The evidence is that there is a natural division between the part called the determiner phrase and the part which follows—the noun. Whenever we insert an adjective in a noun phrase, we automatically insert it just after the part called the determiner phrase, showing that it sticks together as a unit, distinct from the noun. For example, we say *all of the large boxes,* not **all large of the boxes,* or **all of large the boxes.*

DETERMINER PHRASES

The determiner phrase is a complex structure in its own right. Its complexity can be illustrated by the fact that people learning English as a foreign language often have great difficulty with determiners, but native speakers of English use them without thinking about them. The relationship between determiners and the various nouns they can occur with is very close. Determiners answer such questions as *which one(s), how much,* or *how many* about nouns. There are many restrictions on the use of determiners; not every determiner can occur with every noun. Thus, we say *a book* and *some books; some water* but not **a water.*

What is known is that a great variety of material can occur before the noun, and that it is ordered; that is, when several items appear before a noun, they occur in a definite order. Among the

*An asterisk will be used throughout to indicate that a group of words is ungrammatical.

kinds of determiners are those known as *articles: the, a/an,* and *some.* (*The* is considered definite and the others indefinite.) The article *the* can be preceded in the noun phrase by such items as *a lot of, some of, one of, a few of, many of,* etc.—all marked by *of.* This group is sometimes known as **pre-articles,** or **pre-determiners.** We have, for example, *a lot of the students* but not **the a lot of students.*

There are also determiners, such as *this, these, that,* and *those,* which do not occur when the articles do. These are called **demonstratives** and include the meaning of the article plus *here* or *there.* For example, *this book* means *the book here.* Following the article and the demonstrative are **post-determiners,** which include both cardinal (*one, two, three,* etc.) and ordinal (*first, second, third,* etc.) numerals, as in *the three boys; the seventh car.* Numerals also occur in the predeterminers, as in *three of the books;* and *a third of the crop.*

Although it is difficult to sort out the different kinds of determiners and to formulate the rules that govern their use, obviously there are rules, and speakers of English are able to use them without being aware of them. We treat the determiners occurring before nouns as a unit in this series and make no attempt to distinguish among the various kinds. You as a teacher, though, should be aware of them. And some students might be challenged to try to sort out the complexity and to define the way the various kinds of determiners occur. All the facts they need exist in their heads. They have only to think of as many examples as possible of how they use determiners and how they hear them used, and then to try to find the regularities that exist.

Still another kind of determiner is the **null determiner.** This term is used to account for the absence of a visible determiner in such noun phrases as these:

> Bill is my friend.
> Voters rejected the measure.
> Snow was unexpected in June.

Although there are no visible determiners before the underlined nouns in these sentences, their absence is significant in the interpretation of the sentences. *The voters rejected the measure,* or *some voters rejected the measure* and *the snow was unexpected* have different interpretations when the determiners are included, and we wouldn't say **the Bill is my friend.* Moreover, certain nouns do not occur freely with visible determiners. For example, it would be unusual to say **a grass covered the hill.* Because the absence of a visible determiner helps to classify nouns (some can occur without a visible determiner) and also figures in the interpretation of sentences, it is useful to have a term and a symbol to indicate the absence of a determiner. We use the term *null determiner* and the symbol *ø.*

13

PRONOUNS

Another kind of noun phrase consists of a **pronoun.** Traditionally, pronouns have been defined as "words used in place of nouns." There are several kinds of pronouns, which are listed here for your information.

1. Personal pronouns are so named because they refer to first person—the person speaking (*I* or *we*); second person—the person being spoken to (*you*); and third person—the person or thing being spoken about *(he, she, it, they)*. They can also be distinguished by number (*I* or *we; he* or *they,* etc.) and gender (*he, she,* or *it*). Each of them have two or three forms—subjective, objective, possessive—depending on whether they are used before nouns, following verbs and prepositions, or to show possession.

subject forms	*object forms*	*possessive forms*
I	me	my, mine
you	you	your, yours
he	him	his
she	her	her, hers
it	it	its
we	us	our, ours
they	them	their, theirs

Only the subjective forms of these personal pronouns are discussed in *Blueprint for Language.* The objective form is discussed in *Inside Language* and the possessive in *Language—Beneath the Surface.*

2. Indefinite pronouns include *one, someone, some, something, somebody, someone, any, anything, anyone, anybody, everyone, everybody, everything.* With the exception of *one,* these pronouns have determiners built right into them. *Someone,* for example, consists of the indefinite pronoun *one* plus the determiner *some.*

3. Relative pronouns—*who, which,* and *that*—are discussed on pp. 45–47 of this Introduction and introduced in the student texts in *Language—Beneath the Surface.* They replace noun phrases in forming relative clauses.

4. Interrogative pronouns—*what, who* and *which*—are found in questions.

Instead of replacing nouns, pronouns, for the most part, replace the determiner phrase plus the noun. For example, *The boys went swimming* becomes *They went swimming.* So one kind of noun phrase consists of a determiner phrase plus a noun. Another kind consists of a pronoun. Normally when one occurs the other doesn't. This fact can be stated symbolically as a phrase structure rule:

$$NP \rightarrow \begin{Bmatrix} DP + N \\ Pro \end{Bmatrix}$$

The braces are used in writing phrase structure rules to indicate that either one or the other of the items enclosed can occur, but not both together. This is another kind of relationship that sentence parts have to each other—an either-or relationship.

The information in the phrase structure rule can also be illustrated on a branching diagram. It can be used to extend the diagram:

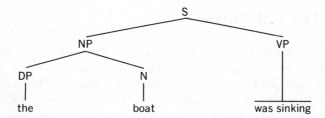

The diagram, as we have just indicated, can be used to illustrate the structure of a sentence like *The boat was sinking,* where the noun phrase consists of the determiner phrase *the* plus the noun *boat,* and the verb phrase is *was sinking.*

The rule for what a noun phrase consists of provides for a choice, either *DP + N* or *Pro.* Therefore, it also provides for a different diagram:

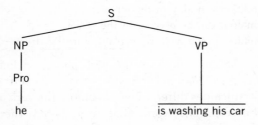

In both the diagrams above, the line drawn over the parts of the *VP* indicates that they all belong to *VP,* the symbol just above them.

Note: For the most part, pronouns replace the whole determiner phrase plus a noun, thus constituting the whole noun phrase. However, sometimes pronouns occur with what we have called predeterminers, as in *one of us is here.* In such cases, the pronoun seems to replace just the article plus the noun, not the whole determiner phrase. *One of the boys* becomes *one of them.* To include such

15

possibilities in the rule, it would be necessary to break down the determiner phrase into its various subordinate kinds of determiners. We make no attempt to do so in these books because it is quite possible to talk about the structure of the sentence without making this sort of detailed analysis. We simply refer to the determiners as a unit. You need to know, however, that the rule is not complete. The same will be true of many rules. They will be complete only as far as parts are identified. In describing language it is important to realize that we can continue to discover new information about the internalized rules speakers follow which may make it necessary to revise rules at some later time.

The Verb Phrase

Turning to the verb phrase part of the basic sentence structure, we can most simply describe it also as consisting of two parts— the **main verb phrase** and the **auxiliary verb phrase.** The main verb phrase is the part that includes the verb and whatever follows it. The main verb phrase can be identified by constructing a paradigm (a list of possible forms) in which the parts before the verb change but the rest of the verb phrase remains the same. Notice the part of the verb phrase that is the same in each of the following sentences:

> The children play in the street.
> The children played in the street.
> The children are playing in the street.
> The children have played in the street.
> The children have been playing in the street.
> The children can play in the street.
> The children can be playing in the street.
> The children could have been playing in the street.

In each of the sentences the verb phrase includes the verb *play* and *in the street. Play in the street* is the main verb phrase. The verb phrase also includes different words before the verb and different endings on the verb. The words that come before the verb in the verb phrase *(are, have, can, be, been,* and *could)* are often called **auxiliary** or **helping verbs.** Together with the endings found on the verb itself *(-ed, -ing)* they make up what is called the *auxiliary verb phrase.* Notice that although the verb is part of the main verb phrase, the parts of the auxiliary verb phrase cluster around the verb and determine the form it can take. Every verb phrase includes a verb, and it may occur in several forms—the root form, the present or past tense form, and the present or past participle form—depending on the auxiliary verb phrase that occurs with it.

The verb phrase, then, can be broken down into two distinct parts: the auxiliary verb phrase and the main verb phrase. This can be written as the following phrase structure rule:

VP → Aux + MVP

Aux stands for auxiliary verb phrase and **MVP** is used to represent the main verb phrase. Since most of the auxiliary verb phrase occurs first, *Aux* is listed first in the rule. In deciding how to write any rule, it is necessary to find the way which results in the simplest grammar. It is simpler to list the auxiliary material first. To try to write a rule which puts part of the auxiliary before the main verb phrase and part of it right after the verb leads to unworkable complications. This rule allows us to extend the branching diagram to illustrate the structure of the verb phrase as well as the noun phrase. For example, it can be used to illustrate the structure of a sentence such as *The children will play in the street:*

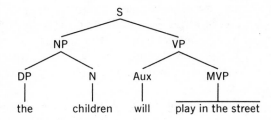

THE AUXILIARY VERB PHRASE

At the outset, the auxiliary material seems to have great variety and complexity. Actually, it can be broken down into four clearly identifiable parts which occur together in a predictable way, thus illustrating both the economy and the simplicity of a rule of language.

Tense

The first part of the auxiliary verb phrase is a part called *tense.* It is found as part of the first word in the verb phrase in basic sentences, and it appears in one of two forms, past tense or present tense, as we can see in the following examples:

He <u>walks</u> home.
He <u>walked</u> home.
He <u>is</u> walking home.
He <u>was</u> walking home.
He <u>has</u> walked home.
He <u>had</u> walked home.
He <u>will</u> walk home.
He <u>would</u> walk home.

17

In the first pair, the verb is the first word in the verb phrase and there are only two forms it can take: *walks,* the present tense form, or *walked,* the past tense form. In the other examples, various helping verbs, which will be identified in the next few pages, are first in the verb phrase, and in each case they can occur in only two forms—the past tense or the present tense.

Tense, then, has two forms, past and present. We can express this fact symbolically by using **Tns** for tense, **Past** for past tense, and **Pres** for present tense. Only one of the two forms will occur at one time in a given word. That is, they have an either-or relationship:

$$\text{Tns} \rightarrow \begin{Bmatrix} \text{Pres} \\ \text{Past} \end{Bmatrix}$$

Tense in traditional grammar was considered an indicator of time. It was applied to the various combinations of parts that occur in the auxiliary verb phrase. In addition to simple present and past tense, there were the perfect tenses, which contain the auxiliary *have* (as in *He has gone*); and the progressive tenses, which contain the auxiliary *be* (as in *He is going*); and even "future" tenses formed with *will* and *shall.*

A careful examination of verb phrases in English, however, shows clearly that tense and time are not necessarily related. In a sentence like *Tomorrow we finish the chapter,* we find so-called present tense, but we interpret the sentence as having something to do with the future. The same is true of *I am going next year.* A sentence like *He is allergic to grass seed,* while containing the present tense, is obviously not related to any specific time. Examples abound. It seems apparent that *tense* should not be confused with the semantic notion of *time* in a careful analysis of the syntax of the sentence.

We get a more accurate—and, incidentally, much simpler—description of the auxiliary system in the verb phrase if we use the term *tense* to refer only to the two forms which the first word in the verb phrase may take.

Past Tense of Verbs

Verbs are classified as regular or irregular on the basis of how they form their past tense. Regular verbs are those whose past tense is formed by adding a sound spelled -*d* or -*ed* to the root form. (Sometimes the sound is the *t* sound as in *sulked;* sometimes it is the *d* sound as in *called.*) Irregular verbs are those whose past tense is not formed by the addition of -*d* or -*ed.* Instead they have internal changes in the root form and sometimes various endings.

One of the areas in which there is variation between dialects of English is in the forms of irregular verbs. Some speakers of English invariably use *done* and *sung* as the past tense forms of *do* and *sing* *(He done it* or *They sung the songs).* Here is where usage can touch the discussion of syntax. You may want to discuss the differences with your class. Students should understand what is meant by standard forms and should know what the standard forms are, since there will be occasions when they will be expected to use such forms, even if they don't normally. An interesting fact about English language study is that the dialectal variation in verb forms occurs most frequently with irregular verbs. Most dialects, standard and nonstandard, include the rule that adds *-d* or *-ed* to regular verbs. It might help students to know that the reason they may have trouble with irregular verb forms is that the rules which apply to irregular verbs are not very general, and therefore not so easily acquired.

Present Tense of Verbs

In the present tense, verbs take one of two forms. If the verb follows a plural noun phrase (a plural noun or *they, you,* or *we*) or *I,* the present tense form is just like the root form of the verb. *(The children see the train.)* Though the present tense form looks like the root form, we know that in such cases it is possible to change the verb to its past tense form without changing the rest of the sentence. Thus we know that this form of the verb includes tense.

If the verb follows a singular noun phrase (except for *I* or *you*), its present tense form will end in *-s* or *-es. (The boy sees the train.)* The change in the present tense form of the verb to correspond with the subject *NP's* is one kind of agreement.

Tense and the Verb Be

The most irregular verb of all is the verb *be* which, as we will see, can also occur as a helping or auxiliary verb. Besides the root form, *be* has seven other forms, five of which include tense. Its present tense forms are *am* (which occurs only with *I*), *is* (following singular noun phrases), and *are* (following plural noun phrases).

> I <u>am</u> angry.
> He <u>is</u> angry.
> They <u>are</u> angry.

The past tense forms of *be* are *was* (following singular noun phrases) and *were* (following plural noun phrases).

> He <u>was</u> angry.
> They <u>were</u> angry.

In addition to tense forms, *be* has an *ing* form *(being)* and a past participle form *(been),* both of which will be discussed in connection with the helping verbs *have* and *be*.

19

The Auxiliary Be + ing

A second kind of auxiliary found in the auxiliary verb phrase is the auxiliary verb *be.* Unlike tense, which occurs in every sentence, the auxiliary *be* is an optional part. It may or may not occur. When it does occur, it comes right before the verb in the main verb phrase and has a predictable effect on the main verb. Following the auxiliary *be,* the verb appears in its *ing* form.

They <u>were</u> leap<u>ing</u>
The stars <u>are</u> shin<u>ing</u>.
I <u>am</u> driv<u>ing</u>.

Because the *ing* ending and the auxiliary verb *be* occur together, we symbolize it as the **be + ing** auxiliary. The *ing* form of the verb is traditionally called the **present participle.** It is formed by adding *ing* to the root form of the verb. In case of doubt, then, the root form of the verb can be identified by finding the form to which *ing* is added.

The form *be* takes when it occurs as an auxiliary depends on what else occurs in the auxiliary verb phrase. If no other auxiliary verb occurs, *be* will be the first word in the verb phrase and tense will be part of it; that is, it will have one of its tense forms, present or past:

Pres + be + ing + V

The stars are shining.

Past + be + ing + V

The stars were shining.

The forms *be* will have if there are other auxiliary verbs will be discussed in the following sections.

The Auxiliary Have + en

Another auxiliary verb that can occur in the auxiliary verb phrase is *have.* Like *be, have* can also be a main verb.

Joe Downs <u>has</u> a boat.

When *have* occurs as an auxiliary, it has a predictable effect on the verb or auxiliary verb that follows it. Following *have,* the verb and auxiliary verb occur in their **past participle** form. In traditional grammar this form was also referred to as the third principal part of the verb. We call it the **en form** of the verb, and we symbolize the auxiliary as the **have + en** auxiliary. The reason for using *en,* rather than *ed* which most English past participles end in, is that *ed* is also the past tense ending and therefore would not be distinctive. The *en* ending, though not found in a large number of verbs, is a distinctively past participial ending and so is useful as a general symbol for past participles.

The past participle of regular verbs is formed just like the past tense—by adding *-d* or *-ed* to the root form.

The swallows <u>have</u> finish<u>ed</u>.

The past participles of irregular verbs are formed by a variety of internal changes and endings. Some resemble the past forms of the irregular verbs:

root	past	past participle
think	thought	(have) thought
bring	brought	(have) brought
fight	fought	(have) fought
find	found	(have) found
hear	heard	(have) heard
feed	fed	(have) fed

Some are like the past forms except for the addition of *-n:*

root	past	past participle
freeze	froze	(have) frozen
break	broke	(have) broken
speak	spoke	(have) spoken

Some are like the root except for the addition of *-n* or *-en:*

root	past	past participle
eat	ate	(have) eaten
see	saw	(have) seen
take	took	(have) taken

And for some, the past participle doesn't resemble either the root or the past form:

root	past	past participle
sing	sang	(have) sung
ring	rung	(have) rung
swim	swam	(have) swum

The form *have* takes as an auxiliary depends on what occurs before it. If *have* is the first word in the verb phrase, tense will be part of it and it will be in either its present tense form *(have* or *has)* or its past tense form *(had).*

> The swallows <u>have</u> arriv<u>ed</u>.
> The swallow <u>has</u> arriv<u>ed</u>.
> The swallow <u>had</u> arriv<u>ed</u>.

Have can occur as an auxiliary verb by itself as in the examples above, or it can occur with the auxiliary verb *be.* When it occurs with *be, have* comes first and *be* next. In this case *have,* being first, will carry tense. And since *be* follows *have, have* will cause *be* to appear in its *en* form *(been).* Finally, the verb following *be* will be in its *ing* form.

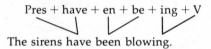

> The sirens have been blowing.

Notice how tense moves back to the word which is *first* in the verb phrase as each auxiliary verb is added:

$$Pres + V$$

Tense as part of verb: He eats watermelon.

$$Pres + be + ing + V$$

Tense as part of *be:* He is eating watermelon.

$$Pres + have + en + be + ing + V$$

Tense as part of *have:* He has been eating watermelon.

Modals

The final kind of optional auxiliary is known as a **modal,** symbolized as **M.** Modals, which constitute a limited group, include *will, shall, can, may,* and *must* (present tense forms) and the corresponding past tense forms *would, should, could, might. Must* has no past tense form.

These nine forms are considered "pure" modals. Three other modals—*dare, need,* and *ought*—will not be discussed in these books. They have been called "decaying" modals because their nature seems to be changing. Though they have many characteristics of the pure modal, *dare, need,* and *ought* are also different. It is more and more common for them to appear with *to,* as in *He ought to go, They need to go. Dare* and *need* now sometimes occur in the same sentence with one of the other modals, whereas the pure modals in most dialects do not. (We say *He will dare to go* but not **He would could go.*) The combination of *be* and *to* is also often considered a modal ("He *is to* go").

Unlike the auxiliaries *have* and *be,* the nine pure modals do not occur as main verbs. They are always auxiliaries. (The main verb *can* is another verb entirely, as can be demonstrated by the fact that it has a different past tense form from that of the auxiliary: *They can peaches every year / They canned peaches every year,* but *He can drive without hands / He could drive without hands.*) And unlike the other auxiliaries and the verbs, the pure modals do not add *-s* in the present after singular nouns *(The man will come to town. / The men will come to town.).*

When a modal occurs in the auxiliary verb phrase, the verb or auxiliary following the modal appears in its root form.

The child was playing in the yard.
but   The child will <u>be</u> playing in the yard.

The fishermen pulled in salmon every few minutes.
but   The fishermen could <u>pull</u> in salmon every few minutes.

Modals are always found combined with tense, because when they appear, they are the first element in the verb phrase. Consideration of the modals makes very apparent why tense should be thought of only as a choice between two forms rather than as an indicator of time. Modals seem even less related to time than other verbs or auxiliaries, although they do have a choice of two forms. With the possible exception of *could,* it is difficult to think of any of the modals as denoting past time, yet they do have a past tense form. In traditional grammar, modals have been associated with statements of condition contrary to fact and with statements of desire or obligation. The modals *will* and *shall* have also been said to denote "future tense." But English, unlike some languages, has no special verb form to denote future.

This lengthy discussion of the parts of the auxiliary verb phrase can be summed up in a symbolic statement or rule which shows what the parts are and how they are related:

Aux → Tns + (M) + (have + en) + (be + ing)

Notice that only tense must occur in every sentence. The other parts of the auxiliary verb phrase are optional. This is indicated by the parentheses around them. This rule shows that tense occurs first and that it may then be followed by a modal, or the auxiliary *have,* or the auxiliary *be,* or by any combination of them; or it may be the only part of the auxiliary verb phrase that occurs.

23

The information in this rule can be used to extend the diagram which represents the structure of sentences. For purposes of illustration we will use it in showing the structure of the sentence *The boy must have been eating the watermelon.*

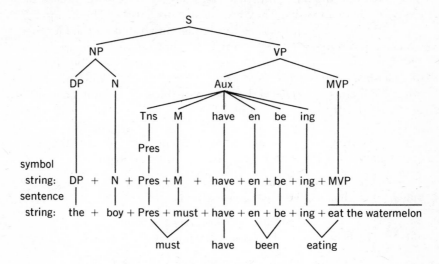

The first string of symbols at the bottom of the diagram is called a **symbol string.** The string of words below the symbols is a **sentence string.** The symbol string represents the parts of sentences with a particular kind of structure. It can represent the structure of many separate sentences having this structure. The sentence string represents the parts of one particular sentence—*The boy must have been eating the watermelon.* It shows the parts of this sentence in essentially the order in which they occur in the sentence. This is a sentence in which all the parts of the auxiliary verb phrase occur. The diagram above the symbol string represents the hidden or invisible structure of the sentence and shows how the various parts are combined in units. The parts higher up in the diagram are said to dominate those lower down. For example, *S* dominates *NP* and *VP;* they are part of *S.* In turn, *NP* dominates *DP* and *N,* and *VP* dominates *Aux* and *MVP.* The diagram shows how the structure of a sentence is a hierarchy consisting of parts within parts within parts.

The symbol string includes three symbols *(Pres, en,* and *ing)* which precede the parts to which they are attached in the sentence. *Pres* becomes part of the next word in the surface structure of the sentence. The past participle ending, represented by *en,* is part of the word following *have;* and the present participle ending, represented by *ing,* is part of the word following *be.* In a complete grammar we would describe the transformation (or change) that moves these parts to a position following the next word. (See pp. 32–33.) Notice, however, how in these books we simply connect the parts that are combined in the words of the sentence. Students have no trouble understanding that the two underlying parts are combined in the actual word.

$$\underbrace{Pres + must}_{must} + \underbrace{have}_{have} + \underbrace{en + be}_{been} + \underbrace{ing + eat}_{eating}$$

THE MAIN VERB PHRASE

The final part of basic sentence structure to be described is the main verb phrase, the part that includes the verb and whatever may follow it. Verbs in English are characterized by the kinds of parts that can follow them and by the kinds of transformations they can enter into.

Verbs Followed by Predicates

Because of its unique characteristics, the verb *be* belongs to a class of verbs of which it is the only member. Some of the unique features of *be* have already been discussed in connection with tense (p. 19). It is the only verb that has five tense forms. In addition, as a main verb, it reverses with the subject *NP* in yes-or-no questions, whereas other verbs, with one partial exception, do not. *(The car is here. / Is the car here?)* In British English and for some American speakers, the verb *have,* as a main verb, also reverses with the subject *NP. (You have a dog. / Have you a dog?)*

The term **predicate** (symbolized as *Pr*) is given to the part that follows *be* in the main verb phrase; a predicate can be an adjective, a noun phrase, or a place adverbial. An adjective is a word like *large* that can follow the verb *be* and can also appear before a noun in a noun phrase *(the large cat).* A place adverbial is a sentence part that answers the question *In what place?* That a predicate can be one of these three parts can be stated as a phrase structure rule:

$$Pr \longrightarrow \begin{Bmatrix} Adj \\ NP \\ Place \end{Bmatrix}$$

One distinguishing feature of *be* is that it must be followed by a predicate.

The man is angry.   *(be + Adj)*
The man is a wrestler.   *(be + NP)*
The man is in his office.   *(be + Place)*

25

When an *NP* follows the verb *be,* it must have the same number as the *NP* that precedes *be;* that is, they must both be plural or both be singular. (The *boys* are *athletes.* / The *boy* is an *athlete.*)

There are a few verbs in English which share one or another of the characteristics of *be.* These verbs are often called *linking verbs.* A few, like *become* and *remain* (and often *stay*), occur with either a noun phrase or an adjective following, but they do not reverse in yes-or-no transformations:

> He remained a friend.   (verb + noun phrase)
> He remained tired.   (verb + adjective)
> *Remained he tired?

When a noun phrase follows these verbs, the number restriction with the noun phrase before the verb holds *(He remained a friend,* not **He remained friends).* Some linking verbs are followed only by adjectives:

> The cake tastes <u>good</u>.
> The flower smells <u>sweet</u>.
> The child grew <u>tall</u>.

Verbs Followed by NP's

By far the largest number of verbs in English are verbs that are followed immediately by noun phrases. Some verbs, such as *fix, make,* and *discover,* must be followed by noun phrases. But for a far larger number, such as *eat, read, write, sing,* and *drink,* the noun phrase is optional. Though it occurs in the deep structure it may be deleted from the surface structure. *(The boys are eating dinner. / The boys are eating.)* Noun phrases following these verbs are not predicates, in the sense in which we have defined "predicates," because they cannot be replaced by an adjective *(*The boys are eating large).* And the noun phrase following verbs like *eat* or *fix* need not correspond in number to the noun phrase preceding the verb *(The boys saw an elephant).*

The noun phrases following such verbs are, for the most part, direct objects, and the verbs are often called **transitive verbs.** Both the verbs and the direct objects are identified by the fact that the sentences in which they occur can become passive sentences. For example, *The boys saw an elephant* can become *An elephant was seen by the boys.* In such sentences the direct object noun phrase belongs to the main verb phrase. In this way it differs from the subject noun phrase that precedes the verb, which is a constituent of

S, one of the two main parts of a sentence. The difference in structure can be illustrated on a diagram.

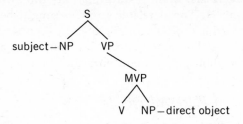

There is a small group of verbs that cannot be followed directly by noun phrases, even in the underlying structure. Most of them are complete without anything following them. In traditional grammar they have been called **intransitive verbs:**

> Buffalo have <u>vanished</u>.
> The dogs were <u>barking</u>.
> The packages <u>arrived</u>.

Indirect Objects

A small class of verbs, such as *give, donate, make, read,* and *tell,* occur not only with a direct object but with an indirect object as well. The indirect object is a noun phrase that in the surface structure is often found preceding the direct object noun phrase.

> He gave <u>the dog</u> a bone.

But it can also occur with a preposition following the direct object:

> He gave a bone <u>to the dog</u>.

We assume that this is how it occurs in the underlying deep structure. When two noun phrases follow the verb, a good way to test for whether the first is an indirect object is to see if it can also be used with a preposition following the direct object. *(He gave the dog a bone. / He gave a bone to the dog.)* Another way the indirect object can be identified is that sentences with indirect objects have two interchangeable passives. *(A bone was given to the dog by him. / The dog was given a bone by him.)*

Adverbials in the Verb Phrase

Finally a variety of different kinds of adverbials occur following the verb. Some of them are parts of the main verb phrase. A few are more correctly described as parts of the verb phrase, coordinate with *MVP.* Adverbials are usually identified by the questions

27

which they answer. Those that are related to *When?* are time adverbials; those that answer the question *Where?* (In what place?) are called place adverbials. Manner adverbials are those related to *How?* (In what manner?). Those related to *Why?* might be called reason adverbials. Adverbials often consist of only one word (*here, now, then, quickly,* etc.) but more often they consist of a prepositional phrase (a preposition plus a noun phrase).

Time and Place Adverbials

Time and place adverbials (symbolized as **Time** and **Place**) occur freely in almost any sentence. Though they follow the verb in the main verb phrase, they aren't dependent on what verb occurs. Thus they differ from the other parts of the main verb phrase we have discussed and can be considered constituents of the verb phrase itself, coordinate with the auxiliary verb phrase and the main verb phrase.[1]

Other Adverbials

Manner adverbials occur quite freely with both transitive and intransitive verbs and with a few linking verbs (*He became tired easily*). They do not occur with *be.* There are also a few verbs which are followed by *NP*'s that cannot occur with manner adverbials. Some examples are *weigh, cost,* and *have.*

> *The package weighed three pounds quickly.
> *My car cost $1000 carefully.
> *They have two dogs thoughtfully.

Such verbs are called **mid verbs.** They are characterized by the fact that they do not occur with manner adverbials or in passive sentences. *They have two dogs* cannot become **Two dogs are had by them.*

---

[1]*Note:* In the first three books in *Concepts in Communication, Time* and *Place* are discussed simply as parts that follow the verb in the main verb phrase; in *Language—Putting It All Together* they are first described as part of the *MVP.* In the early books there is no reason for showing that these adverbials are better described as parts of *VP.* However, later in the fourth book the rule is revised and they are specifically identified as constituents of *VP* and added to the rule:

VP → Aux + MVP + (Place) + (Time)

Since either or both *Time* and *Place* may or may not occur, they are placed side by side in parentheses.

The boy was playing at home at three o'clock.

The *Place* element which occurs with the verb *be,* however, is a *Pr* and therefore part of *MVP.* (See p. 25.)

Adverbs of reason, which we don't deal with in *Concepts in Communication,* should probably also be considered part of the *VP,* coordinate with *Time* and *Place.* (Examples are: I swim *for exercise.* He hid *because of fear.*) Such adverbials seem to occur freely in almost any verb phrase.

There are a number of other adverbials, some of which are restricted in the verbs they can occur with. As such they help to categorize the verbs; that is, verbs can be classified according to whether or not they can occur with a particular adverb. When one occurs, the other can also occur.

Directional adverbials are adverbials of the kind just mentioned. They are related to the question *Toward what place?* and occur with a limited set of verbs. Among them are such verbs as *drive, shoot, send, run,* and *put.*

> Bob drove the car <u>to the coast</u>.
> He shot the arrow <u>at the target</u>.
> The garage sent a repairman <u>to the wreck</u>.
> We ran <u>to the store</u>.
> Gerry put the book <u>on the table</u>.

With most of these verbs, the directional adverbial is optional, but with *put* it seems to be necessary. There are also directional adverbials related to the question *From what place?* (He came *from Philadelphia.* The bus has arrived *from Chicago.*)

Frequency adverbials are related to the question *How often?* Examples of such adverbials are *frequently, every three hours, now and then, often.* (He took his medicine *every three hours.*)

Adverbials of duration are related to the question *For how long?* (The play lasted *for three hours.* Our visitors stayed *for two weeks.* We will remain here *forever.*)

Adverbials of means, or instrumental adverbials, are related to the question *How?* meaning *By what means?* (He mowed the lawn *with a hand mower.* They traveled to Rome *by train.*)

One other kind of adverbial is the **sentence adverbial**, such adverbials as *certainly, surely, positively,* etc. These seem to be related to whole sentences *(It is certain. It is sure. It is positive.)* which are reduced by a transformation. They are, therefore, not part of the basic sentence structure.

The kinds of parts that occur in the main verb phrase can be summarized in a phrase structure rule. The part that must occur in every main verb phrase, of course, is the verb *(V).* Immediately following the verb can be either a predicate or a noun phrase that isn't a predicate, depending on what the verb is. In any given sentence, one or the other may occur, but not both together. They have an either-or relationship. They are also optional; that is, they do not have to occur in every verb phrase. This relationship can be symbolized with braces and parentheses. With some verbs an indirect object *NP* as well as a direct object *NP* occurs. In the basic structure

29

the indirect object consists of a preposition *(Prep)* plus a noun phrase. This should be enclosed in the braces with the direct object *NP*. The phrase structure rule will then look like this:

$$MVP \rightarrow V + \left(\begin{Bmatrix} Pr \\ NP \end{Bmatrix} + (Prep + NP) \right)$$

The main verb phrase may also include a whole group of adverbials which occur optionally, either alone or in various combinations. If all those that we have discussed were included in the phrase structure rule, it would look like this:

$$MVP \longrightarrow V + \left(\begin{Bmatrix} Pr \\ NP \end{Bmatrix} + (Prep + NP) \right) +$$
$$(Man) + (Dir) + (Freq) + (Dur) + (Means)[1]$$

We should point out that the order in which the adverbials are listed is somewhat arbitrary. There are obviously certain restrictions on the order in which they occur and on which ones can occur together, as well as on the verbs they can occur with. But there is also considerable freedom in moving them about. Many can occur at the beginning of a sentence or before the verb *(**Quickly** he slammed the door. / He **quickly** slammed the door.).* We don't attempt, in *Concepts in Communication,* to sort out the restrictions, but students interested in language might enjoy trying to figure out what they are, and experimenting with what they feel can and cannot be said (for example, *He slammed the door quickly,* but not **He slammed quickly the door*).

We have now developed seven phrase structure rules:

$$S \longrightarrow NP + VP$$

$$NP \rightarrow \begin{Bmatrix} DP + N \\ Pro \end{Bmatrix}$$

$$VP \longrightarrow Aux + MVP + (Time) + (Place)[2]$$

$$Aux \longrightarrow Tns + (M) + (have + en) + (be + ing)$$

$$Tns \rightarrow \begin{Bmatrix} Pres \\ Past \end{Bmatrix}$$

[1]*Note:* In *Blueprint for Language* we talk about the parts of the main verb phrase but do not formulate a rule. In *Inside Language* we formulate a rule which includes *Man* but not the other adverbials. In *Language—Putting It All Together* we talk about the other optional adverbials in an enrichment section where problems are posed. They are all included in the discussion here only for your information.

[2]*Time* and *Place* are included in the rule formulated in *Blueprint for Language.*

$$MVP \longrightarrow V + \left(\left\{ \begin{matrix} Pr \\ NP + (Prep + NP)^1 \end{matrix} \right\} \right) + (Man)$$

$$Pr \longrightarrow \left\{ \begin{matrix} Adj \\ NP \\ Place \end{matrix} \right\}$$

These rules account for most of the basic parts and the basic relationships found in the underlying structure of the sentences of English, and they account for a great variety of sentence structures. Two of the possible structures provided for by these rules are:

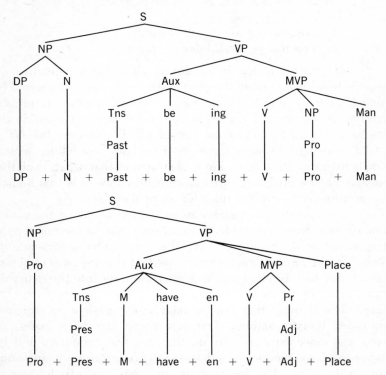

It should not, of course, be assumed that the rules we have described constitute a complete description. A complete grammar would have more extensive rules, but for the most part they would be modifications of the rules we have formulated here. And the ones we have formed here are adequate to account for the sentences we will describe in *Concepts in Communication;* they illustrate most of the basic ingredients and basic relationships found among the parts of the language. They show that the language consists of a limited number of parts which are organized economically according to a limited number of rules.

[1]*(Prep + NP)* is not included in the rule as formulated for students in the first three books in the series.

Transformations

It should be obvious that although the structure of many sentences can be accounted for by the phrase structure rules, they are all structures of simple sentences—the ones we call basic sentences. The rules will not account for such sentences as the following:

The paper has not arrived.
Has the paper arrived?
Where is the paper?
The boy who was here brought the paper.
The boy and his dog were here.
We asked the boy to bring the paper.
We knew that he would bring the paper.

If we were to try to account for all of these different kinds of sentences by modifying the phrase structure rules, they would become hopelessly complex. For example, the rules we have formulated describe sentences that consist of *NP + VP*. But in a question that can be answered by *yes* or *no,* part of the *VP* precedes the *NP*. It would be difficult to write a rule to show both possibilities without simply listing all the various kinds of structures that occur, in all their possible orders. Such a list would not explain how it is that humans can acquire very early the rules for using their language.

Fortunately, a simpler way to account for all of the various kinds of sentences is possible. If we assume that, in their underlying deep structure, all sentences have the basic sentence structure described by the phrase structure rules, we find that the basic structures can be modified, or changed, in predictable ways into the many different kinds of sentences found in the surface structure of the language. The changes that can be made in the basic deep structures are called **transformations.** Transformations can delete parts, add parts, and move parts around; and the parts that are moved or deleted are the constituents of the basic sentence structure. Transformations make it possible, for example, to show how a basic structure can be changed to become a question or a negative or a passive. No new phrase structure rules are needed—just a description of the transformations, that is, of the regular ways sentences differ from the basic structure. Transformations operate on single basic sentence structures as well as on combinations of basic structures. The surface structure is said to be **derived** by transformations from the deep structure.

THE AFFIX TRANSFORMATION

A transformation that applies to all sentences is the **affix** transformation. The phrase structure rules describe structures that are essentially the structures of basic sentences—simple affirmative sentences without noun modifiers or compound parts. The deep and surface structures are essentially alike. They include the same parts, which have the same relationships and occur in essentially the same order. The only exceptions are three parts of the auxiliary verb phrase (*tense, en,* and *ing*), which are slightly out of place. These three parts (*tense, en,* and *ing*) don't always attach to the same word. But *tense* always is part of the first word in the verb phrase; *en* is always part of what follows *have;* and *ing* is always part of what follows *be.* We can indicate this relationship most simply and economically by putting *tense* first in the rule and listing *en* with *have,* and *ing* with *be.* Listing the parts in this order, however, leaves *tense, en,* and *ing* slightly out of place. But since they don't always attach to the same word in a sentence, but always attach to whatever word happens to follow, this is the simplest way to do it.

A complete grammar would include a transformation describing how these parts, called *affixes,* move to the ends of the verbs that follow. If we use **Af** to stand for the three kinds of affixes, we can illustrate the change in this way:

For example:

$$Af + V \Rightarrow V + Af \qquad Af + V \Rightarrow V + Af$$
$$\text{Past} + \text{call} \quad \text{called} \qquad \text{ing} + \text{call} \quad \text{calling}$$

The double arrow is the symbol used in describing transformations. It means "the structure on the left becomes, by a regular change, the structure on the right." Since this transformation must occur in the derivation of all sentences, we don't bother to describe it each time. Instead we simply indicate the fact that the affixes combine with the next word in this way:

$$\text{Past} + \text{have} \qquad \text{ing} + \text{ring}$$
$$\text{had} \qquad \text{rung}$$

TRANSFORMATIONS OF SINGLE BASIC SENTENCE STRUCTURES

Yes-or-No Questions

In any basic sentence structure the subject noun phrase is followed by one of the following parts of the auxiliary verb phrase: tense combined with a modal (*Tns + M*); tense combined with the auxiliary verb *have* (*Tns + have*); tense combined with the auxiliary verb *be* (*Tns + be*); or tense combined with the main verb (*Tns + V*). In a yes-or-no question, on the other hand, these parts of the

33

auxiliary verb phrase precede the subject *NP* rather than follow it. The difference can be illustrated by the following pairs of sentences:

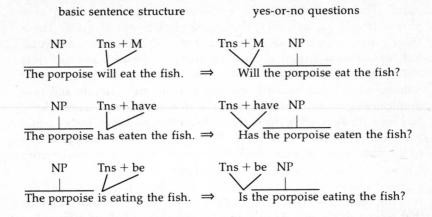

basic sentence structure   yes-or-no questions

Notice that in each case a simple reversal occurs. The tense-carrying part of the auxiliary reverses with the subject *NP*. This simple transformation accounts for the surface structure of yes-or-no questions. If we assume that the statement and the related questions have the same basic underlying structure, the same parts, the same relationships among the parts, then to describe a question we need only describe this basic structure and show how it is changed (transformed) into the surface structure of a question. To show explicitly, in the description of the deep structure, how we understand a question rather than an affirmative, we use the symbol *Q* to represent **question element.** A description of the deep structure of a question, then, is just like the deep structure of the related affirmative except that it also includes *Q.*

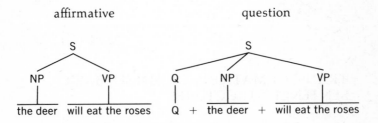

affirmative   question

Since the part that reverses with the subject *NP* is always the tense-carrying part of the auxiliary verb phrase, we use the symbol **Aux**ᴛ to represent it. This gives us a concrete way to represent the group of parts that moves, and to describe the transformation which occurs whenever the deep structure includes *Q:*

       Q + NP + Auxᴛ ⇒ Auxᴛ + NP

In the basic structure that includes tense as its only auxiliary, the related question includes a form of *do.*

$$\underset{\text{The porpoise}}{NP} \quad \underset{\text{ate the fish.}}{Tns + V} \quad \Rightarrow \quad \underset{\text{Did}}{Tns + do} \quad \underset{\text{the porpoise eat the fish?}}{NP}$$

Do occurs because when tense alone reverses with the subject *NP*, it is moved away from a verb to which it can attach. *Do* is then added for tense to combine with. In the underlying structure, tense is combined with the main verb, but in the question it is combined with *do.*

$$\underset{\text{the porpoise}}{Past + V} \quad \underset{\text{ate the fish}}{} \Rightarrow \underset{\text{did}}{Past + do} \quad \underset{\text{the porpoise eat the fish}}{V}$$

The transformation that adds *do* in such cases is called the **do-support transformation** *(T$_{do\text{-}support}$).* It can be symbolized as

Tns $\Rightarrow$ Tns + do

(when tense occurs with no verb to attach to)

The question transformation not only gives us a very simple way of describing questions, but it also has another advantage. By showing that statements and their related question have the same basic underlying structure, we have a way to explain how we know they are related.

Wh-questions

Yes-or-no questions aren't the only kinds of questions. In English there is also a whole set of questions beginning with what we call **Wh-words:** *where, when, what, who, why, how.* In part, these questions are like yes-or-no questions in that the tense-carrying part of the auxiliary verb phrase *(Aux$_T$)* comes before the subject *NP.* But in addition these questions begin with one of the *Wh*-words:

<u>Where</u> has John gone?
<u>What</u> are they looking at?
<u>When</u> will they arrive?
<u>How</u> did Mac find you?

Each of these questions is related to a yes-or-no question or to an affirmatative statement. For example, *Where has John gone?* is related to *John has gone someplace* and to *Has John gone someplace?*

Notice that each statement and yes-or-no question includes an indefinite word like *someplace, sometime,* whereas the *Wh*-question includes related *Wh*-words. *Someplace* is related to *where; some-*

thing to *what;* etc. Both words are indefinite. The only difference is that *Wh*-words inevitably appear at the beginning of their own sentence structure. We assume that the deep structure of the yes-or-no question and the related *Wh*-question are alike except for the *Wh*-word and the related indefinite word. The difference can be illustrated on diagrams:

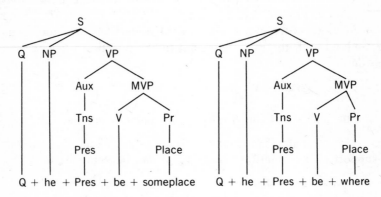

Q + he + Pres + be + someplace   Q + he + Pres + be + where

In each, the question transformation *(TQ)* moves *Pres + be* ahead of the subject *NP,* resulting in the following strings:

> Pres + be + he + someplace
> Pres + be + he + where

The first is a string representing a yes-or-no question *(Is he someplace?)* but in the second another transformation must move *where* to the beginning. *(Where is he?)*

The transformation that moves the *Wh*-word to the beginning of its own basic structure applies to any sentence which contains a *Wh*-word that isn't already at the beginning. It is called the **Wh-word repositioning transformation** or *T*repos *Wh-word*. When a *Wh*-word occurs as the object of a preposition, the preposition may or may not come to the front along with the *Wh*-word. For example, the deep structure *Q+ you are talking to who* can become either *Whom are you talking to?* or *To whom are you talking?*[1]

---

[1]A word should be said about questions like *Who called?* and *What has happened?* in which the *Wh*-word is at the beginning of the sentence in the deep structure as well as in the surface structure. In describing such sentences it might at first seem logical to bypass the *TQ* and *T*repos *Wh-word* transformations and treat these questions as exceptions. To do so, however, would make the rules more complicated since they would have to indicate the exceptions. Moreover, it would leave us no way to show how such questions are alike and how they are different from their related statements and yes-or-no questions, or how they are like other questions. We find instead that applying the *TQ* and *T*repos *Wh-word* transformations to the deep structure *Q + who + has called* results in the surface structure *Who has called?* In other words, the transformations produce the right results for all questions, indicating that they are indeed general transformations.

Negatives

Negative sentences normally include *not* after the tense-carrying part of the auxiliary verb phrase—the parts we group together under the symbol *Auxт*. For example:

$$Aux_T$$
$$|$$

The crow might <u>not</u> steal the corn.

$$Aux_T$$
$$|$$

The crow has <u>not</u> stolen the corn.

$$Aux_T$$
$$|$$

The crow is <u>not</u> stealing the corn.

$$Aux_T \ + \ do$$

The crow did <u>not</u> steal the corn.

It is not easy to describe where *not* occurs in a phrase structure rule because it may occur after any one of the four kinds of parts that introduce verb phrases. Instead of one rule for the auxiliary verb phrase (described on pp. 34–35), it would be necessary to have at least four rules, one for each possibility. Such a description would not show that negatives have related affirmatives. A simpler way is to show that affirmatives and their related negatives have the same underlying structure but that a transformation adds *not* to the negative. We need only indicate that in the deep structure of the negative, there is a **negative element, *(Neg):***

affirmative   negative

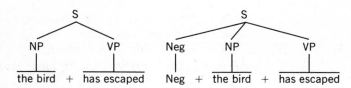

Any deep structure which includes *Neg* must have *not* added after *Auxт*.

Neg + the bird + has escaped ⇒ the bird has not escaped

This is called the **negative transformation *(TNeg).***

Negatives in whose deep structure tense is the only auxiliary include a form of *do (The crow did not steal the corn)*. The addition of *do* can be explained as it was for questions beginning with *do*, by noting that when *not* is added to such structures, it separates tense from a verb. We then must add *do*. The $T_{do\text{-}support}$ transformation (p. 35) applies to such cases and to all cases where tense is separated from a verb to combine with.

the crow + Past + not + steal ⟹ the crow + Past + do + not + steal

did

Note: The **contraction transformation** *(T_contr)* usually applies to such sentences, changing *did not* to *didn't*.)

Negative Questions

Among the sentences of English are negative questions *(Hasn't the crow stolen the corn?).* Their underlying structure includes both a negative element *(Neg)* and a question element *(Q)*. Both T_Q and T_{Neg} are needed to show how such sentences are derived. Applying T_Q first and T_{Neg} second results in *Hasn't the crow stolen the corn?* First *has* and *the crow* are reversed, and then *not* is added after *has*. Applying T_{Neg} first and T_Q second produces a different form. First *not* is placed after *has,* but then T_Q moves *has* ahead of *the crow,* resulting in *Has the crow not stolen the corn?* This is a possible English question but not a common one in American usage. (*Note:* Negative questions with *do* also require the $T_{do\text{-}support}$ transformation in their derivation. This transformation is always applied last.)

Passive Sentences

Sentences in which the subject *NP* of the deep structure is also the subject *NP* of the surface structure are said to be in the **active** voice. For example, in *The robber broke the lock,* the robber is the subject *NP,* the first main part of the sentence, and is dominated by *S*.

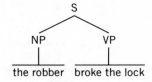

Sentences in the active voice that have direct object *NP's* following the verb and that can occur with manner adverbials have related **passives** *(The robber broke the lock. / The lock was broken by the robber.).*

By observing a number of active sentences and their related
passives, we can see that each passive is formed by a process of regular change in the structure of the active. In each passive,

1. the subject *NP* of the active follows the verb + *by;*
2. the object of the active is in the subject position;
3. a form of *be* is inserted before the main verb, which then
   takes its past participle form.

The *by* + *NP* of a passive sentence is often called the **agent.**
To indicate in the deep structure of a passive that it will have a different surface structure from the active, we take advantage of the
fact that all passives include verbs that can occur with manner adverbials, that is, the constituent *Man* can occur in all passives. By assuming that *Man* can include *by* + *agent* we have a way to describe
the deep structure of a passive and to show how it is like and how
it is different from the deep structure of its related active.

A deep structure with *by* + *agent* requires the passive transformation, which adds *be* + the past participle (*be* + *en*) before the
verb and moves the subject *NP* to the agent's position and the direct
object *NP* to the subject position:

$$NP^1 \quad + \text{Past} + \quad V \quad + \quad NP^2 \quad + \text{by} + \text{agent}$$

the robber + Past + break + the lock + by + agent $\Rightarrow$

$$NP^2 \quad + \text{Past} + \text{be} + \text{en} + \quad V \quad + \text{by} + \quad NP^1$$

the lock + Past + be + en + break + by + the robber

was   broken

The passive transformation is a good example of how transformations can simplify the grammar and in doing so explain how
we know two sentences with different surface structures can mean
the same thing. Passives are just the reverse of actives; all the restrictions on what can occur before and after a particular verb in an active
sentence are reversed in the passive. By describing the two as having
the same basic underlying sentence structure, we need describe the
restrictions only once—in the deep structure. This simplifies the description, and it also explains why we know that the two mean the
same thing—they are derived from the same basic sentence structure.

Imperatives

Imperative sentences, which give commands or make re-
quests, take several forms: *Shut the door. Don't shut the door. You*   **39**

will shut the door. You won't shut the door. You shut the door. Don't you shut the door. Do shut the door. The most common are imperatives like *Shut the door* and *Don't shut the door,* which have no visible subject. It is generally agreed that the subject *you* is understood in such sentences. Evidence actually exists that not only *you* but also *will* exists in the deep structure of imperatives. This is revealed by adding tag questions or reflexive pronouns[1] to the imperative. Such tag questions always include *will* or *will not——won't (Shut the door, won't you?);* and the reflexive pronoun that occurs is either *yourself* or *yourselves (Shut the door yourself).*

We can assume, then, that the deep structures of all imperatives can be symbolized as *Imp + (Neg) + you + Pres + will + V.* Because there are no restrictions on the verb or what follows the verb in imperatives, this fact of the deep structure is symbolized as *MVP.* The symbol *(Neg)* is included in the description of the deep structure because imperatives can be negative as well as affirmative. The symbol **Imp** stands for the **imperative element.** Like *Q* and *Neg* it is a symbol used to represent an abstract element which is understood in our interpretation of a sentence.

Some imperatives, such as *You will shut the door* and *You won't shut the door,* have the same surface structure as statements; that is, they are ambiguous. The symbol *Imp* used in the description of the deep structure distinguishes the imperatives from the statements. (On the surface the imperatives usually have a different pronunciation, which reflects the element symbolized as *Imp* in the deep structure.)

For the other five forms of the imperative, a transformation reverses *Pres + will* and *you* (Imp + (Neg) + you + Pres + will + MVP ⟹ Imp + Pres + will (not) + you + MVP). This is, in effect, the *T$_Q$* transformation, which obviously has broader application than just deriving questions.[2] It also applies to deep structures with *Imp.* If the deep structure of the imperative includes *Neg,* the negative transformation is also applied. Imperatives that include *do,* lack *will.* We conclude that *will* is deleted from such imperatives but that tense is not deleted. Left alone, tense requires the addition of *do (T$_{do\text{-}support}$).* These transformations *(T$_Q$, T$_{Neg}$, T$_{delete\ will}$, T$_{do\text{-}support}$)* account for the derivation of *Don't you shut the door.*

Another transformation deletes *you,* thus accounting for *Do shut the door* and *Don't shut the door.*

---

[1]Reflexive pronouns are personal pronouns which include *self* or *selves.* They replace an *NP* identical to an *NP* that occurs earlier in the same basic sentence structure (John hurt John ⟹ John hurt himself).

[2]The T$_Q$ transformation—that is, the simple reversal of *NP* and *Aux$_T$*—occurs in many kinds of sentences. For example, in a sentence such as *John is riding the bus* and *Bill is riding the bus, T$_Q$,* together with a transformation that deletes everything beyond *Aux$_T$* in the second half of the compound and substitutes *so,* results in *John is riding the bus and so is Bill.*

A third transformation deletes *Pres + do,* resulting in *You shut the door* and *Shut the door.*

This description of the derivation of imperatives helps to account for the fact that an imperative can have several different surface structure forms. It illustrates how applying transformations in a certain order simplifies the description of the grammar, and it illustrates how general many transformations (such as T_Q, T_{Neg}, $T_{do\text{-}support}$) are. They apply to many cases.

In describing the deep structure of questions, imperatives, and negatives, we have identified three elements that may occur, in addition to *NP* and *VP,* in the deep structure of sentences. To make explicit the phrase structure rule that indicates what the various parts of *S* are, we should add *Q, Imp,* and *Neg.* Since a sentence may be either a question or an imperative but not both together, we place these parts in braces and also in parentheses because they are optional. Because any sentence may include *Neg,* this symbol is also listed as an optional coordinate part:

$$S \rightarrow \left(\left\{ \begin{matrix} Q \\ Imp \end{matrix} \right\} \right) + (Neg) + NP + VP$$

The rule indicates that in forming sentences we always choose an *NP* and a *VP* and may optionally choose to make the sentence a negative and either an imperative or a question.

TRANSFORMATIONS OF COMBINED BASIC SENTENCE STRUCTURES

Many sentences result from combinations of two or more basic sentence structures, and some transformations operate on such combinations. In some sentences the basic structures that have been combined are obvious. In others, the combination of basic structures is apparent only in how we interpret the sentences. For example, in *The large box fell from the moving truck* we understand: *The box fell from the truck. The box was large. The truck was moving.*

There are two ways in which sentences can be combined—in a coordinate relationship and in a dominant-subordinate relationship. In the first case, the basic sentence structures are simply added onto each other. In the second, one structure is embedded in another as a subordinate part.

41

Compound Sentences and Sentences with Compound Parts

Compound sentences, such as *The bus stopped and the children got off,* are the most obvious examples of two or more basic sentences being combined in a coordinate structure (S + S ⇒ S + and + S). One is simply joined to the other with a coordinating conjunction *(and, yet, but, for, or, nor).* There is little or no restriction on the use of *and* to join basic structures; there are some semantic restrictions on the structures that can be joined with *but, for,* etc. *(*Joe arrived first, but Jim arrived first* is not a normal English sentence.)

Basic sentence structures combined coordinately also underlie sentences with compound parts. For example, the deep structure of *Lions and tigers roam at liberty,* is *Lions roam at liberty* and *Tigers roam at liberty.* Because each basic structure includes the same *VP (roam at liberty),* one *VP* can be deleted, leaving *Lions and tigers roam at liberty.* Underlying *Jean plays tennis and swims* is *Jean plays tennis* and *Jean swims.* Because both have the same subject *NP,* one *NP* can be deleted, leaving *Jean plays tennis and swims.*

Deletion transformations are very common. They account for what is understood but doesn't actually appear in the surface structure. A general rule governing deletion is that we can delete from the deep structure any element that we can reconstruct (understand) in the surface structure when it isn't there.

Transformations of Sentences Within Sentences

There are three places where one basic sentence structure can be embedded in another. One place is in the determiner phrase. This kind of embedding underlies various kinds of noun modifiers. Another place is in the *NP.* A third place is in the main verb phrase.

Noun Modifiers

Various kinds of noun modifiers are derived from sentences embedded in another sentence. Among such noun modifiers are the following:

adjectives before nouns (a <u>strange</u> cloud)
place adverbials (the skeleton <u>in the closet</u>)
appositives (George <u>the baker</u>)
restrictive relative clauses (the money <u>which I found</u>)
present participial modifiers (a <u>drenching</u> rain)
past participial modifiers (a <u>broken</u> window)

Underlying each modifier we understand a whole basic sentence. Because the close relationship between a noun modifier and

the noun it modifies is much like the relationship between a determiner and its noun, we assume that noun modifiers derive from an
S which is actually part of the determiner phrase. We assume, that is,
that the *DP* includes regular determiners *(Det)*, which invariably appear before nouns, and that it may also include an embedded *S*, a
fact represented by the following rule:

DP → Det + (S)

This relationship can also be illustrated on a diagram:

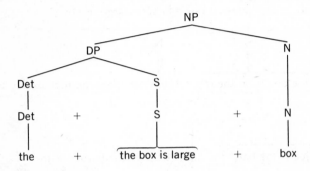

Notice that the embedded sentences underlying noun modifiers include a noun phrase identical to the noun phrase in which they are
embedded. For example, in the diagram above, the embedded sentence includes the noun phrase *the box,* and this sentence is embedded in the identical determiner phrase *the box* in the dominant sentence. As you can see, this description of the deep structure underlying a noun modifier reflects the relationship we understand, but it
does not represent a grammatical surface structure sentence. In surface structure sentences a whole basic sentence structure does not
occur between a determiner and its noun.

Two very general transformations are needed to change the
deep structures of noun modifiers to surface structure—a deletion
transformation and a repositioning transformation. The deletion
transformation applies to sentences embedded between *Det* and *N*
and which include *be,* either as a main verb or as an auxiliary verb.
The transformation, called the **be-deletion transformation** (*T*delete be)
deletes everything up to and including *be,* leaving only what follows
be in the embedded sentence.

Various kinds of parts can follow *be.* When *be* is the main
verb it is followed by a predicate which may be either an adjective,
a place adverbial, or a noun phrase. When *be* is an auxiliary verb
it is followed by a verb in its *ing* form (*ing* + *V*). Or the embedded
sentence with *be* may itself be a transformed sentence. For example,
it may be a sentence like *The book is John's,* in which case *be* is
followed by a possesive noun phrase, symbolized as *NP + Poss.* Or

43

the embedded sentence may include the past participle form of the verb as in a passive sentence (*en* + *V*). So, *T$_{delete be}$* may leave either an adjective, a place adverbial, an *NP*, a possessive noun, or a present or past participle form of a verb. But this transformation is optional. If it isn't applied, the whole embedded sentence is left between the determiner and the noun.

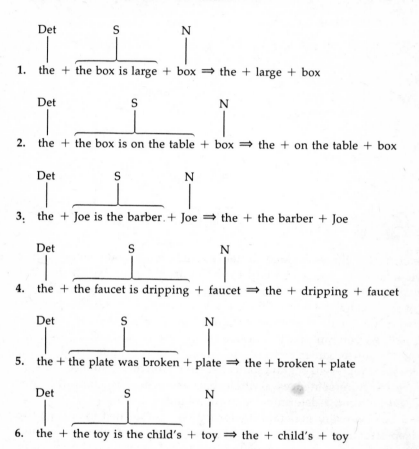

1. the + the box is large + box ⟹ the + large + box

2. the + the box is on the table + box ⟹ the + on the table + box

3. the + Joe is the barber + Joe ⟹ the + the barber + Joe

4. the + the faucet is dripping + faucet ⟹ the + dripping + faucet

5. the + the plate was broken + plate ⟹ the + broken + plate

6. the + the toy is the child's + toy ⟹ the + child's + toy

In the first, fourth, fifth, and sixth examples above, the transformation that deletes *be* is all that is needed to change the deep structure to surface structure. But when what is left after *T$_{delete be}$* is a place adverbial, as in sentence 2, or a noun phrase as in sentence 3, or when nothing has been deleted from the embedded sentence, another transformation moves the embedded part to a position after the noun phrase where it occurs in the surface structure.

> the + the barber + Joe ⟹ Joe the barber
> the + on the table + book ⟹ the book on the table
> the + the cat stole the canary + cat ⟹ the cat + the cat
> stole the canary.

The transformation that moves the embedded sentence is called the **sentence repositioning transformation** *(T$_{repos\ S}$)*.

Two additional transformations which produce relative clauses must be applied when the whole embedded *S* is repositioned. One uses a relative pronoun (*that, who, which*) to replace the noun phrase that is identical to the noun phrase in which it is embedded.

$$\overset{\displaystyle S}{\overline{\text{the cat} + \overbrace{\text{the cat stole the canary}}}} \Rightarrow \text{the cat} + \overbrace{\textit{that} \text{ stole the canary}}$$

This transformation is called the **Wh-word transformation** *(T$_{Wh\text{-}word}$)*. Relative pronouns are *Wh*-words.

In some embedded *S*'s, the noun phrase that is replaced by a relative pronoun is not at the beginning of the *S*. In that case, it must be moved there. This transformation is the same transformation that is used in moving the *Wh*-words in *Wh*-questions to the beginning.

$$\text{the canary} + \overbrace{\text{the cat ate the canary}}^{\displaystyle S} \Rightarrow$$

$$\text{the canary} + \overbrace{\text{the cat ate }\textbf{which}}^{\displaystyle S} \Rightarrow$$

$$\text{the canary} + \overbrace{\textbf{which} \text{ the cat ate}}^{\displaystyle S}$$

The transformations that account for relative clauses can also account for clauses that have traditionally been called adverbial clauses. Examples are *He locked the door when he left* and *Jim left the car where he found it*. Such sentences are related to the following sentences with relative clauses: *He locked the door at the time at which he left* and *Jim left the box at the place at which he found it*. In the first sentence, the relative clause modifies a noun which is itself part of a time adverbial *(at the time)*. In the second, the relative clause modifies a noun which is part of a place adverbial *(at the place)*. The noun phrases that have been replaced by relative pronouns are *the time* in the first and *the place* in the second.

at the time $\Rightarrow$ at which
at the place $\Rightarrow$ at which

We assume that the adverbial clauses are derived from the same deep structure as the relative clauses, but that instead of a noun within the place or time adverbial being replaced by a relative pro-

45

noun, the whole time or place adverbial is replaced by the *Wh*-words *when* or *where*

> he left at the time ⇒ he left when
> he found it at the place ⇒ he found it where

Because they are *Wh*-words, *when* and *where* then move to the beginning of their clauses. *(He locked the door at the time when he left./ He left the box at the place where he found it.)* A further deletion can then delete *at the time* and *at the place.*

Though they aren't discussed in *Concepts in Communication,* we assume that other adverbial clauses can be derived in much the same way by applying the transformations used in deriving relative clauses.

Nonrestrictive Relative Clauses

Noun modifiers can be either restrictive or nonrestrictive. Restrictive modifiers restrict the interpretation of the noun phrase, usually indicating *which one* of many possibilities. For example, *the car that is outside is mine* indicates *which* car is mine. Nonrestrictive modifiers add information but don't restrict the interpretation. In *My car, which is a Plymouth, is four years old,* the clause *which is a Plymouth* merely adds information. Actually, most noun modifiers can be interpreted either restrictively or nonrestrictively. When a sentence containing a nonrestrictive clause is pronounced, there is usually a slight pause to set off the nonrestrictive clause from the rest of the sentence. In writing such a sentence, we indicate that the clause is intended to be nonrestrictive by setting it off by a comma or commas.

In a few cases there are other clues as to whether a clause is restrictive or nonrestrictive. Clauses modifying proper nouns are nonrestrictive except when a visible determiner is used before the proper noun.

> Bill, whom I went to school with, has become famous. (nonrestrictive)
> The Bill that I went to school with has become famous. (restrictive)

Most people use the relative pronoun *that* only in restrictive relative clauses. *Who* and *which* are used in both restrictive and nonrestrictive clauses.

To account for the difference in interpretation between a restrictive and a nonrestrictive modifier, we assume that restrictive modifiers derive from sentences embedded in determiner phrases (see pp. 42–44). Since nonrestrictive modifiers simply add information in much the same way as the second clause in a compound sentence does, we assume that sentences with nonrestrictive clauses derive from the same kind of deep structure as a compound sentence. We assume further that another transformation moves the sentence underlying the nonrestrictive clause into the noun phrase just ahead of the noun it modifies. It is called the **nonrestrictive S transformation** ($T_{nonres\ s}$).

$$\overbrace{\text{this boy talks well}}^{S^1} + \overbrace{\text{this boy is two}}^{S^2} \Rightarrow$$

$$\overbrace{\left[\overbrace{\text{this} + \text{this boy is two}}^{S^2} + \text{boy talks well} \right]}^{S^1}$$

After the nonrestrictive S transformation has been applied, the same transformations used in deriving all relative clauses take over ($T_{repos\ s}$, $T_{Wh\text{-}word}$, and $T_{repos\ Wh\text{-}word}$).

$$\overbrace{\text{this} + \text{this boy is two}}^{S^2} + \text{boy talks well} \Rightarrow$$

$$\text{this boy} + \overbrace{\text{this boy is two}}^{S^2} + \text{talks well} \Rightarrow$$

$$\text{this boy} + \overbrace{\text{who is two}}^{S^2} + \text{talks well}$$

Noun Clauses

Another kind of sentence structure includes clauses known as noun clauses. These are clauses that function as noun phrases. Unlike relative clauses, which can occur in almost any noun phrase, noun clauses are restricted in their occurrence. Often they begin with an introductory *that*, which should not be confused with the relative pronoun *that*. In fact, the *that* introducing noun clauses has no other function in the structure of the sentence than to introduce the clause.

Noun clauses can occur as subjects of sentences with the main verb *be* when *be* is followed by abstract adjectives (such as *fantastic*) or by noun phrases (such as *a fact*) (see p. 48). Or noun clauses may occur as subjects of verbs such as *surprise* that require animate objects. Or they may occur as direct objects of cognitive verbs such as *know, perceive, think,* and so on.

That he would lie is strange. (subject of *be*)
That he would lie surprised me. (subject of *surprise*)
I knew that he would lie. (object of *know*)

47

We assume that noun clauses are derived from sentences embedded right after *N* or *Pro* in the noun phrase. In this way they are distinguished from sentences embedded directly in the determiner phrase.

$$\text{NP} \rightarrow \begin{Bmatrix} \text{DP} + \text{N} \\ \text{Pro} \end{Bmatrix} + \text{(S)}$$

deep structure of
noun modifier

deep structure of
noun clause

Basic sentence structures that become noun clauses are embedded only in noun phrases that have a noun or pronoun with the feature *abstract*. Examples are *fact*, *idea*, *theory*, and the abstract pronoun *it*. The abstract *it* is sometimes called an expletive. It does not refer to a noun phrase that occurs earlier. Having no meaning, it simply fills the position of a noun phrase. The abstract *it* is often deleted from the surface structure, particularly when it is in the subject *NP*. However, if the noun clause is moved to the end of the sentence, *it* is left to fill the subject position *(It surprised us that he would lie.).* The noun clauses in the sentences above are derived in the following way:

it + he would lie + is strange ⇒
 it + that he would lie + is strange ⇒
  that he would lie + is strange

it + he would lie + surprised us ⇒
 it + that he would lie + surprised us ⇒
  that he would lie + surprised us

I knew it + he would lie ⇒
 I knew it + that he would lie ⇒
  I knew + that he would lie

Verb Complements

In addition to *S*'s embedded in *DP*'s and *NP*'s, *S*'s are also embedded in the *MVP* with certain verbs, such as *consider, elect, appoint, find, know, believe, want,* all of which occur with direct object *NP*'s. The *S*'s embedded in this position become verb complements. They have subject *NP*'s identical to the direct object *NP*'s of the *MVP* in which they are embedded, and they often include

be, either as the main verb or as an auxiliary verb with *ing*. For example, the deep structure of *I consider John to be a friend* can be represented on this diagram:

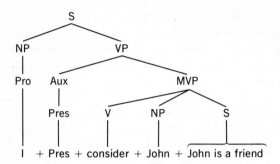

The deep structure of *I found the child playing in the closet* can be
represented on this diagram:

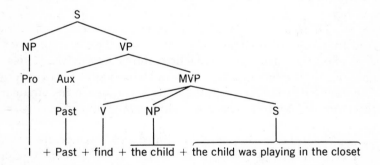

If the embedded *S* has no auxiliary except tense, a transformation deletes the subject *NP* and changes tense to *to*.

I consider John + John is a friend ⟹ I consider John to be a friend

If the main verb in the embedded *S* is *be*, *to be* can usually be deleted:

I consider John + to be a friend ⟹ I consider John a friend

If the embedded *S* includes the auxiliary *be* + *ing*, a transformation deletes everything up to and including the *be* (but not the
ing):

I found the child + he was playing in the closet
I found the child + playing in the closet

49

The Lexicon

FEATURES OF WORDS

The phrase structure rules identify the basic constituents of sentences (the kinds of parts that occur). Transformations show how these constituents can be moved around or deleted or changed. But in the sentences of the language, the constituents are represented by words and parts of words. Therefore, a grammar is also concerned with describing words.

The words of the language are sometimes referred to as the **lexicon,** and a speaker's internalized knowledge of his language includes knowledge about his lexicon (the words he knows and uses). When we know a word, we know what it means, how to pronounce it, and where it can occur in a sentence. This kind of knowledge can be described in terms of features. Every word consists of a whole set of features or characteristics, and although words may share many of the same features, every word is distinct in the combination of features it has. In at least one feature every word differs from all other words. This is what enables us to distinguish one word from another.

There are several kinds of features that characterize words. And there are restrictions on what words can occur together that depend on these features. **Syntactic features** determine where a word goes in the structure of a sentence and what words it can occur with. The noun *smoke* occurs with the null determiner in the singular, but the noun *car* doesn't. The noun phrase *the boy* can be replaced by the relative pronoun *who* and the personal pronoun *he;* the noun phrase *the tree* can be replaced by *which* and *it.* The word *see* occurs as a verb, the word *boy* as a noun. The verb *fix* must be followed by a noun phrase, the verb *arrive* cannot be.

Words also have **semantic features.** They are the features that determine the meaning we give to words. For example, both *man* and *boy* share the semantic feature [masculine], but only *man* has the combination of this feature and the feature [mature]. Semantic features also place certain restrictions on the words that can occur together. Though sentences consist of noun phrases and verb phrases, not every noun can occur with every verb. For example, the noun *snow* cannot occur with the verb *laugh.*

The way we pronounce words is determined by the **phonetic features** of the sounds we combine and the rules for putting the sounds together. For example, the words *bat* and *pat* are distinguished only by the difference of one sound feature in the initial sounds. The sound /b/ is voiced whereas the sound /p/ is not. Yet all speakers of English are aware of this difference.

THE STRUCTURE OF WORDS

Though we think of words as the units of language, actually words consist of smaller units called **morphemes,** and just as there are syntactic rules for putting larger units of the sentence together, there are rules for putting morphemes together to form words. Morphemes have a deep and a surface structure, which aren't always alike. Some deep structure morphemes are abstract elements in the deep structure. *Past* is such an abstract morpheme. In the surface structure it may take several forms: the sound spelled *-d* or *-ed* or the change in form found in irregular verbs *(went, drove)*.

Some morphemes can stand alone as individual words. They are known as root morphemes. Some morphemes must be combined with other morphemes; the morphemes *-ly* and *-ed* are examples. There are restrictions on how morphemes are put together. For example, the morpheme *re-* must occur before the root of a word, but the morpheme *-ly* occurs at the end.

By describing the lexicon as consisting of morphemes, we simplify the description because there are fewer morphemes than words. Morphemes are used and reused in forming many words. For example, the morpheme *-ing* is found in all present participle forms of verbs. Instead of listing every present participle verb in describing the lexicon, it is more economical to list the root verbs and *-ing* and to note the rule that combines them.

A complete grammar, then, would include a description of the syntax, a description of the rules for pronouncing words and sentences, and a description of how sentences are interpreted. It would also include a description of the lexicon, that is, of the morphemes and the rules for combining them, and of the features that characterize them.

INSTRUCTIONAL RESOURCES

We have included here a variety of available films and filmstrips to supplement the language material. It is always wise to preview audio-visual materials prior to their use in the classroom.

Films

Debt to the Past—Language and Communication (16 min., color, 1962, Moody Institute of Science). Describes our heritage of spoken and written language and its role in the communication of ideas. Emphasizes the importance of developing skill in language. Traces three stages of written language development — the pictographic, ideographic, and phonetic.

Definition of Language (30 min., b/w, 1957, Indiana University). Explains the relationship between language and culture. Tells whether one language is older, better, or more difficult to learn than another. Discusses language patterns and how they affect the learning of a language.

Do Words Ever Fool You? (12 min., color or b/w, 1973, Coronet). Consists of two parts: 1) a game which alerts us to word foolers, words in disguise (homonyms and homophones), general words (that leave room for misinterpretation), extreme words (that need comparisons to make sense), and word associations (that involve feelings); and 2) a "remedy booth" which offers aids such as the dictionary and careful attention to usage.

English Language Series, The (11–13 min. each, color or b/w, Coronet). Contains four 16mm films, two of which are appropriate for this year's study: *Story of Its Development*—Traces the history of English from the time of the Celtic, Roman, Nordic, and Saxon tribes. Shows the constant growth and change in the English language exemplified by developments wrought by church monks, William the Conqueror, Chaucer, Shakespeare, and the printing press. *How It Changes*—Describes how our language is constantly changing by the addition of words, changes in the spelling, pronunciation, and meaning of words, and changes in the rules of grammar. Shows how changes keep our language alive and flexible and make it a useful tool for communication through examples ranging from the writing of Captain John Smith to Noah Webster's Dictionary of 1828 to recent additions to our language.

Hiding Behind the Dictionary (29 min., b/w, Indiana University). Explains how meanings of words are learned; provides examples of how words are inferred. Tells us that a writer of a dictionary is a historian not a law giver.

How English Changed in America (12 min., color or b/w, 1973, Coronet). Traces the Americanization of English—its pronunciation, vocabulary, and figures of speech—from the time of the Pilgrims to the landing of astronauts on the moon.

How Words Are Made (12 min., color of b/w, 1973, Coronet). Reviews, by means of a dream-fantasy, the three basic ways in which words are made. A fictitious character invents some words to illustrate the principles involved, then dreams up examples of real words formed by compounding, by adding prefixes and suffixes to base words, and by shortening words, including the formation of blends and acronyms.

How Words Get New Meanings (12 min., color or b/w, 1973, Coronet). Shows how old words may change meaning slightly to fit new ideas and inventions. Also illustrates how words may change in meaning by becoming more general or specific, more positive or negative.

Nature of Language, The (28 min., color, 1966, Stuart Finley). Examines current knowledge about language from the viewpoint of the scientific linguist. Features staff members of the Center for Applied Linguistics.

Varieties of English (12 min., color or b/w, 1973, Coronet). Demonstrates how people living in different English-speaking countries speak English differently—how even within the United States the language varies from state to state, sometimes even from one section of a city to another. Shows that people in specialized occupations often use language differently. And reveals a variety of pronunciations, words, meanings, figures of speech, and vocabularies, by having students listen to these differences.

Filmstrips

Holt English Language Filmstrips (color, sound, 1972, Holt, Rinehart and Winston, Inc.). Contains a series of six filmstrips designed to supplement *Concepts in Communication.* Can all be used at any level above the ones for which they were designed, to provide an overview or review of the basic elements of the language program. The *Introduction* is intended to stimulate students' thinking about the miracle of language and to help them consider language as an entity. (Designed for use with Chapter 1 of *Blueprint for Language.*) *The Basic Sentence* provides an overview of phrase structure rules that govern the noun phrase and verb phrase. (Designed for use with *Blueprint for Language*—after phrase structure rules have been introduced.) *Writing Systems* gives students an overview of several writing systems: picture writing, pictographs, ideographs, logographs, syllabaries, hieroglyphics, and alphabets. (Designed for use with Chapter 9 of *Inside Language*.) *Yes-or-No Questions and Negatives* provides help in applying transformations to declarative sentences to produce the surface structures of yes-or-no questions and negative statements. (Designed for use with *Inside Language*.) *Embedding* provides practice in embedding and recognizing embedded sentences; also gives review of phrase structure rules needed for embedding. (Designed for use with *Language—Beneath the Surface*.) *The Origins and Early History of English* traces the development of English from its earliest beginnings to modern times, concentrating on Old and Middle English. This filmstrip is designed to provide an introduction to the study of language history and may be used at any level where language study is taught, either as introduction or summation. (Designed for use with the last three books in the series.)

Interesting Facts About Your Language (color, sound, 1967, Society for Visual Education). Illustrates the process by which words are acquired from other languages and discusses the development of the dictionary, the meaning of proverbs, and the use of language in the form of codes. (From the Linguistic Background of English Series, Group 1.)

SOURCES OF MATERIAL

Films

Coronet Films, 65 East South Water Street, Chicago, Illinois 60601

Indiana University, Audio Visual Center, Bloomington, Indiana 47401

Moody Institute of Science, Educational Film Dept., 12000 East Washington Blvd., Whittier, California 90606

Stuart Finley, Inc., 3428 Mansfield Road, Falls Church, Virginia 22041

Filmstrips

Holt, Rinehart and Winston, Inc., 383 Madison Avenue, New York, New York 10017

Society for Visual Education, Inc., 1345 Diversey Parkway, Chicago, Illinois 60614

PERFORMANCE OBJECTIVES FOR
LANGUAGE—BENEATH THE SURFACE

The student should be able to

1. Explain the difference between linguistic competence and linguistic performance.

2. Define the terms *deep structure* and *surface structure* and explain how they are related.

3. Distinguish between phrase structure rules and transformations and explain the purpose of each.

4. Demonstrate an understanding of recursiveness and show why language is recursive.

5. State the two ways in which basic sentence structures can be combined.

6. Identify the deep structure of compound sentences and sentences with compound parts and show how their surface structure is derived from the deep structure.

7. Recognize the following kinds of noun modifiers and identify the deep structure of sentences in which they are found: adjectives, place adverbials, appositives, relative clauses, and possessives.

8. Represent, either on a branching diagram or a sentence string, the deep structure of sentences with any of the noun modifiers listed in 7 above and explain the transformations by which their surface structure is derived.

9. Explain how the various noun modifiers are alike and how they differ in their deep structure and in their derivation.

10. Identify various syntactic features that distinguish nouns and verbs.

11. Describe in general how English dictionaries have developed and how modern dictionaries differ from earlier ones.

Chapter 1

Language: Discovering Relationships

PERFORMANCE OBJECTIVES

The student should be able to

1. Explain what is meant by linguistic competence.

2. Make clear what linguistic competence enables us to do.

3. Explain why we need three different kinds of rules to describe language.

4. Explain what is meant by *syntax* and *syntactic rules*.

5. Identify noun phrases with the null determiner; the past and present tense forms of verbs, both regular and irregular; the present and past participle forms of verbs, both regular and irregular; the parts of the auxiliary verb phrase in a sentence; manner, time, and place adverbials; the tense-carrying word in a sentence.

6. Distinguish between a phrase structure rule and the description of a transformation.

7. Describe and express as a phrase structure rule the constituency of a basic sentence (*S*), a noun phrase, a verb phrase, and an auxiliary verb phrase.

57

8. Construct diagrams representing the basic deep structure of basic sentences.

9. Explain what happens in the following transformations: the question, the negative, and the passive.

10. Explain why some questions and negatives include *do*.

SYNOPSIS

The chapter consists of the following sections:

1. The introductory section (pages L3–4) reminds students of their complex language, which they were able to learn, without realizing that they were doing so, at a very early age.

2. Linguistic Competence (pages L4–7) defines linguistic competence—what we know that enables us to use language—and discusses and illustrates by four exercises how it enables us to recognize sentences, to produce and understand sentences we have never heard or used, to recognize synonymous sentences, and to recognize ambiguity in sentences.

3. What Are the Internalized Rules Like? (pages L7–8) points out that three kinds of rules—phonological, semantic, and syntactic—are needed to describe our use of language.

4. What Kind of Syntactic Structure Do Sentences Have? (pages L8–11) discusses that sentences consist of parts within parts (a hierarchy) and, in a subsection "Deep and Surface Structure," explains that, because we understand much that doesn't actually occur in a sentence, we assume that a sentence has two structures, a deep structure that includes all that we understand and a surface structure that is the structure of the sentence we actually produce.

5. Describing Language (pages L11–15) discusses phrase structure rules as rules that name the basic ingredients of sentences and give the recipes for making sentences. It explains the four kinds of symbols used in writing phrase structure rules ($\rightarrow$, $+$, $(\ )$, and $\{\ \}$) to show the kinds of relationships the various parts have to each other. It then identifies the parts of a basic sentence and the parts found in a noun phrase. Students are asked to write phrase structure rules expressing the make-up of a basic sentence and of a noun phrase. And they learn how the rules are related to branching diagrams by constructing diagrams for a number of sentences.

6. The Verb Phrase (pages L15–20) identifies the two main parts of the verb phrase—the main verb phrase and the auxiliary verb phrase—and the parts that each of these two parts consist of. A subsection "The Auxiliary Verb Phrase" begins with the part that occurs immediately preceding the verb *(be + ing)* when all four parts appear and then takes up each of the other parts in the order in which it precedes the verb. Students are asked to put the information about the auxiliary verb phrase into a phrase structure rule.

7. **Forms of Verbs** (pages L20–24) is concerned with the root form of verbs and the past and present and the two participle forms of both regular and irregular verbs. The section includes two exercises, in one of which students are asked to identify the various parts found in the verb phrase, in the other, to represent the deep structure of sentences on branching diagrams, which by this time are fairly detailed.

8. **Transformations** (pages L24–29) distinguishes between basic and transformed sentences and describes three transformations: the question, the negative, and the passive. Students are shown how questions, negatives, and passives derive from the same basic sentence structure as are related affirmative active statements.

9. **Review** (page L29) includes a set of questions about the basic concepts developed in the chapter.

TEACHING THE CHAPTER

1. Become familiar with the "Teacher's Introduction," pages 1 through 41, as preparation for teaching the chapter, and refer to it when you have questions.

2. This chapter is intended for use both as a review for students who may have studied transformational grammar in earlier books in this series and as an introduction for students new to this grammar. For the latter it will be necessary to go more slowly and to augment each section with additional exercises. Even for students familiar with the grammar it is suggested that the chapter be taught a section at a time over a period of several days. Considerable time should be spent on the sections that deal with the various parts of the sentence.

3. Students are asked to express the relationships of the parts in terms of phrase structure rules. If adequate time has been spent in preparation of these exercises, they should present no particular problem.

4. The exercises are all integral parts of the sections in which they are found and are intended to be used to reinforce such sections. In the keys to the exercises you will find suggestions as to the use of each exercise. Those exercises designated for class discussion are intended only as guides in teaching the material in the sections in which they are found. Those designated as class exercises

can be worked out by the students right in class, either individually or in groups, and then discussed. Those indicated to be written assignments are intended for out-of-class work to be done by the students individually. In general, they provide practice and reinforcement for the various concepts that have been explained in class.

5. The explanatory material in the sections both preceding and following the exercises is meant to be taught and discussed. You will find it helpful to use the chalkboard or overhead projector to illustrate various structures discussed in the chapter, and to use additional sentences as illustration, some of which you can ask students to supply.

KEY TO THE EXERCISES

EXERCISE 1—*page L5 (a class exercise)*

PURPOSE: To demonstrate the creative nature of language and to stimulate discussion.

Make up some sentences you have never used before. Then trade your sentences with a classmate and see if you can understand each other's sentences. What do you think makes it possible for you to understand sentences that you have never seen before? What makes it possible for you to produce new sentences whenever you need to?

Discuss this exercise as part of the introductory section of the chapter and of the section on "Linguistic Competence." Have some of the students' sentences shared with the class.

Students may not arrive at the answers to the questions, but the exercise should stimulate thought. In other words, students should begin to understand that we unconsciously know the rules for making sentences.

EXERCISE 2—*page L6 (for class discussion)*

PURPOSE: To demonstrate that we can recognize sentences that mean the same thing though they appear to be different.

Which sentences in each of the following groups mean exactly the same thing?

1. The baseball broke his tooth.
    His tooth broke the baseball.
    His baseball hit the tooth.
    His tooth was broken by the baseball.

2. Red carnations are very fragrant.
    Carnations that are red are very fragrant.
    Fragrant carnations are very red.
    Carnations that are very red are fragrant.

3. Geoffrey's bicycle has a flat tire.
    The flat tire on the bicycle is Geoffrey's.
    The bicycle that is Geoffrey's has a flat tire.
    The flat tire is on Geoffrey's bicycle.

4. Marla pleases everyone easily.
    Marla was easy to please.
    It was easy to please Marla.
    Everyone pleased Marla easily.

5. The stork on the roof is behind the chimney.
    The stork on the roof has a nest behind the chimney.
    The nest behind the chimney is on the roof.
    The stork that is on the roof has a nest behind the chimney.

> **Have students discuss briefly how they can tell which are
> the synonymous sentences. Though they may not arrive
> at a satisfactory answer, their thinking about the question
> will motivate the study of language.**

EXERCISE 3 – *page L7 (for class discussion)*

> **PURPOSE: To demonstrate that we can recognize am-
> biguity in sentences.**

Try to write sentences that express at least two different interpretations for each of the sentences below.

1. Time flies.

    Time passes quickly.
    Record the speed or duration of flies. (An imperative sentence
    referring either to a play in baseball or to insects.)

2. I saw the man in the park with the binoculars.

    I saw the man in the park who had the binoculars.
    With the binoculars, I saw the man in the park.
    I saw the man in the park where the binoculars were.

61

3. Annoying bus drivers will be forbidden.

    It is forbidden to annoy bus drivers.
    Bus drivers who are annoying will be forbidden.

4. He hit the man in the house.

    He hit the man who was in the house.
    While he was in the house, he hit the man.

> Following the discussion of this exercise, discuss the section "What Are the Internalized Rules Like?" Ask students to explain the difference in meaning between *Carson fed the parakeet* and *The parakeet fed Carson* and to make clear how they are able to recognize the difference.
>   Things to stress:
> 1. The three kinds of rules.
> 2. The terms *syntax* and *syntactic rules*.

EXERCISE 4—*page L13 (an individual written assignment)*

> **PURPOSE: To help students learn how to write phrase structure rules and to reinforce their understanding of the basic constitutents of S and NP.**

Rewrite each of the following statements in the form of a phrase structure rule. (Use the symbols →, +, and { }, and *S* for sentence, *NP* for noun phrase, *VP* for verb phrase, *DP* for determiner phrase, *N* for noun, and *Pro* for pronoun.)

1. A sentence consists of a noun phrase and a verb phrase.

    S → NP + VP

2. A noun phrase consists either of a determiner phrase plus a noun or of a pronoun.

    $$NP \rightarrow \begin{Bmatrix} DP + N \\ Pro \end{Bmatrix}$$

> Before having students do this exercise individually, carefully discuss the sections "What Kind of Syntactic Structure Do Sentences Have?" and "Describing Language," perhaps using the chalkboard or an overhead projector to demonstrate the various points being made. You might, for example, want to illustrate the structure of *The kingfisher dived* with a diagram like those on pages 8–9 of the student text.
>   Points to stress:
> 1. The structure of a sentence, consisting as it does of parts within parts (a hierarchy).

2. Our ability to understand something that doesn't actually appear in a sentence.
3. The difference between deep and surface structure.
4. How we can illustrate the form of the phrase structure rules.
5. How we can explain what is meant by a noun phrase, verb phrase, determiner phrase, noun and pronoun. (Depending on the background of your students, you may need to use even more examples than those given to provide practice.)
6. The subject noun phrase as the first main part of a basic sentence.

EXERCISE 5—*pages L14–15 (a written assignment)*

PURPOSE: To reinforce the students' ability to identify the noun phrase, the verb phrase, and the parts of the noun phrase in a basic sentence, and to represent their structure on a branching diagram.

Decide what the two main parts of each of the following sentences are. Then decide if the *NP* consists of a determiner phrase plus a noun or of a pronoun. Finally construct diagrams to show the structure of each sentence. For example:

A raccoon disappeared into the bushes.

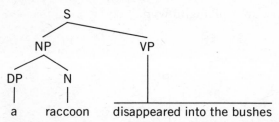

(Note: Sometimes a part of a sentence has not been completely broken down into its subordinate parts, as is the case with the *VP* in the diagram above. We then draw a line over the part to show that everything under the line belongs to the part indicated by the symbol right above the line.)

1. The deer have eaten the roses.

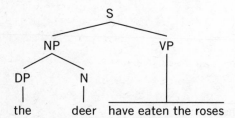

63

2.   All of the players were discouraged.

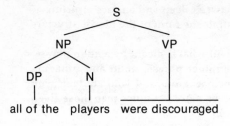

3.   A boat went through the pass.

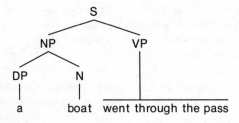

4.   Many people are walking to work.

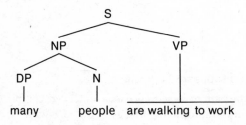

5.   Rain kept us inside.

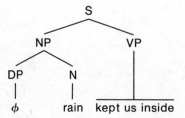

6. We will return soon.

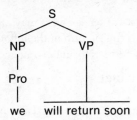

> You may wish to discuss that some verb phrases include noun phrases. Have students try to identify them, but in each case emphasize which is the subject noun phrase of the sentence.

EXERCISE 6—*page L17 (a written assignment)*

> **PURPOSE:** To reinforce the students' understanding of what the auxiliary verb phrase consists of.

A. Using the symbols *MVP, Aux,* and *VP,* express the following statement in the form of a phrase structure rule:

> The verb phrase consists of the auxiliary verb phrase and the main verb phrase.
>
> **VP → MVP + Aux**

B. How would you show the relationship of the *VP,* the *MVP,* and the *Aux* on a diagram?

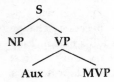

> This exercise should be assigned following a careful discussion of the material in the section "The Verb Phrase." You may want to use additional examples to illustrate the various constituents identified in that section and to provide practice in identifying them.

EXERCISE 7—*page L20 (a written assignment)*

> **PURPOSE:** To reinforce the students' understanding of what the auxiliary verb phrase consists of.

A. Using the symbols *Aux, Tns, M, have + en,* and *be + ing,* express the following statement in the form of a phrase structure rule.

> The auxiliary verb phrase always consists of tense and it may also include the following: a modal; *have* plus the *en* form of the following verb; and the auxiliary *be* plus the *ing* form of the following verb.

Aux → Tns + (M) + (have + en) + (be + ing)

B. How would you indicate the relationship of *Aux, Tns, M, have + en,* and *be + ing* on a branching diagram?

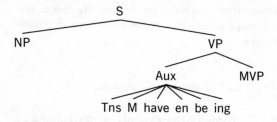

C. Using *Pres* for present tense and *Past* for past tense, write a phrase structure rule showing that *Tns* consists of one or the other.

$$\text{Tns} \rightarrow \begin{Bmatrix} \text{Pres} \\ \text{Past} \end{Bmatrix}$$

> **Prepare for this exercise by carefully discussing the section on "The Auxiliary Verb Phrase." You may need to use additional examples to provide practice in identifying the various parts of the auxiliary verb phrase. Put on the board sentences that include only tense (for example: *Jack wrote a song. The bell rings softly.*). Then ask students to add a form of *be,* making the necessary change in the verb, to add *have,* and finally to add a modal. Take time to discuss each part of the auxiliary and its effect on the rest of the sentence and also discuss where it occurs in relation to the rest of the sentence. (See pages 17 through 25 in the "Teacher's Introduction.")**

EXERCISE 8—*page L22 (a written assignment)*

> **PURPOSE: To provide practice in identifying the verb phrase, the main verb phrase, and the parts of the auxiliary verb phrase.**

Find the verb phrase in each of the following sentences. Then identify the main verb and whatever follows it. Finally, identify

the auxiliary verb phrase and indicate if tense is past or present.
(Remember that to find tense you must look at the first verb in the
verb phrase.) For example:

> The woodpecker was breaking acorns.
>
> VP: was breaking acorns
> MVP: break acorns
> Aux: past tense and be + ing

1. The horns were blowing.

   VP: were blowing
   MVP: blow
   Aux: past tense and be + ing

2. The runner broke all records.

   VP: broke all records
   MVP: break all records
   Aux: past tense

3. Fog has hidden the dock.

   VP: has hidden the dock
   MVP: hide the dock
   Aux: present tense and have + en

4. Some ducks have been swimming in the pond.

   VP: have been swimming in the pond.
   MVP: swim in the pond
   Aux: present tense, have + en, and be + ing

5. George should finish first.

   VP: should finish first
   MVP: finish first
   Aux: past tense and the modal *shall*

6. You should be hearing soon.

   VP: should be hearing soon
   MVP: hear soon
   Aux: past tense, the modal *shall*, and be + ing

> **This exercise should follow a discussion of the material
> that precedes it in the section "Forms of Verbs." It rein-
> forces not only what is covered in that section but in the
> several preceding sections. The exercise will help you
> determine if more practice in identifying the various
> parts of the verb phrase is needed. If it is, provide addi-
> tional sentences for practice. The following could be used:**
> **1. The possum is eating the tomatoes.**
> **2. A cloud has hidden the sun.**
> **3. Many boats will be going through the pass.**

4. A fish jumped from the water.
5. A mouse has been nibbling the cheese.
6. They may have been sleeping.

Things to stress:
1. That in identifying the main verb phrase, the root form of the verb is given.
2. How regular and irregular verbs differ.

EXERCISE 9—*page L24 (a written assignment)*

> PURPOSE: To provide practice in identifying the various parts found in basic sentence structure and in determining their relationship by means of branching diagrams.

Construct branching diagrams for some of the following sentences. Try to choose those that will give you practice in identifying and diagraming sentences with different kinds of parts.

1. The raccoon has been turning on the faucet for the hose.

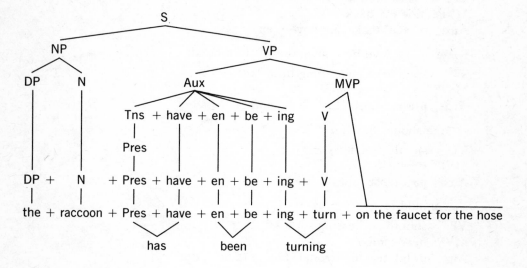

2. Fog rolled through the valley.

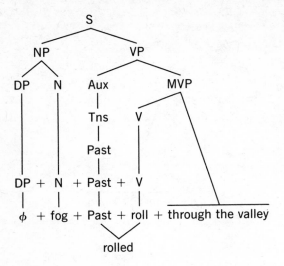

3. One of the cats has found a mouse.

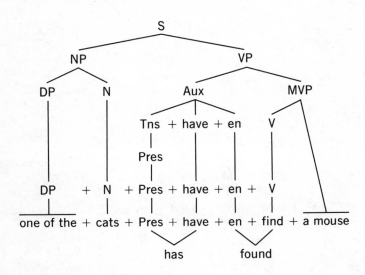

4. They are playing tennis on Monday.

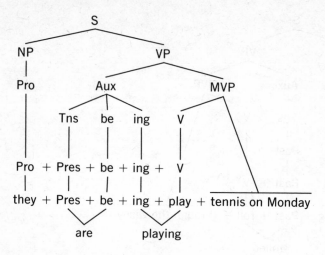

5. George should feed his dog.

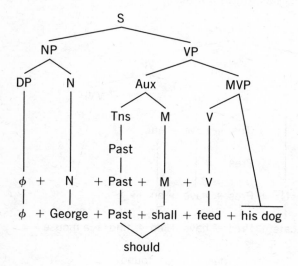

6. A pheasant was running across the road.

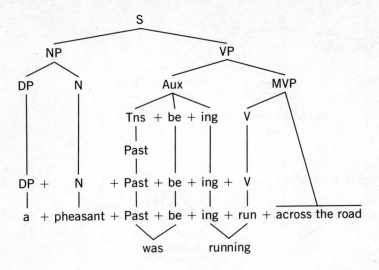

7. Some students have mowed the lawn.

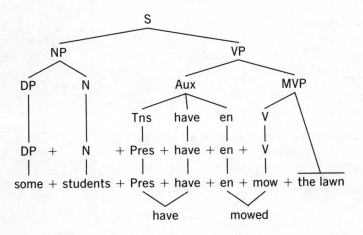

8. You might be receiving a surprise.

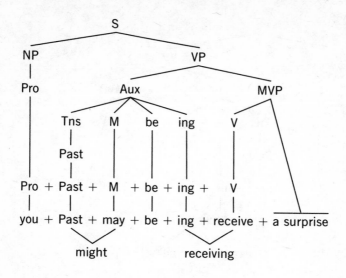

9. Birds have been staying here all winter.

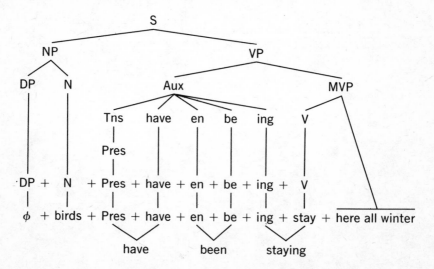

10.   The automobile is a polluter.

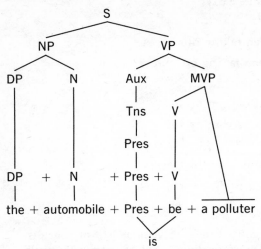

the + automobile + Pres + be + a polluter

Assign the sentences on the basis of the needs of your class, using enough of them to give the students an opportunity to identify a wide variety of sentence parts. The diagrams on page 23 of the student text should be used as a model. One way to cover all the sentences would be to divide the class into small groups and to allot a different sentence to each group. All diagrams could then be put on the board, providing for a general discussion.

EXERCISE 10—*page L26 (a written assignment)*

PURPOSE: To help students identify the part of the auxiliary verb phrase that reverses with the subject *NP* in forming questions.

Write the yes-or-no question related to each of the following statements and identify the part that moves in forming the question. For example:

Mary is taking the bus to school.
Is Mary taking the bus to school?
Is: Pres + be

1.   All the leaves have fallen.

Have all the leaves fallen?
Have: Pres + have

2.   Most of us are going to the game.

Are most of us going to the game?
Are: Pres + be

3. The team will leave early.

   Will the team leave early?
   Will: Pres + will

4. Someone has been taking our paper.

   Has someone been taking our paper?
   Has: Pres + have

5. The boats should be coming in.

   Should the boats be coming in?
   Should: Past + shall

6. The dog was sleeping in the closet.

   Was the dog sleeping in the closet?
   Was: Past + be

> This exercise can be done in class as part of your discussion of "Transformations," but each student should do it by himself. Be sure that students realize that the part that moves in each case includes tense, either *Past* or *Pres.*
>
> *Note:* You may want to use sentences 2, 4, 5, and 6 to review the various forms *be* may take, and sentences 1 and 4 to review the forms of *have.*

Supplementary Material

If students are new to transformational grammar, it will be worthwhile to spend considerable time discussing the following points:

1. That the part that moves in forming each question is the part that includes tense.
2. That the symbol used to refer to the parts that move in forming questions is *Auxт*.
3. That a phrase structure rule identifies parts and shows what they consist of, whereas a transformation describes how one structure can be changed to become another structure.

For further practice, have students write related yes-or-no questions to an additional list of statements. (See pages 33–35 of the "Teacher's Introduction.")

EXERCISE 11—*pages L27–28 (for discussion)*

PURPOSE: To help students perceive how a negative sentence differs from its related affirmative.

A. Study the following pairs of sentences and try to describe the transformation that will change each of the basic sentence structures into the structure of a negative sentence.

1. The deer have eaten the roses. ⟹ The deer have not eaten the roses.
2. The truck was delivering the papers. ⟹ The truck was not delivering the papers.
3. George may win the race. ⟹ George may not win the race.
4. The bus turned over. ⟹ The bus did not turn over.

In the first three pairs of sentences the affirmative can be changed to the negative by adding *not* after the first word in the verb phrase. In the fourth *did* is added as well as *not*.

B. In the fourth pair of sentences in section A, what other change besides the addition of *not* was made in the basic structure? *Did* **was added.**   Can you explain why it was necessary to make this second change?   **Actually, *not* is added after the tense-carrying part of the auxiliary verb phrase, that is, after tense plus a modal, tense plus *have*, tense plus *be*, or simply tense alone if there is no other auxiliary. Adding *not* after tense separates it from a verb and *do* is added for tense to combine with. This is what happened in the fourth pair of sentences.**

> **This exercise should follow a careful discussion of the question transformation on pages 25–27. Students should especially understand the parts that reverse with the subject *NP* and why the *do*-support transformation is necessary for sentences in which tense is the only auxiliary. This exercise should help them see that the same set of parts is involved in the negative transformation, and that *Tdo-support* is necessary in negatives for the same reason that it is necessary in questions. If they understand the question transformation, they should be able to do this exercise with no trouble.**

EXERCISE 12 — *page L28 (a written assignment)*

> **PURPOSE: To help students see how the structure of a passive sentence differs from the structure of its related active.**
>
> The dog broke the chain ⟹ The chain was broken by the dog.
>
> (The above pair of sentences from the student's book are those referred to in this exercise and are repeated here for the teacher's convenience.)

Try to describe the change or transformation that can change the first sentence in the pair above into the second or passive sentence. What was added in the passive sentence?   **A form of the verb *be* and the preposition *by* were added to the passive sentence.**   Were any parts moved? If so, what parts and where?   **The subject *NP* moved to the end of the sentence after *by*, and the direct object *NP* moved to the subject position.**   What form does the verb have in the first sentence?   **Its past form.**   What form does it have in the second?   **Its past participle or *en* form.**

> **You may wish to put the active and passive sentences on the board for the class to focus on during your discussion.**

> **Supplementary Material**

> You may also want to put some other pairs of active and passive sentences on the board to help students see that the change from active to passive is a regular change. (See pages 38–39 of the "Teacher's Introduction.")

> The following pairs are suggested for your use:

> The boys found the money. ⟹ The money was found by the boys.

> The dog has buried the bone. ⟹ The bone has been buried by the dog.

> The divers found the treasure. ⟹ The treasure was found by the divers.

> Shane will write the letter. ⟹ The letter will be written by Shane.

> **Things to discuss:**
> 1. **That the actives and their related passives are synonymous sentences.**
> 2. **And that showing that they derive from the same basic structure explains how we know they are synonymous.**

REVIEW — *page L29 (to be used to fit the needs of the class)*

> **PURPOSE: To serve as a guide for reviewing the essential concepts.**

1. What is meant by linguistic competence? **The total of the internalized knowledge that enables us to use language, that is, to produce sentences and to understand them.**

2. What do we mean when we say that the rules of language are internalized? **That we know the rules and are able to use them unconsciously but are not generally aware of them.**

3. What are some things a speaker's linguistic competence enables him to do? **To produce a sentence at will, including sentences he has never heard or used before; to recognize when sentences are synonymous or closely related; to recognize whether a sentence belongs to the language (that is, whether it has been produced by the rules of the language) or whether it does not; to recognize ambiguity in a sentence; and to understand a great deal that doesn't actually appear in a sentence.**

4. What is meant by the terms *syntax* and *syntactic rules*? *Syntax* **is the structure of a sentence. It includes the order in which the parts occur and the relationships between the parts.** *Syntactic* *rules* **are the rules determining the order in which parts occur, what parts occur together, and what the relationships between the parts are.**

5. Why is the structure of a sentence said to be a hierarchy? **Because the structure consists of parts within parts within parts. The larger parts consist of subordinate parts which in turn consist of still more subordinate parts.**

6. What is the difference between deep and surface structure? **Deep structure is the structure that includes all that we understand a sentence to mean. It includes all of the parts and explicitly describes all of the relationships between the parts. Surface structure is the structure of the sentence that is actually pronounced. It may or may not include everything that is involved in our interpretation of the sentence.**

7. What does a grammar attempt to do? **A grammar attempts to describe the rules that are followed in producing and understanding sentences, that is, to make explicit what we know implicitly.**

8. What are phrase structure rules? **Rules used in identifying the basic ingredients of a sentence and in showing how these ingredients are related.** What kinds of relationships can they describe? **How one part consists of subordinate parts; how parts are combined in a coordinate relationship or an either-or relationship; and which parts are optional as opposed to essential.**

77

9. In a grammar, what is the purpose of phrase structure rules?   **To describe the parts and relationships found in the deep structure.** What is the purpose of transformations?   **To show how the deep structure becomes (or is related to) surface structure.**

> *Note:* **The answers given above are intended as guides for the teacher. It is not expected that students will word their answers in the same way.**
>
> **These review questions cover the essential concepts developed in the chapter, the concepts that underlie transformational grammar. They are probably best handled in class discussion, though you may want students to think about them individually in preparation for talking about them in class.**
>
> **The questions don't, of course, cover any of the specific rules and relationships discussed in the chapter. It is expected that the teacher will see that students have a grasp of these rules before going on to Chapter 2.**

One and One Make One: Compounds

PERFORMANCE OBJECTIVES

The student should be able to

1. Explain what is meant by *recursiveness*.

2. Explain that one way to make sentences longer is to add two basic sentence structures together.

3. Identify compound sentences and sentences with compound parts.

4. In a sentence with compound parts indicate what kind of parts are compound (e.g., *NP*'s, nouns, verbs, *VP*'s, etc.).

5. Indicate what basic sentences are found in the deep structure of compound sentences and sentences with compound parts.

6. Represent the deep structure of compound sentences and sentences with compound parts on diagrams and show how the deep structure becomes surface structure.

7. Identify some coordinating conjunctions.

8. Name the parts that have been deleted from the deep structure of sentences with compound parts.

9. Identify the compound sentences from whose deep structure parts can be deleted.

SYNOPSIS

The chapter consists of the following sections:

1. **The introductory section** (pages L31–33) helps students explore the fact that the rules of language make it possible to produce an infinite number of sentences by using a limited set of rules. Not that a speaker is ever able to produce an infinite number of sentences, even though he has the knowledge of how to do so. A system which can produce an infinite number of products by using a limited set of parts and a limited set of rules is said to have *recursiveness.*

2. **One Way to Make Sentences Longer** (pages L34–37) consists of four exercises through which students discover that two basic sentence structures can be joined together with a coordinating conjunction to form a compound sentence. This knowledge of how to describe each of the basic sentence structures then enables the students also to describe the compound structure.

3. **Sentences with Compound Parts** (pages L37–43) and **Other Kinds of Compounds** (pages L43–47) are concerned with describing sentences with compound parts. Students discover that such sentences are related to and derive from the same deep structure as compound sentences. They also discover something about the conditions under which parts can be deleted from the deep structure. Deletion can occur when speakers are able to replace the deleted parts from clues that are left in the surface structure. In the case of compound sentences, a part can be deleted if each part of the compound includes the same part.

4. **Can You Figure It Out?** (page L48) poses some questions about why there are no restrictions on the parts that can be joined by *and* but definite restrictions on the parts that can be joined by other coordinating conjunctions. For example, we don't say* "John but Bill were here."

5. **Review** (page L48) includes questions about the important concepts of the grammar that are introduced in this chapter.

TEACHING THE CHAPTER

1. Read pages 41–42 in the "Teacher's Introduction" to this guide as background for teaching the chapter.

2. This chapter should present no teaching problems. The subject matter may at first seem very elementary and obvious, for naturally compound sentences can be described as consisting of two basic sentences. The concepts that underlie the description, however, are fundamental to an understanding of transformational grammar. If students grasp them here they will have little trouble with subsequent chapters. It will be worthwhile, therefore, to explore each section with your students and to help them realize that:

a. Basic sentence structures can be joined to form other longer sentences.
b. Sentences which mean the same thing can be described as having the same deep structure. If we know, therefore, what the deep structure of one of them is, we know what the deep structure of the other one is. There are specific steps (transformations) which change the deep structure into different kinds of surface structure.
c. If a sentence includes identical parts, one of the identical parts can be deleted. The presence of the other part will enable speakers to understand what has been deleted.
d. More broadly speaking, anything that can be put back into a sentence, when it doesn't appear in the surface structure, can be deleted.

3. Most of the exercises of the chapter are intended as teaching exercises, that is, they are to be used simply to guide discussion or are to be worked out right in class to demonstrate the particular point being made. Largely inductive, they present data and then ask questions about such data that will lead to conclusions about the structure and derivation of compound sentences and sentences with compound parts.

4. Exercises dealing with the same point form units and should be taught together. For example, Exercises 1 and 2 are discussion exercises to be used in introducing the chapter. Exercises 3–6 form a unit concerning the deep structure of compound sentences. Exercises 7–9 form a unit leading to an explanation of how sentences with compound parts are derived. Exercise 10 is a reinforcement exercise providing practice, and Exercises 11 and 12 are concerned with parts that can be deleted in forming sentences with compound parts. Exercises 13–15 extend the technique of describing sentences with compound subject *NP*'s to sentences with other compound parts.

5. Although it is important to begin to develop the concepts listed in item 2 above, it is also important for students to be able to describe in some detail the deep structure of compound sentences and sentences with compound parts. The use of branching diagrams is particularly useful for helping them identify the kinds of parts that are compound and the kinds that are deleted and for comprehending the kind of deep structure involved. Exercises 5, 6, 8, and 14 call for the construction of diagrams. We have provided detailed diagrams in the key that follows. It is, of course, quite possible to make more general diagrams in which the two main parts are not completely broken down. Use your own judgment about how detailed the diagrams should be. Requiring a detailed diagram at this point may be good practice for your students in analyzing the various parts of a sentence. In illustrating the deep structure of a sentence in which only a part of the *VP* is compound, it is of course necessary to break the *VP* down in order to isolate the part that is compound, *e.g., Mary has been visiting Helen and Doris.* The compound part is a subordinate part of the *MVP*.

KEY TO THE EXERCISES

EXERCISE 1 — *pages L31–32 (for discussion)*

PURPOSE: To stimulate thought and discussion.

A. How could you make the following sentence longer?

The dog barked at the mailman.

Now is there any way you can make your new sentence longer? And can you make that one longer? Could you keep on making new sentences, each one longer than the last?

B. Why don't people make sentences longer and longer and longer? Why isn't there a book, for instance, made up of just one long sentence? What stops us from lengthening a sentence endlessly?

Have students make the sentence longer and longer, and put their suggestions on the board. While answers to the questions will vary, students should come to realize that there is a way to continue to make sentences infinitely long.

EXERCISE 2 — *page L33 (for discussion)*

PURPOSE: To consider how a limited number of rules can produce an infinite number of sentences.

A. Do you think it is possible to learn an infinite number of rules? Give reasons for your answer.   **It is not possible. For one thing, we don't live long enough.**

B. How is it possible to make an infinite number of sentences by using a limited number of rules?

Answers will vary. The best answer, however, is that the rules are such that they can be reused indefinitely.

> Discuss this exercise as part of your general discussion of the introductory section of the chapter.
>   Things to stress:
> 1. We know how to make an infinite number of sentences.
> 2. We aren't, however, actually able to make an infinite number.
> 3. We must know only a limited number of rules.
> 4. Therefore, it must be possible to make an infinite number of sentences with a limited number of rules.
> 5. The ability of a system to use and reuse parts endlessly is called *recursiveness*.

EXERCISE 3 — *page L34 (for discussion)*

PURPOSE: To focus attention on compound sentences.

A. Study the following sentences and try to describe how they are alike in structure.

1. I called Mary and she came home quickly.
2. Linda whispered in class and the teacher scolded her.
3. Hank stepped on the starter and the car shot forward.
4. Helen cooked the dinner and Barbara washed the dishes.
5. The house was shaking and we ran outside.

In each there are two basic sentences joined by *and*.

B. In what way are the sentences in section A different from sentences like the following:

1. The gopher ruined the lawn.
2. The horse cantered gently.
3. I called Mary.
4. She came home quickly.

The sentences in A consist of two basic sentences. Those in B have only one basic sentence each.

C. Could you show the structure of the sentences in section A on a branching diagram of the kind you know how to make? **No.**

Some students may see that it will take two diagrams of the kind they can make to show the structure of each of the sentences in A.

83

> This exercise and Exercises 4, 5, and 6 should be taught
> as a unit.

EXERCISE 4 — *page L35 (for discussion)*

> PURPOSE: To demonstrate that the compound sentences
> in column I consist of two separate basic sentences joined
> by *and*.

A. The sentences you looked at in Exercise 3 are reprinted below in
column I. In column II below is another group of sentences. Pick
out the sentences in column II that you feel are most closely
related to each of the sentences in column I. Then try to describe
how they are related.

I	II
1. I called Mary and she came home quickly. **a, f**	a. I called Mary.
	b. Barbara washed the dishes.
2. Linda whispered in class and the teacher scolded her. **m, i**	c. Helen cooked the dinner.
	d. Hank stepped on the starter.
3. Hank stepped on the starter and the car shot forward. **d, j**	e. The house was shaking.
	f. Mary came home quickly.
	g. John came home quickly.
4. Helen cooked the dinner and Barbara washed the dishes. **c, b**	h. We ran outside.
	i. The teacher scolded Linda.
5. The house was shaking and we ran outside. **e, h**	j. The car shot forward.
	k. The teacher scolded Barbara.
	l. Linda scolded the teacher.
	m. Linda whispered in class.
	n. Mary ran outside.

B. Now try to make a statement about one possible way to make
sentences longer by using parts of sentences over again.

Two sentences can be joined by *and* to make a longer sentence.

EXERCISE 5 — *pages L35–36 (a written assignment to be done in class and then discussed)*

> PURPOSE: To reinforce the concept that a compound
> sentence consists of two separate sentences, neither of
> which is part of the other.

A. Look again at sentence 3 from Exercise 4:

Hank stepped on the starter and the car shot forward.

And look at the two sentences related to it, sentences d and j:

Hank stepped on the starter.
The car shot forward.

Show the basic underlying structure of sentence d and of sentence j by drawing a branching diagram for each one.

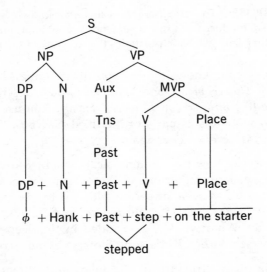

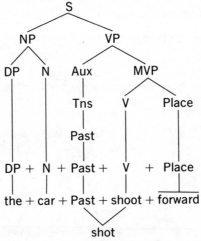

B. What do you think the underlying structure of sentence 3 would include? **Both the structure of sentence d and the structure of sentence j.**

85

C. Does sentence 3 include anything not found in sentences d and j?   **Yes.**   If so, what is it?   **The word *and*.**

EXERCISE 6 — *pages L36–37 (a written assignment to be done in class and then discussed)*

PURPOSE: **To help students realize that knowledge of how to produce one kind of sentence is used in producing another sentence which includes the structure of the first.**

A. How does your knowledge of how to describe sentences like *Birds sing, Flowers bloom,* and so on, help you to describe a related sentence like *Birds sing and flowers bloom*?   **You use both of the first two sentences as parts of the third. So you are, in reality, using the same rules over again.**

B. You have seen how two sentences can be joined to make a sentence longer than either one of them. Can you make *Birds sing and flowers bloom* even longer by adding a third sentence in the same way?   **Yes.** Try it.   **Birds sing and flowers bloom and trees bud.**   What would be included in the deep structure of your new sentence?   **Birds sing. Flowers bloom. Trees bud.**

C. Show the deep structure of the following sentences by constructing a branching diagram for each one.

   1.   Larry sings ballads and Jane plays the guitar.

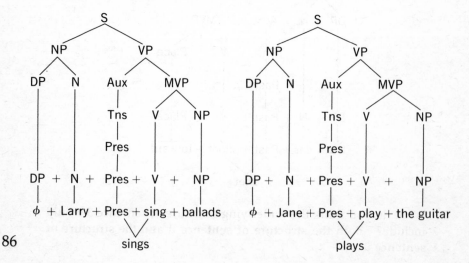

86

2. The mouse ran by and the cat grabbed it.

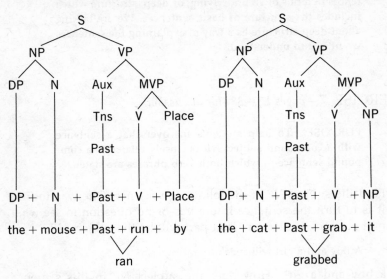

3. The boys ordered hamburgers and the girls ordered hot dogs.

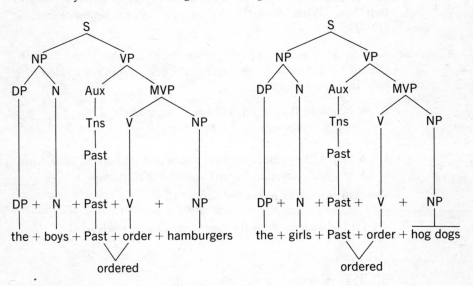

Use the questions as the basis for discussion, but have the students construct the diagrams. Emphasize that in making sentences we use the basic structures of two sentences to make a third sentence.

To show how the two parts are combined in the deep structure, they should be constructed side by side.

Note: Avoid the implication that speakers make sentences out of other sentences, that is, by actually putting sentences together and then changing them. What the

87

grammar claims is that we can describe such longer sentences in terms of an underlying, or deep, structure which includes the structure of basic sentences. We are talking about deep structure as a way of explaining the sentences we utter and understand.

EXERCISE 7 — *pages L37–38 (for discussion)*

PURPOSE: To help students discover that a sentence with a compound subject *NP* is closely related to a compound sentence in which both verb phrases are stated.

A. Find the subject *NP* of the following sentence. One way to find it is to turn the sentence into a yes-or-no question to see what part reverses with *Auxт*. That part will be the subject *NP*.

A boy and a girl will speak tomorrow.

a boy and a girl How does the subject *NP* in this sentence differ from the *NP* in *A boy sat there*? It has two *DP's* and two *N's*. What does the *NP* in the second sentence consist of? *DP + N*

B. Now find the sentence in the following group that is most closely related to *A boy and a girl will speak tomorrow*. Try to describe how the two are related.

1. A boy said that a girl will speak tomorrow.
2. The girl will speak to the boy tomorrow.
3. The girl will speak before the boy.
4. A boy will speak tomorrow and a girl will speak tomorrow.
5. A boy will come and a girl will speak tomorrow.

The two sentences mean the same thing.

Let the students draw the conclusions by themselves.

EXERCISE 8 — *page L38 (for discussion)*

PURPOSE: To help students discover that sentences can be described as having the same deep structure.

A. The following two sentences mean the same thing, but they do not look exactly alike.

1. A boy will speak tomorrow and a girl will speak tomorrow.
2. A boy and a girl will speak tomorrow.

B. Draw a diagram that shows the deep structure of sentence 1.

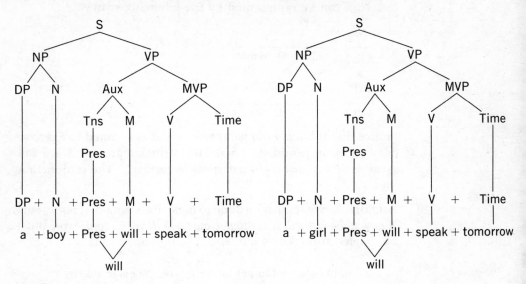

C. Sentence 1 includes all the parts shown on your diagram. What else does it include?   **The conjunction *and*.**

D. If sentence 1 and sentence 2 mean the same thing, what diagram will show the deep structure of sentence 2?   **The diagrams which show the deep structure of sentence 1.**   What is missing from the surface structure of sentence 2 that is found in sentence 1? **The verb phrase *will speak tomorrow* following *the boy*.**

> You could have a volunteer(s) put the diagrams for part B on the board. The two parts should be put side by side so that they can be examined when the surface structure of sentence 2 is being discussed. This will help students see that, though the two sentences look different, their deep structures are the same. It will also help them see what transformation is needed to produce sentence 2 from this deep structure.

EXERCISE 9 — *page L39 (for discussion)*

> **PURPOSE:**   To identify the steps involved in changing the deep structure of a sentence with compound parts to surface structure.

A. Study the diagram you made for Exercise 8 and decide what part of the deep structure is missing from *A boy and a girl will speak tomorrow*.   **The verb phrase of *A boy will speak tomorrow*.**

89

B. The sentences in the deep structure of *A boy and a girl will speak tomorrow* can be represented by the following strings:

NP   VP
a boy + will speak tomorrow

NP   VP
a girl + will speak tomorrow

Notice that these are the sentences you diagrammed in Exercise 8. What must be added to make the strings represent *A boy will speak tomorrow and a girl will speak tomorrow*? **The conjunction *and*.**

C. And finally, what must be done to make the string that represents *A boy and a girl will speak tomorrow*? **Will speak tomorrow must be deleted from *A boy will speak tomorrow*.**

> It would be useful to put the strings on the board side by side. Have students decide on each step. Be sure they see that the strings are the ones found at the bottom of the diagrams they constructed for Exercise 8.
> After having students read the material that follows the exercise, in which the compound transformation is described, discuss it thoroughly with them.

EXERCISE 10 — *page L41 (a written assignment)*

> PURPOSE: To provide practice in identifying the deep structure of sentences with compound parts and in showing how it is changed to surface structure.

A. Write the sentences found in the deep structure of each of the following sentences. Label the subject *NP* and the *VP* in each. Then show how the deep structure sentences become the surface structure. Remember that a double arrow ($\Rightarrow$) is used to show that one string is changed to another string. For example:

The taxis and the buses run at night.

deep structure:

NP   VP   .   NP   VP
the taxis run at night + the buses run at night $\Rightarrow$

adding *and*:

NP   VP   NP   VP
the taxis run at night + and + the buses run at night $\Rightarrow$

deleting:

NP   NP   VP
_____
the taxis + and + the buses run at night

1. The pilot and the stewardess made preparations.

    deep structure:

    NP   VP   NP   VP
    _____
    the pilot made preparations + the stewardess made preparations ⟹

    adding *and*:

    NP   VP
    _____
    the pilot made preparations + and +

    NP   VP
    _____
    the stewardess made preparations ⟹

    deleting:

    NP   NP   VP
    _____
    the pilot + and + the stewardess made preparations

2. Helen and Barbara washed the dishes.

    deep structure:

    NP   VP   NP   VP
    _____
    Helen washed the dishes + Barbara washed the dishes ⟹

    adding *and*:

    NP   VP   NP   VP
    _____
    Helen washed the dishes + and + Barbara washed the dishes ⟹

    deleting:

    NP   NP   VP
    _____
    Helen + and + Barbara washed the dishes

3. The owl and the pussycat went to sea.

    deep structure:

    NP   VP   NP   VP
    _____
    the owl went to sea + the pussycat went to sea ⟹

91

adding *and:*

NP   VP   NP   VP

the owl went to sea + and + the pussycat went to sea $\Rightarrow$

deleting:

NP   NP   VP

the owl + and + the pussycat went to sea

4.   Buttercups and daisies grow in Oregon.

deep structure:

NP   VP   NP   VP

buttercups grow in Oregon + daisies grow in Oregon $\Rightarrow$

adding *and:*

NP   VP   NP   VP

buttercups grow in Oregon + and + daisies grow in Oregon $\Rightarrow$

deleting:

NP   VP   VP

buttercups + and + daisies grow in Oregon

5.   An elephant and a tiger escaped last night.

deep structure:

NP   VP   NP   VP

an elephant escaped last night + a tiger escaped last night $\Rightarrow$

adding *and:*

NP   VP

an elephant escaped last night + and +

NP   VP

a tiger escaped last night $\Rightarrow$

deleting:

NP   NP   VP

an elephant + and + a tiger escaped last night

B. Compare the final surface structure string for each sentence with the deep structure strings and name the kind of part that has been deleted from each deep structure. **The first verb phrase has been deleted in each case.**

Go over the example with your students to make sure they understand how to do the exercise.

EXERCISE 11 — *page L42 (a written assignment to be done in class and then discussed)*

PURPOSE: To help students discover that there are rules for deleting parts: that those parts that are repeated elsewhere in a sentence can be deleted.

A. Rewrite each of the following sentences, deleting whatever parts you think could be left out.

1. Bud will work in the beanfields and Joe will work in the beanfields.
    Bud and Joe will work in the beanfields.

2. Trains go to the city and planes go to the city.
    Trains and planes go to the city.

3. Cars went by all night and trucks went by all night.
    Cars and trucks went by all night.

4. The man came from California and the woman came from California.
    The man and the woman came from California.

5. The grass turned green overnight and the leaves turned green overnight.
    The grass and the leaves turned green overnight.

B. How are your rewritten sentences related to the original sentences?
    They have the same deep structure as the original sentences.

C. Can you tell when a sentence has had parts deleted from the deep structure?   **Yes, when we understand parts that don't actually appear in the surface structure, we know that they have been deleted from the deep structure.**   Do you know what parts have been deleted?   **Yes, the parts that we understand without their actually appearing in the surface structure.**   In the sentence *The ring and the necklace will be in the safe,* for instance, what was in the deep structure that doesn't appear in the sentence you see here?   **The verb phrase *will be in the safe* following *the ring*.**   How do you know?   **We understand it even though it does not appear. We understand it because it appears elsewhere in the sentence.**

Before discussing the exercise, have students do section A and think about sections B and C. Try to help them conclude that what is left out is related to something that is left in and that the sentences with parts deleted have the same meaning as the sentences with the parts left in. Because we understand one, we understand the other.

EXERCISE 12 — *pages L42–43 (for class discussion)*

PURPOSE: To help students see that nothing can be deleted in compound sentences that do not have identical parts.

A. Decide if parts could be deleted from any of the following sentences without changing their meaning, and explain why you think so.

1. The cat sat on the fence and the dog barked at her.
2. Randy took a long hike and Pete took a long hike.
3. The child held still and the chipmunk ate out of her hand.
4. Rain is falling and the wind is blowing.
5. A siren sounded and the cars stopped.
6. Ducks fly south early and geese fly south early.
7. The door blew open and the rain came in.

In sentences 2 and 6, parts can be deleted from the deep structure because parts of these compound sentences are identical. Such sentences will then become *Randy and Pete took a long hike* and *Ducks and geese fly south early.*

B. Explain when it is possible to delete parts of the deep structure of a sentence and when it isn't.   A part of the deep structure of a compound sentence can be deleted if that part is found someplace else in the sentence.

Students should be led to see that if anything were left out of sentences 1, 3, 4, 5, and 7, there would be no clue to our understanding of what had been left out. Students should also conclude that only those parts can be deleted that are repeated in some way in what remains in the surface structure. In other words, only those parts can be deleted that can be replaced by a speaker of English.

EXERCISE 13 — *pages L43–44 (for discussion)*

PURPOSE: To demonstrate that compound sentences with identical subject *NP's* can have one *NP* deleted.

A. Which of the following sentences is most closely related to *The wind whistled and sang*? How are the sentences related?

1. The wind whistled and the bird sang.
2. The wind whistled around the house.
3. **The wind whistled and the wind sang.**
4. The wind sang and the boy whistled.

They mean the same thing.

B. What basic sentences are in the deep structure of the sentence you picked out in section A? *The wind whistled / The wind sang.*

C. What is in the deep structure of *The wind whistled and sang*? *The wind whistled / The wind sang.* How do we know? **We understand that** *the wind* **is the subject of** *sang* **as well as of** *whistled.*

D. What is missing from the surface structure of *The wind whistled and sang* that was in the deep structure? *The wind* before *sang.* What part of the sentence is it? **The subject** *NP.* What kind of part is *whistled*? **A verb phrase. (In this case the verb phrase includes only tense and the verb.)** What kind of part is *sang*? **A verb phrase.**

> **All of the students should be involved in drawing the conclusions that in these sentences the subject *NP*'s are identical and that therefore one can be deleted, leaving a compound verb phrase. Like the sentences in the previous exercises, the deletion occurs because the meaning doesn't change and because the part deleted is repeated in the part that remains.**

EXERCISE 14 — *page L45 (a written assignment)*

> **PURPOSE: To provide practice in identifying the deep structure of sentences with compound parts as well as in showing how the deep structure is related to the surface structure.**

A. Write the sentences found in the deep structure of each of the following. Then show how the deep structure was changed to become the surface structure. Tell what kind of a sentence part is involved in each change. (If you have trouble identifying the parts, construct branching diagrams of the deep structure sentences.) For example:

Clara and Heidi climbed the mountain.

95

deep structure sentences:

Clara climbed the mountain ⎱ ⟹
Heidi climbed the mountain ⎰

adding *and*:

Clara climbed the mountain and Heidi climbed the mountain ⟹

deleting a VP:

Clara and Heidi climbed the mountain.

1. Sarah washed and dried the dishes.

   Sarah washed the dishes ⎱ ⟹
   Sarah dried the dishes ⎰

   Sarah washed the dishes and Sarah dried the dishes ⟹
   Sarah washed and dried the dishes

   The repeated *NP* has been deleted.

2. The Scouts raised and lowered the flag.

   The Scouts raised the flag ⎱ ⟹
   The Scouts lowered the flag ⎰

   The Scouts raised the flag and the Scouts lowered the flag ⟹
   The Scouts raised and lowered the flag

   The repeated *NP* has been deleted.

3. The plane crashed and burned in the field.

   The plane crashed in the field (or simply The plane crashed) ⎱ ⟹
   The plane burned in the field ⎰

   The plane crashed (in the field) and the plane burned
   in the field ⟹
   The plane crashed and burned in the field

   The repeated *NP* and the first occurrence of the place ad-
   verbial have been deleted, if we assume that the deep struc-
   ture included the place adverbial in both basic sentences.

4. Flowers wither and die in the desert.

   Flowers wither in the desert ⎱ ⟹
   Flowers die in the desert ⎰

   Flowers wither in the desert and flowers die in the desert ⟹
   Flowers wither and die in the desert

   The second *NP* and the first place adverbial have been
   deleted.

B. Show the deep structure of each of the following sentences by
   constructing a branching diagram. (Be sure to include the symbol
   string as well as the sentence string in each diagram.) Then show

how the deep structure has been changed to the surface structure.
What kinds of sentence parts have been deleted?

1. The tourist has caught and weighed the salmon.

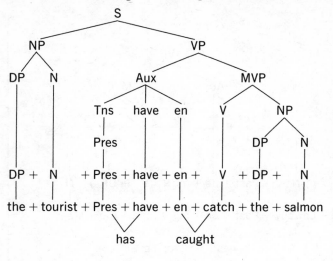

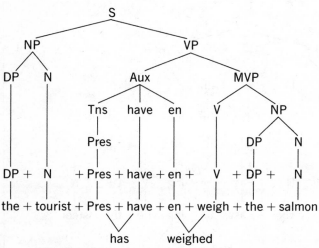

adding *and:*

> the tourist has caught the salmon + and +
> the tourist has weighed the salmon ⟹

deleting:

> the tourist has caught and weighed the salmon

**The sentence parts that have been deleted are: the second
subject *NP*, the *NP* following the verb in the first basic sentence structure; and *has (tense + have)* in the second basic**   97

sentence. (Notice that the *en* part of *have + en* remains. It is part of *caught*.)

2. The cowboy was roping and tying the steer.

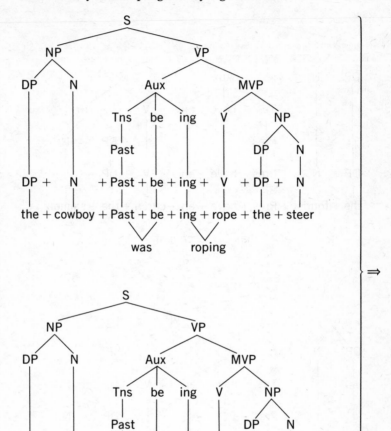

adding *and*:

> the cowboy was roping the steer + and +
> the cowboy was tying the steer

deleting:

> the cowboy was roping and tying the steer

The sentence parts deleted are: the second subject *NP*, the *NP* following the first verb; and *was (tense + be)* in the sec-

ond basic sentence. (Notice that the *ing* part *of be + ing* remains in the sentence as part of *tying*.)

After the students, individually, have completed the exercise, it should be discussed. In section A, sentence 3, be sure that they see that the compound part is only the verb (with tense included). Diagrams may be needed in section A to help them identify exactly what has been deleted.

The easiest way to identify the parts that are deleted in section B would be to have volunteers put the diagrams on the board. Such diagrams should be placed side by side so that it would be easy to add *and* between them. Then, simply by reading through the string, students could circle the parts that are deleted, together with the symbols that indicate what parts they are.

EXERCISE 15—*pages L45–46 (a written assignment)*

PURPOSE: To provide practice in identifying the deep structure of sentences with compound parts and in identifying the parts that are compound and the parts that have been deleted.

A. Write the sentences found in the deep structure of each of the following. Then cross out the parts that are deleted when the deep structure is changed to surface structure. Name the kind of sentence part that is compound in the surface structure. For example:

The plane shook and bounced above the river.
The plane shook ~~above the~~ river.
~~The plane~~ bounced above the river.
compound part: verb

1. Bozo ran and kicked the ball.

    Bozo ran.
    ~~Bozo~~ kicked the ball.
    compound part: verb phrase

2. John and Bob painted the Blarney stone.

    John ~~painted the Blarney stone.~~
    Bob painted the Blarney stone.
    compound part: subject NP

3. The swallows dip and soar over the field.

    The swallows dip ~~over the field~~.
    ~~The swallows~~ soar over the field.
    compound part: verb

99

4. David threw the rock and hit Goliath.

    David threw the rock.
    ~~David~~ hit Goliath.
    compound part: verb

5. Bridget stuffed and roasted a turkey.

    Bridget stuffed a ~~turkey.~~
    ~~Bridget~~ roasted a turkey.
    compound part: verb

6. Mrs. Plushbottom poured coffee and tea.

    Mrs. Plushbottom poured coffee.
    ~~Mrs. Plushbottom poured~~ tea.
    compound part: NP following verb

7. Our grandparents lived peacefully and happily.

    Our grandparents lived peacefully.
    ~~Our grandparents lived~~ happily.
    compound part: manner adverbial

8. We saw them yesterday and the day before.

    We saw them yesterday.
    ~~We saw them~~ the day before.
    compound part: time adverbial

9. Peter became violent and abusive.

    Peter became violent.
    ~~Peter became~~ abusive.
    compound part: adjective following verb

B. In all of the sentences above, are the compound parts the same
kind of sentence part or are they different? **They are the
same kind.**

This exercise should help students see that almost any
kind of sentence part can be compound. It would be useful
to have students name the parts that have been deleted
as well as the parts that are compound in the surface structure. In sentences 1 and 4, for instance, only the subject
NP has been deleted. In 2, an entire verb phrase has been
deleted. In 3, a subject *NP* and a place adverbial have been
deleted, leaving a compound verb (with tense). In 5, one
of the subject *NP*'s and an *NP* following the verb have
been deleted. In 6, 7, 8, and 9, a subject *NP*, *Aux*, and the
verb have been deleted, leaving what follows the verb.

EXERCISE 16—*page L46 (an assignment to be written, then discussed)*

> **PURPOSE:** To reinforce the concept that identical parts can be deleted from the deep structure of compound sentences, leaving a sentence with compound parts.

Write a statement in which you explain how a deep structure that consists of two sentences with some identical parts can become a surface structure with compound parts joined by *and*.

When a deep structure consisting of two coordinate S's includes some of the same parts in each of the S's, one of the identical parts can be deleted, leaving a sentence with a compound part joined by *and*.

> **Requiring students to describe what they have been doing should reinforce their understanding and should indicate to you whether or not more work is needed. Their wording will not be the same as the suggested answer above, but it should include the same information. Be sure to discuss the section that follows the exercise in the student text. Have students look at the symbolic statements of the transformations and be certain that they understand what they mean.**

EXERCISE 17—*page L47 (a written assignment)*

> **PURPOSE:** To demonstrate that when sentences with compound parts are derived from two S's in the deep structure, it is sometimes necessary to make some changes in the surface structure to bring about agreement between the parts.

What sentences are found in the deep structure of each of the following? What changes must take place for the deep structure to become surface structure? (Note especially whether the nouns are singular or plural, and note also the form of the part of the word that shows tense.)

1.   Mutt and Jeff are characters in a comic strip.

  Mutt is a comic strip character.
  Jeff is a comic strip character.

  The sentences are joined by *and*; then the verb phrase of the first is deleted. When this happens, the singular verb *is* must be changed to the plural *are* since the common subject is considered plural. For the same reason, *character* must become *characters*.

101

2. Jack and Jill have fallen down.

   Jack has fallen down.
   Jill has fallen down.

   The sentences are joined by *and;* then the verb phrase of the first is deleted. Again the singular verb *has* must be changed to the plural verb *have* since the compound subject is plural.

3. The stars and the moon were shining in the sky.

   The stars were shining in the sky.
   The moon was shining in the sky.

   The sentences are joined by *and;* then the first verb phrase is deleted. The singular verb *was* in the part that is left is changed to *were* because the subject is now compound.

4. The calico cat and the gingham dog sit on the table.

   The calico cat sits on the table.
   The gingham dog sits on the table.

   The sentences are joined by *and;* then the first verb phrase is deleted. The verb *sits* must be changed to *sit* since the subject is compound in the surface structure.

   Ask students to do the exercise and to write their conclusions individually. Then discuss it with them. The kinds of changes needed to make the verb phrase agree with the plural subject in each of the sentences and to change *character* to *characters* in the first sentence are transformations that occur in the surface structure to achieve agreement. Such transformations occur last in the derivation of the sentences.

REVIEW — *page L48 (the basis of a review discussion)*

   PURPOSE: To guide your discussion of the important concepts of the chapter.

1. Is there a limit to the number of sentences that we know how to make? **No.**

2. Is there a limit to the number of rules speakers use in making sentences? **Yes.**

3. How do we create new sentences? **By using the rules we already know.**

4. What is one way to make a sentence longer? **By adding another sentence connected to the first with *and.***

5. What is the difference between deep and surface structure? **Deep structure contains everything we understand in a sentence; surface structure contains only what we hear or speak.**

6. When two sentences mean the same thing but look different, what do we suspect about their deep structure? **That their deep structure is the same.**

7. Explain how compound parts get into sentences? **In the deep structure they are actually found in separate sentences, parts of which are deleted, leaving the compound part.**

> The questions in this review exercise deal with fundamental concepts of the grammar which have been demonstrated in the chapter. They do not cover any of the specific material about compound sentences and compound parts, nor about how such sentences are derived from their deep structures. Make certain that your students have achieved an understanding of these techniques before leaving the chapter. (See the statement of objectives on pages 79–80 of this guide.)

Chapter 3

Sentences Within Sentences: Adjectives

PERFORMANCE OBJECTIVES

The students should be able to

1. Explain the relationship between a determiner phrase and the noun with which it appears.

2. Explain how determiners differ from and how they are like prenominal adjectives.

3. Identify the deep structure of sentences with prenominal adjectives and represent that deep structure either with a sentence string or on a branching diagram.

4. Explain how the deep structure of a sentence with a prenominal adjective must be changed to become surface structure.

5. Explain how the deep structure of a sentence with a prenominal adjective differs from the deep structure of a compound sentence or a sentence with compound parts.

SYNOPSIS

The chapter consists of the following sections:

1. **The introductory section** (pages L51–52) reminds students of the concepts developed in the previous chapter: how com-

pound sentences and sentences with compound parts are formed by combining basic sentences; the difference between a basic sentence and one that is not basic (the surface structure of a basic sentence is essentially like the deep structure).

2. **Another Look at Determiners** (pages L52–55) reviews various kinds of determiner phrases and their relationship to the noun with which they occur. It also introduces prenominal adjectives and distinguishes them from regular determiners (adjectives occur after certain verbs, such as *be*, as well as before nouns; determiners always occur with nouns in noun phrases).

3. **Other Ways to Join Sentences** (pages L55–58) leads students to recognize that sentences with prenominal adjectives actually derive from two basic sentences. The relationship between the two can be represented by showing that the sentence with the adjective is embedded within the other sentence just before the noun that the adjective modifies.

4. **Adjectives Before Nouns** (pages L58–60) discusses how prenominal adjectives differ from and how they are like determiners.

5. **Adding Another S to the Diagram** (pages L61–63) is concerned with how the deep structure of a sentence with a prenominal adjective can be represented on a branching diagram, and with what changes must be made in such a deep structure to derive the sentence with the adjective before the noun (everything but the adjective is deleted from the embedded sentence).

6. **What Parts Can be Deleted** (pages L63–65) reiterates that parts can be deleted if speakers of the language can understand from the surface structure what the deleted parts are, and emphasizes that knowledge of the structure of basic sentences enables us to describe the deep structure of sentences in which two basic sentences have been combined. Finally, it distinguishes between the kind of deep structures that underlie sentences with compound parts and those that underlie sentences with prenominal adjectives, that is, between sentences in which two basic sentences have been combined coordinately and those in which one sentence has been embedded within another.

7. **Review** (page L65) again poses questions that relate to the important concepts of the chapter rather than to specific details in the description and derivation of sentences with prenominal adjectives. The questions emphasize the difference between deep and surface structure, the purpose of phrase structure rules and transformations, the difference between adjectives and determiners, and the two ways sentences can be combined.

TEACHING THE CHAPTER

1. This should be one of the most challenging chapters in this text to teach. It is certainly one of the most important, because it deals with sentences in which the deep structure is quite different from the surface structure and introduces the notion of sentences being subordinate to other sentences. A thorough understanding of these concepts is important for understanding subsequent chapters.

2. As preparation for teaching the chapter, read again pages 42–45 in the "Teacher's Introduction," and use these pages for reference when needed. Also work through the chapter in the student text with the key to the exercises in hand.

3. The chapter is primarily inductive in nature. Many of the exercises, usually intended to be used right in class as part of the discussion, supply data for analysis as well as questions to guide this analysis and to help students discover the deep structure of sentences with prenominal adjectives. There are also follow-up exercises for consolidation, reinforcement, and practice.

4. The exercises should be considered integral parts of the sections in which they occur. Often the particular concepts developed in the exercises are summarized and reinforced by the explanation that follows.

5. In dealing with sentences in which the deep structure differs from the surface structure—especially those sentences in which one basic structure is embedded in another—you will find the chalkboard or overhead projector a very useful aid. If the sentence parts can be illustrated on a diagram or sentence string, it is easier usually to visualize the relationship of such parts and also to identify what must be done to change the deep structure to surface structure.

KEY TO THE EXERCISES

EXERCISE 1—*page L53 (a class exercise)*

PURPOSE: To demonstrate that determiners are related to questions like *Which? How much?* and *How many?*

A. Match each sentence in column I with the question most closely related to it in column II.

I		II
1. That boy broke the window.	e	a. How many trees are dying?

2. Some of the trees are dying.   a
3. He found three books.   d
4. Lots of popcorn is needed.   b
5. These books will help.   c

b. How much popcorn is needed?
c. Which books will help?
d. How many books did he find?
e. Which boy broke the window?

B. List the words in column II that ask questions. **How many? How much? Which? How many? Which?** To what part of the sentences in column I are these question words related? **The determiner phrases.**

C. What do determiners like those in the sentences of column I tell about the noun in the noun phrase? **They identify or limit the nouns which follow them. They tell** *which* **or** *how much* **or** *how many* **about the nouns.**

> Use the questions in sections B and C to discuss the function of determiners. Determiners like *the, a, some,* and φ have a special relationship to the nouns they accompany, though they aren't so obviously related to *which, how much,* or *how many.* They indicate whether a noun is definite or indefinite and are also related to whether the noun is count or mass.

EXERCISE 2 — *page L54 (for discussion)*

> PURPOSE: To demonstrate that other words besides determiners can appear in the noun phrase just before the noun.

A. Compare the sentences in each of the following pairs.

1. The dragon puffed smoke.
   The green dragon puffed smoke.
2. The cat hissed.
   The angry cat hissed.
3. The trout fought fiercely.
   The large trout fought fiercely.
4. The man runs a store.
   The funny man runs a store.
5. The crackers taste strange.
   The stale crackers taste strange.

B. How do the two sentences in each pair differ? **The second sen-**   107 tence gives additional information. It includes a word not found in the first sentence.

C. List the word in the second sentence of each pair that isn't found in the first sentence, and describe its position in the second sentence. *Green, angry, large, funny,* and *stale* **are found between a determiner and a noun.**

D. What kind of sentence part do we ordinarily expect to find in this position? **We usually find determiners occurring just before nouns.**

E. Do the words you listed in section C always appear before nouns? **No.** Can these words be found someplace else in a sentence? If so, give some examples. **These words can also appear after verbs.** *The man is funny. The water was green.* Can you remember what such words are called? **Such words are called adjectives.**

> **Remind students that adjectives can be identified by their ability to appear both after verbs such as *be* and before nouns.**

EXERCISE 3—*page L55 (a class exercise)*

> **PURPOSE:** **To help students realize that sentences with prenominal adjectives are related to sentences in which the adjective appears after the verb *be*.**

A. For each sentence in column I, pick out the two sentences in column II that you feel are most closely related to it.

I		II
1. The purple lilac needs water.	**b, g**	a. The geese were wild.
2. The little boy ran across the street.	**e, h**	b. The lilac needs water.
3. Three of the angry children were throwing rocks.	**d, j**	c. A pig was wallowing in the mud.
4. A fat pig was wallowing in the mud.	**c, i**	d. Three of the children were throwing rocks.
5. The wild geese flew overhead.	**a, f**	e. The boy was little.
		f. The geese flew overhead.
		g. The lilac is purple.
		h. The boy ran across the street.
		i. A pig was fat.
		j. The children were angry.

B. Try to explain how the sentences you picked out in column II are related to the sentences in column I.   **Each sentence in column I contains two of the sentences in column II. In other words, both of the related sentences in column II would be found in the deep structure of the column I sentences.**

> Section A should probably be done individually and section B used as a guide to discussion. Reinforced in the following two exercises will be the concept that underlying a prenominal adjective is a sentence in which the adjective follows the verb *be*. The paragraph following the exercise also reiterates this fact.

EXERCISE 4 — *page L57 (a written assignment)*

> PURPOSE: To reinforce the fact that in sentences with prenominal adjectives we really understand a sentence with an adjective following the verb *be* and therefore assume that such a sentence exists in the deep structure.

A. Now look more closely at sentence 1 of Exercise 3 and at the two sentences that are closely related to it.

    1. The purple lilac needs water.
      b. The lilac needs water.
      g. The lilac is purple.

Show the deep structure of sentences b and g by drawing a branching diagram of each.

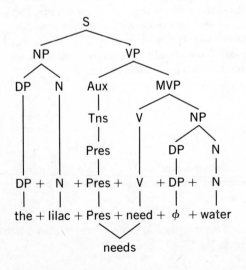

109

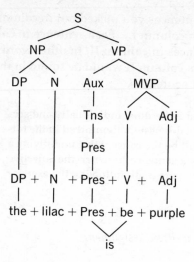

B. Answer these questions.

1. In sentence g, what relationship does *purple* have to *lilac*? **Purple tells something about *lilac*. Together, *the* and *purple* tell which *lilac*.**

2. In sentence 1, what relationship does *purple* have to *lilac*? **Together with *the*, it tells which *lilac*.**

3. How many basic sentence structures do you find in the deep structure of *The purple lilac needs water*? **Two.** What are they? *The lilac needs water* **and** *The lilac is purple.*

You may wish to have a student or students put the two diagrams on the board for discussion.

In discussing the questions in section B, students should realize that the relationship between *purple* and *lilac* is the same in the two sentences. Whether they can explain the relationship is not as important as realizing that it is the same. They should also realize that in sentence 1 they understand both sentences b and g.

EXERCISE 5 — *page L57 (a class exercise)*

PURPOSE: To reinforce that in *The purple lilac needs water* the structure of one sentence has become part of another.

A. Look once more at *The purple lilac needs water* and at the two sentences related to it.

110

   b.   The lilac needs water.
   g.   The lilac is purple.

In *The purple lilac needs water,* has *The lilac is purple* been added onto *The lilac needs water*?   **No.**

B.   Write the sentence *The purple lilac needs water.*

   1.   Underline the part of sentence b you find in it.   **All of sentence b should be underlined:** *The purple lilac needs water.*

   2.   Put two lines under the part of *The purple lilac needs water* that is found in sentence g but not in sentence b.   *The purple lilac needs water.*

   3.   What parts of *The purple lilac needs water* are found in both sentence b and sentence g?   *The* **and** *lilac.*

   4.   Has b become a part of g? Or has g become a part of b?   **Sentence g has become part of sentence b.**

   Students should have time to think about and to do this exercise individually before it is discussed. It is important to contrast the kind of relationship found between the two sentences here and the kind found in compound sentences.

   Students should look at the paragraphs that follow the exercise to see how one sentence can be written inside of another. They should, of course, understand that *the +* *the lilac is purple + lilac needs water* is only a way of representing the relationship that we understand. Ask the class to think about what must be done to this representation to change it into the grammatical sentence *The purple lilac needs water.*

EXERCISE 6 — *page L58 (a written assignment)*

   PURPOSE: To provide practice in identifying the deep structure underlying prenominal adjectives.

Decide what sentences are found in the deep structure of each of the following. Write down each pair of deep structure sentences in a string that shows how they are related. Underline any parts that have been deleted in the surface structure. For example:

   The little bird is eating seed.

   the + the bird is little + bird is eating seed

111

1. The good weather helps the farmer.
   the + the weather is good + weather helps the farmer

2. The crafty fox faded into the bushes.
   the + the fox was crafty + fox faded into the bushes

3. The yellow light will be satisfactory.
   the + the light is yellow + light will be satisfactory

4. The old king led the army.
   the + the king was old + king led the army

5. George sold a valuable possession.
   George sold a + a possession was valuable + possession

> Putting an additional example on the board may help students understand what they are to do. For example:
>
> The dry leaves rustled underfoot.
>
> **the + the leaves were dry + leaves rustled underfoot**
>
> Be sure to comment on the adjective that occurs before the word *possession* in sentence 5. Students should understand that an adjective can occur before a noun in any noun phrase no matter where it occurs in a sentence.

EXERCISE *7 — page L59 (a guide for discussion)*

> PURPOSE: **To identify the difference between prenominal adjectives and the determiners that occur before nouns.**

A. Determiners have a special relationship to the nouns they occur with. What are some of the questions determiners answer about nouns?   **Which? How much? How many?**

B. Which of the following questions is answered by *purple* in *The purple lilac needs water*?

   Where is the lilac?
   Who will water the lilac?
   Which lilac needs water?

   Can you make a general statement about how adjectives are related to the nouns that follow them?   **They answer the question *Which?* or *How much?* or *How many?* about the nouns.**

C. In what two positions can adjectives occur?   **Either before nouns or after verbs.**

112 D. Think of five sentences in which adjectives come before nouns

and write them down. Now write five related sentences in which the same adjectives follow the verb.

Answers will vary. The following are possibilities if you need them for illustration: *The cranky dog snarled at the postman. The dog was cranky. A brilliant pheasant flew out of the grass. A pheasant was brilliant. The bird uttered a shrill cry. A cry was shrill.*

> In discussing the questions, emphasize that determiners tell *which* about the nouns they occur with and so do prenominal adjectives. The paragraph that follows the exercise reiterates the concept that prenominal adjectives derive from a sentence embedded in the determiner phrase of another sentence.

EXERCISE 8 — *page L60 (a class exercise)*

> **PURPOSE:** To help students summarize what they have learned about the deep structure of prenominal adjectives by putting it in the form of a phrase structure rule.

Using the symbol *Det* to stand for determiner and *S* to stand for a basic sentence structure, write a phrase structure rule to show that *DP*'s consist of determiners but may also include other basic *S*'s. Remember that all *DP*'s must contain determiners but do not necessarily contain other *S*'s. How can you show these facts in your rule? **DP → Det + (S)**

> Before assigning this exercise for individual work, you may wish to review what is involved in writing a phrase structure rule: the arrow means "consists of"; parentheses show an optional item. Remind students that phrase structure rules describe the deep structure, that is, they describe what we understand in a sentence.

EXERCISE 9 — *page L62 (a class exercise)*

> **PURPOSE:** To show students how the deep structure of a sentence with a prenominal adjective can be represented on a branching diagram.

The diagram of the deep structure of *The lilac needs water* looks like this:

113

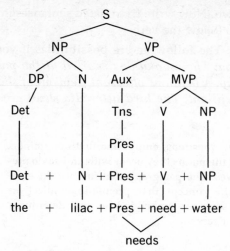

Change this diagram to make it represent the deep structure of *The purple lilac needs water*. First decide where the diagram of the deep structure of *the lilac is purple* should fit into this diagram. Then copy this diagram and include the diagram of *the lilac is purple*. Remember that an *S* can be part of a *DP* in another *S*.

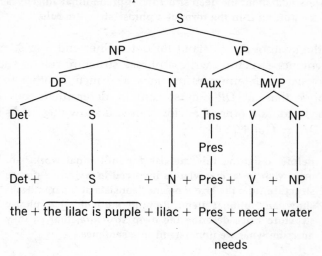

The section preceding the exercise should be assigned and discussed before students do the exercise. They should understand that in a compound sentence two S's are joined together but that neither becomes part of the other. This is one kind of relationship between sentences which are combined. In the other kind of relationship, one deep structure sentence becomes part of another.

Students, individually or perhaps in groups, should attempt to construct the diagram, after which someone should then put it on the board. Two colors of chalk to represent the two S's would emphasize the structure and the relationship of the two. It should be seen by the class that the diagram, as well as the string at the bottom, contains all of the parts of both S's, but that it does not represent a grammatical sentence. You may wish to ask the students what needs to be done to make it represent a grammatical sentence. Then have them look at the transformation that follows the exercise.

Note: It is not necessary to break down the verb phrase in the dominant sentence nor the embedded S unless you feel your students need the practice.

EXERCISE 10 — *pages L63–64 (a written assignment)*

PURPOSE: To provide practice in identifying the deep structure of sentences with prenominal adjectives and in showing how the deep structure can be changed to represent the surface structure.

A. List the two sentences found in the deep structure of each of the following sentences. Underline the one that is embedded in the deep structure. In the dominant sentence, make an X at the point where the embedding occurs. For example:

The conceited man won the fight.

the X man won the fight
the man is conceited

1. He found a poisonous bat.

    He found a X bat.
    A bat was poisonous.

2. The red dress cost ten dollars.

    The X dress cost ten dollars.
    The dress was red.

3. He threw the wastebasket at the open door.

    He threw the wastebasket at the X door.
    The door was open.

4. Indelible ink ran on the rug.

    X Ink ran on the rug.
    Ink was indelible.

5. Many tall trees grow by the river.

    Many X trees grow by the river.
    The trees are tall.

115

6. The two gray chipmunks begged for food.

   The two ✕ chipmunks begged for food.
   The chipmunks were gray.

7. The teacher punished the lazy pupils.

   The teacher punished the ✕ pupils.
   The pupils were lazy.

8. The early snow stopped the harvest.

   The ✕ snow stopped the harvest.
   The snow was early.

9. The dormant volcano was smoking.

   The ✕ volcano was smoking.
   The volcano was dormant.

10. You will be taking an easy course.

    You will be taking a ✕ course.
    A course is easy.

B. Make deep structure diagrams of sentences 2 and 4 and show what transformations change the deep structure to the surface structure. (Study the diagram you were asked to make for Exercise 9 and the transformation that follows the exercise if you have trouble.)

   2. The red dress cost ten dollars.

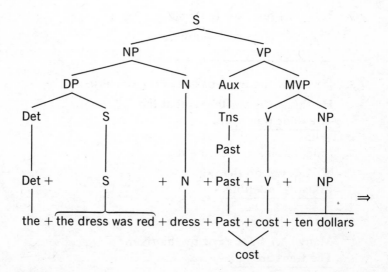

```
Det + Adj +   N
 |     |      |
the + red + dress . . .
```

Note: In this diagram and the one for sentence 4, the *VP* in the embedded sentence need not be broken down. Instead, it can be brought down into the string and a line drawn over *cost ten dollars* and *run on the rug*. Only the part of the transformed string that is changed has been shown. The ellipsis represents the rest.

4. Indelible ink ran on the rug.

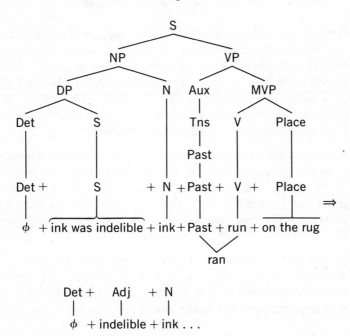

```
Det +   Adj   + N
 |       |      |
 φ   + indelible + ink . . .
```

Discuss the example with your students so that they will understand what they are to do in section A, and perhaps you will also wish to use the diagram constructed for Exercise 9 as a model for the exercises in section B. Caution the students to leave plenty of space for the embedded sentences as they construct their diagrams. First they will need to decide what part of the diagram will include the embedded sentence. You may want to point out that in sentence 4 the place adverbial consists of a preposition plus a noun phrase which can be treated as a unit.

**   *Note:* In sentence 4 some students may suggest that the embedded sentence is *The ink was indelible.* Although**

we usually assume the noun phrase in the embedded sentence is identical to the noun phrase in the dominant sentence, don't make an issue of it at this point. In sentence 2 accept either *The chipmunks* or *The two chipmunks* in the embedded sentence.

EXERCISE 11 — *pages L64–65 (the basis of discussion)*

PURPOSE: To help students draw some conclusions from what has been discussed in the chapter.

A. How does your knowledge of how to describe a sentence like *The lilac needs water* and a sentence like *The lilac is purple* help you describe a sentence like *The purple lilac needs water*? **The deep structure of *The purple lilac needs water* includes both *The lilac needs water* and *The lilac is purple*. Therefore, the same rules can be used to describe it as are used to describe the two basic sentences found in its deep structure.**

B. How does the deep structure of *The purple lilac needs water* differ from the deep structure of *The walrus and the carpenter walked on the beach*? **The second sentence is made from two basic sentences joined by *and*. The first sentence contains a basic sentence — *The lilac needs water* — in which another sentence — *The lilac is purple* — has been embedded.**

C. Which of the following diagrams represents the kind of deep structure found in *The canary and the parakeet flew against the mirror*? Which one represents the kind of deep structure found in *The yellow parakeet talks fluently*?

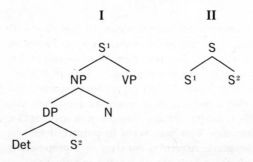

The yellow parakeet talks fluently. **(I)**

The canary and the parakeet flew against the mirror. **(II)**

REVIEW — *page L65 (an individual assignment)*

> **PURPOSE:** To help students identify and to reinforce their understanding of the important concepts of the chapter.

1. What do we call the structure of sentences we hear and speak? **Surface structure.**

2. What do we call the structure of what we understand sentences to mean? **Deep structure.**

3. Which structure do the phrase structure rules describe? **Deep structure.**

4. What do we use to change deep structure to surface structure? **Transformations.**

5. How are determiners related to nouns? **They describe or limit nouns by answering questions like *Which?* or *How many?* or *What kind?***

6. How do adjectives differ from determiners? **In the deep structure they are found in a main verb phrase following the verb.** How are they alike? **They answer the question *Which?* about nouns.**

7. What are two different ways sentences can be combined in the deep structure? **Two sentences can be joined by a conjunction, or one sentence can be embedded in the determiner phrase of another; this is the difference between coordination and subordination.**

> Students should think about, and perhaps write, the answers individually. They should then be discussed. You may wish to use the board again to illustrate the deep structure of embedded sentences. Emphasize that the deep structure is only a way to represent what we understand a sentence to mean.

119

Chapter 4

Family Resemblance: Closely Related Sentences

PERFORMANCE OBJECTIVES

The student should be able to

1. Identify relative clauses and relative pronouns.

2. Identify the deep structure of sentences with relative clauses and represent the deep structure on a branching diagram or sentence string.

3. Illustrate and explain the transformations that change deep structure to the surface structure with a relative clause.

4. Explain what is meant by closely related sentences and why they are useful in identifying deep structure.

5. Explain why a sentence with a prenominal adjective and a related sentence with a relative clause can have the same meaning.

SYNOPSIS

The chapter consists of the following sections:

1. **The introductory section** (pages L67–70) discusses what is meant by closely related sentences (those having the same parts

related in the same way and with the same meaning) and the ability of humans to recognize that such sentences have a common deep structure.

2. Discovering Relative Clauses (pages L70–74) identifies and defines relative clauses, clauses in general, and the difference between a subordinate and a dominant clause. It leads students inductively to discover that sentences with relative clauses can be derived from the same deep structure as a related sentence with a prenominal adjective (for example, *the black cat* . . . and *the cat that is black* . . . have the same deep structure)

3. Relative Pronouns (pages L74–75) identifies relative pronouns *(that, who,* and *which)* and distinguishes the relative pronoun *that* from the determiner *that.*

4. Changing a Noun Phrase to a Relative Pronoun (pages L75–78) describes and illustrates the transformations that change the deep structure of a relative clause to surface structure: the transformation that moves the embedded sentence to a position following the noun and the transformation that replaces a noun clause in the embedded sentence with a relative pronoun.

5. Review (page L79) provides questions dealing with the important concepts of the chapter: the meaning of closely related sentences; how knowing how to describe the deep structure of one helps in describing the deep structure of the other; why closely related sentences have different surface structures; where relative clauses are found in the deep and surface structure, and what a relative pronoun replaces.

TEACHING THE CHAPTER

1. In preparing to teach this chapter you should review pages 42–48 in the "Teacher's Introduction," using them for reference. You should also work through the chapter in the student's text with the key to the exercises in hand. In the key you will find some suggestions for teaching and occasionally some additional background information.

2. The chapter is a continuation of the material introduced in Chapter 3. It is concerned with the very simple and basic idea that a sentence can be embedded, in the deep structure, in a noun phrase of another sentence if it includes a noun phrase identical to the one in which it is embedded. This concept explains a great many superficially different constructions in our language and will be the basis for much of the subsequent work in the language curriculum.

121

3.   The exercises are designed so that the chapter can be taught inductively, if you like to teach in this way. They present data and include questions to help analyze the data. Some exercises are designed only as guides for class discussion, some for use as exercises to be done right in class as part of the presentation, and some for individual, out-of-class assignments for practice and reinforcement. They are all integral parts of the sections in which they are found and should be used in conjunction with the material that precedes or follows them in the sections. Use Exercises 3–8 right in class as teaching exercises around which to build your presentation and with which to present the concepts.

4.   It should be pointed out that the diagrams and strings and transformations that students are asked to construct are only devices to aid in understanding what is included in the deep structure of a sentence (that is, what it is that as speakers of the language we understand) and in grasping the regular and predictable relationship that exists between a given deep structure and its surface structure. You should not be pedantic in insisting that they get every plus sign and every brace, etc., exactly as we represent them in this key. The important thing is to understand the concepts. Careful construction of diagrams, however, is often an aid to understanding and an indication of whether the student's understanding is accurate.

KEY TO THE EXERCISES

EXERCISE 1 — *page L69 (a class exercise)*

PURPOSE: To show students that they can recognize related sentences.

In each of the following groups, three of the sentences are related to each other in a way that the fourth isn't. Pick out the three sentences that are most closely related.

1.   **The blackbird ate the corn.**
      Did the blackbird eat the corn?
      The blackbird is a nuisance.
      What did the blackbird eat?

2.   **The teacher assigned a theme yesterday.**
      The theme was difficult.
      When did the teacher assign a theme?
      What did the teacher assign yesterday?

3.   **The motor worked beautifully.**
      How did the motor work?

What kind of motor do you have?
Did the motor work beautifully?

4. **Lightning hit the tree.**
Did lightning hit the tree?
The tree was hit by lightning.
Does lightning frighten you?

> In discussing the exercise you might ask students why
> they think the sentences are related and emphasize that
> the ability to recognize related sentences is part of our
> internalized (built-in) knowledge of our language even
> if we can't always explain why.
>   *Note:* You should understand that the deep structure
> of the sentences is not identical in these examples—just
> quite similar. But this similarity explains why we can
> recognize the relationship among them. In the exercises in
> the remainder of the chapter, we will work with related
> sentences whose deep structures are identical.

EXERCISE 2 — *page L70 (a written assignment)*

> PURPOSE: To focus attention on a kind of sentence not
> previously discussed and to provide a useful review of
> what has been learned.

A. Study the following sentences. Using the rules you have learned
so far, make a branching diagram to represent the deep structure
of each one.

1. The mockingbird was singing sweetly.

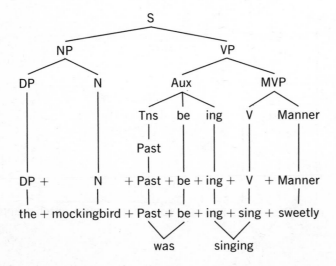

2. Pamela has a golden ring.

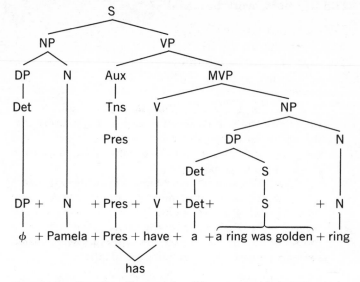

In constructing the diagram for this sentence it is necessary to break down the VP because the embedded sentence occurs in a subordinate part of the VP. Notice also
that the embedded sentence includes a noun phrase
identical to the noun phrase in which it is embedded.

3. He sold some apples that were rotten.

Note: **This is the sentence that students will probably find
difficult to diagram. They will not know what to do with
the relative clause. We include the diagram below for
your information.**

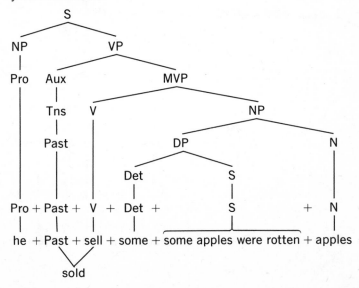

4. The girls and the boys arrived quietly.

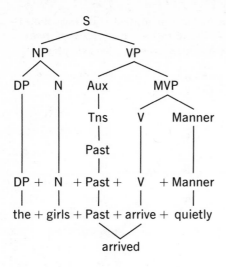

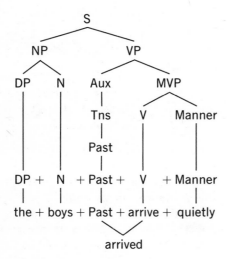

B. Was there any sentence you couldn't diagram? If so, what was different about it?

> In the process of diagramming these sentences students should discover that the rules they have learned will not accomodate sentence 3. You should have them try to decide why they can't diagram it, pinpointing the part that is different from the sentences they have worked with — the relative clause *that were rotten*. This will serve to motivate the next exercise.

125

EXERCISE 3—*pages L70-71 (a class exercise)*

> PURPOSE: To demonstrate to students that the kind of
> sentences they are studying in this chapter are related to
> sentences they have studied in the previous chapter.

A. For each sentence in column I, find the sentence in column II that
seems most closely related to it.

I		II
1. A cheerful dentist pleases children.	**d.**	**a.** Students that are honest will receive rewards.
2. Some hungry dogs roamed about.	**g.**	**b.** My dentist likes children.
3. Icy roads cause accidents.	**h.**	**c.** The house that is white stands on the corner.
4. The dead trees will fall.	**e.**	**d.** A dentist that is cheerful pleases children.
5. Honest students will receive rewards.	**a.**	**e.** The trees that are dead will fall.
6. The white house stands on the corner.	**c.**	**f.** Roaming dogs are mean.
		g. Some dogs that were hungry roamed about.
		h. Roads that are icy cause accidents.

B. In what way are the sentences that you matched together alike?
**Each sentence is matched with another sentence that has the
same meaning.** In what way are they different? **The students
should see here that the sentences in column II use several
words to convey the information contained in just one word in
the sentences in column I. Also, in column II these words
follow rather than precede the noun they are related to.**

C. When two closely related sentences mean the same thing, what
do you suspect about their deep structures? **Their deep structures will be the same.**

> Students should consider section A individually before
> discussing sections B and C. In talking about C, remind
> students that they have already found that compound
> sentences and sentences with compound parts which
> have the same meaning are derived from the same deep
> structure. As much as possible let them arrive at con-
> clusions on the basis of their intuitive knowledge about
> their own use of language.

EXERCISE 4—*page L71 (a class exercise)*

> **PURPOSE: To demonstrate that a sentence with a relative clause following a noun must have the same deep structure as a sentence with an adjective before the noun.**

A. Now look once more at two of the related sentences in Exercise 3—sentence 2 and sentence g:

> **2.** Some hungry dogs roamed about.
> **g.** Some dogs that were hungry roamed about.

What are the two basic sentences in the deep structure of sentence 2? *Some dogs roamed about* and *Some dogs were hungry.* Show how these deep structure sentences are related by constructing a branching diagram of the deep structure of sentence 2.

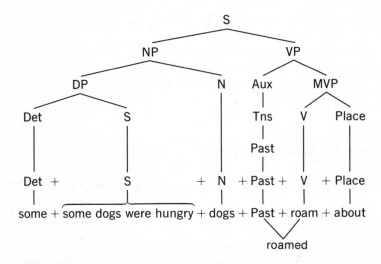

B. If sentence g means the same thing as sentence 2, what do you think would be its deep structure? **The same as the deep structure of sentence 2.** What would the diagram of its deep structure look like? **Like the diagram of the deep structure of sentence 2.**

> Before assigning this exercise, remind students of the relationship between a prenominal adjective and a noun and of the fact that such adjectives come from sentences embedded in the determiner phrase of another sentence. After each student does section A by himself, the diagram should be put on the board. You may want to leave it there to refer to as you proceed to Exercises 5 and 6. Use the questions in section B as the basis of discussion.

127

EXERCISE 5 — *pages L71–72 (the basis of a discussion)*

> **PURPOSE: To help students discover that a relative clause has the same relationship to the noun it occurs with as a prenominal adjective does.**

Look once more at these two sentences and answer the questions that follow.

> **2.** Some hungry dogs roamed about.
>
> **g.** Some dogs that were hungry roamed about.

1. What part of sentence 2 tells you *which* dogs?   ***Some hungry.***

2. Is there a part in sentence g that tells you *which* dogs? If so, what is it?   **Yes:** *some* **and** *that were hungry.*

3. In sentence 2 the word *hungry* is all that is left of the deep structure sentence *some dogs were hungry*. What is left of this deep structure sentence in sentence g?   ***That were hungry.***

> **In comparing the two different surface structures which have been derived from the same deep structure, refer students to the diagram of the deep structure which was constructed in Exercise 4.**

EXERCISE 6 — *pages L72–73 (a class exercise)*

> **PURPOSE: To identify what must be done to change an embedded sentence in the deep structure to a relative clause in the surface structure.**

A. If you look at the sentence string at the bottom of the diagram you constructed for Exercise 4, you will see that the parts of one sentence have been embedded between a determiner and a noun in the other sentence in this kind of arrangement:

some + some dogs were hungry + dogs roamed about

The *S* stands for the whole sentence that is embedded between the determiner and the noun. (The **ellipsis** [. . .] stands for the remainder of the sentence, which isn't involved in this transformation and therefore does not have to be shown here.) What changes must take place for this deep structure to become *Some hungry dogs roamed about*?   ***Some dogs were*** **must be deleted from the embedded sentence;** *hungry* **is left in front of** *dogs.*

B. Now try to describe what changes must take place in the same deep structure for it to become *Some dogs that were hungry roamed about.* Use the following questions as a guide.

1. In sentence 2, what part comes from the embedded sentence?   **The adjective *hungry.***

2. In sentence g, what part comes from the embedded sentence?   **The part *that were hungry.***   How has its position in the sentence changed?   **Instead of preceding the noun, it comes after the noun in the surface structure.**

3. In sentence g, has something been left out of the embedded sentence?   **Yes, the words *some dogs.***   Has something been added?   **Yes, the word *that.***

4. Is there any connection between what has been left out and what has been added? If so, what?   **Yes; the word *that* stands for the words *some dogs.***

This exercise can be taught inductively. Allow students plenty of time to consider their answers. To insure that each student thinks about the questions, you may want to ask the class to write the answers before discussing them. It would be useful to put the deep structure string on the board and to use it as the center of discussion.

The material following the exercise should be carefully discussed. Students should look at the way the transformations are represented and should become familiar with the terms *relative clause, clause, relative pronoun, derives from, dominant* or *main clause,* and *subordinate clause.*

EXERCISE 7 – *page L75 (a class exercise)*

PURPOSE: To provide practice in distinguishing between the relative pronoun *that* and the determiner *that.*

Decide whether the *that* found in each of the following sentences is a relative pronoun or a determiner.

1. I like that picture.   **Determiner.**
2. My friend gave me that record.   **Determiner.**
3. The record that is on the phonograph is new.   **Relative pronoun.**
4. That girl is popular.   **Determiner.**
5. The boys that are on the team will leave early.   **Relative pronoun.**

You could have students read the material preceding the exercise and then have them do the exercise itself right in class.

129

EXERCISE 8 — *page L75 (a class exercise)*

> PURPOSE: To introduce the relative pronouns *who* and *which.*

A. There are other relative pronouns besides *that.* In the following sentences, find the relative clauses and then find some other relative pronouns.

   1. Some dogs which were hungry roamed about.   **Which.**
   2. I have a dentist who is cheerful.   **Who.**
   3. Students who are honest will receive rewards.   **Who.**
   4. The trees which are dead will fall.   **Which.**
   5. A house which is white stands on the corner.   **Which.**

B. Make a general statement about when *who* is used and when *which* is used. What kind of noun phrase does each replace? You will learn more about *who* and *which* in a later chapter.   **Who refers to people and *which* to everything else.**

> Assign the exercise for individual work right in class and then discuss the answers. You need not spend much time on it.
>
> *Note:* The kind of relative clause discussed in this chapter is the restrictive clause — the kind that restricts the interpretation of the noun phrase instead of simply adding information. (See pages 45–47 in the "Teacher's Introduction.") The relative pronoun *that* appears only in restrictive relative clauses. It is therefore used in most of the examples in this chapter. *Who* and *which* can appear in either restrictive or nonrestrictive clauses.

EXERCISE 9 — *pages L76–77 (a written assignment)*

> PURPOSE: To provide practice in identifying the deep structure of related sentences and in showing that they derive from the same deep structure by different transformations.

A. In Exercise 3 you found that the following pairs of sentences are closely related. List the basic sentences that are found in the deep structure of each pair. Write a sentence string that will illustrate the deep structure of each pair. Use the symbol *S* to label the embedded sentence and use the symbols *Det* and *N* to label the parts on either side of the embedded sentence. For example:

   a. The blond girl works at Macy's.
   b. The girl that is blond works at Macy's.

deep structure sentences:

> the girl works at Macy's
> the girl is blond

deep structure sentence string:

Det   +   **S**   +   N . . .

the + **the girl is blond** + girl works at Macy's

1. **a.** A cheerful dentist pleases children.
   b. A dentist that is cheerful pleases children.

   A dentist pleases children.
   A dentist is cheerful.

   Det +   **S**   **+ N**   . . .

   a   + a dentist is cheerful + dentist pleases children

2. **a.** Icy roads cause accidents.
   b. Roads that are icy cause accidents.

   Roads cause accidents.
   Roads are icy.

   Det +   **S**   **+ N** . . .

   φ   + roads are icy + roads cause accidents

3. **a.** The dead trees will fall.
   b. The trees that are dead will fall.

   The trees will fall.
   The trees are dead.

   Det +   **S**   **+ N** . . .

   the + the trees are dead + trees will fall

4. **a.** Honest students will receive rewards.
   b. Students that are honest will receive rewards.

   Students will receive rewards.
   Students are honest.

   Det +   **S**   **+ N**   . . .

   φ   + students are honest + students will receive rewards   131

5. a. The white house stands on the corner.
    b. The house that is white stands on the corner.

The house stands on the corner.
The house is white.

Det +   S   + N   . . .

the + the house is white + house stands on the corner

B. Now, for each pair, show the transformations that produce the two different surface structure sentences. Use symbols to label the parts involved. For example:

Det   +   S   +   N   . . .

a. the + **the girl is blond** + girl works at Macy's ⟹

deletion: S

Det + **Adj** + N   . . .

the + **blond** + girl works at Macy's

Det   +   S   +   N   . . .

b. the + **the girl is blond** + girl works at Macy's ⟹

moving the embedded S:

Det + N +   S   . . .

the + girl + **the girl is blond** + works at Macy's ⟹

replacing with a relative pronoun:

S

Det + N + Rel Pro   . . .

the + girl + **that is blond** + works at Macy's

Det +   S   + N   . . .

1. a. a + **a dentist is cheerful** + dentist pleases children ⟹

deletion:

S

Det + Adj + N   . . .

a + cheerful + dentist pleases children

132

Det +   S   +   N   . . .
  | ⌒‿‿‿‿‿⌒ |

b.   a   + a dentist is cheerful + dentist pleases children ⟹

moving the embedded sentence:

Det + N   +   S   . . .
  | | ⌒‿‿‿⌒

a   + dentist + a dentist is cheerful +

                          pleases children ⟹

replacing with a relative pronoun:

                          S
                ⌒‿‿‿‿‿‿‿⌒

Det + N + Rel Pro   . . .
  | | |

a   + dentist +   that   is cheerful +

                          pleases children

Det +   S   +   N   . . .
  | ⌒‿‿‿‿‿⌒ |

2.   a. ϕ + roads are icy + roads cause accidents ⟹

deletion:

              S
              |

Det + Adj +   N   . . .
  | | |

ϕ +   icy   + roads cause accidents

Det +   S   +   N   . . .
  | ⌒‿‿‿‿‿⌒ |

b. ϕ + roads are icy + roads cause accidents ⟹

moving the embedded sentence:

Det +   N   +   S   + . . .
  | | ⌒‿‿‿⌒

ϕ + roads + roads are icy + cause accidents ⟹

replacing with a relative pronoun:

                    S
                    |

Det +   N   + Rel Pro   . . .
  | | |

ϕ + roads +   that   are icy + cause accidents   133

Det + S + N . . .
  | |

3. a. the + the trees are dead + trees will fall ⟹

deletion:

                   S
                   |
Det + Adj + N . . .
  | | |
the + dead + trees will fall

Det + S + N . . .
  | |

b. the + the trees are dead + trees will fall ⟹

moving the embedded S:

Det + N + S . . .
  | |
the + trees + the trees are dead + will fall ⟹

replacing with a relative pronoun:

                   S
Det + N + Rel Pro . . .
  | | |
the + trees + that are dead + will fall

Det + S + N . . .
  | |

4. a. ϕ + students are honest + students will receive
                                        rewards ⟹

deletion:

                   S
                   |
Det + Adj + N . . .
  | | |
ϕ + honest + students will receive rewards

Det + S + N . . .
  | |

b. ϕ + students are honest + students will receive
                                          rewards ⟹

moving the embedded sentence:

Det +   N   +   S   . . .

φ + students + students are honest +
                        will receive rewards ⟹

replacing with a relative pronoun:

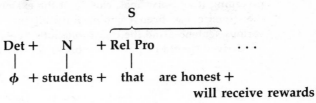

S

Det +   N   + Rel Pro   . . .

φ + students +   that   are honest +
                        will receive rewards

Det +   S   + N . . .

5. a.   the + the house is white + house stands on the
                                  corner ⟹

deletion:

S

Det +   Adj   +   N   . . .

the +   white   + house stands on the corner

Det +   S   + N   . . .

b.   the + the house is white + house stands on the
                                corner ⟹

moving the embedded S:

Det +   N   +   S   . . .

the + house + the house is white + stands on the
                              corner ⟹

replacing with a relative pronoun:

S

Det +   N   + Rel Pro   . . .

the + house +   that   is white +
                      stands on the corner   135

This exercise more or less sums up everything that should have been learned in the previous chapter and up to this point in this chapter. Doing the exercise will give students a chance to compare the two different surface structures that can develop from a deep structure in which a sentence is embedded in a determiner phrase. In preparation for the exercise, students should study the paragraphs preceding it and also look closely at the example. After the exercise has been completed by all the class, the various sentences and the transformations by which they are derived should be put on the board for discussion.

EXERCISE 10 — *page L78 (a written assignment)*

PURPOSE: To provide practice in identifying and representing the deep structure of sentences with prenominal adjectives and relative clauses and in showing how the deep structure can be transformed to surface structure.

Construct a diagram to illustrate the deep structure of each of the following sentences and then show the transformations that change each deep structure sentence string to its surface structure sentence.

1.   The new combo played at the dance.
2.   The students that were late must stay after school.
3.   That brilliant star is Venus.
4.   The girl that has measles missed the party.

1.   The new combo played at the dance.

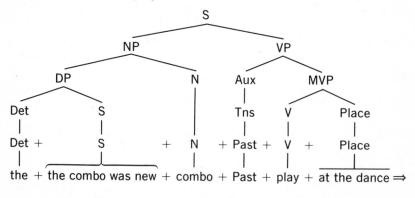

2. The students that were late must stay after school.

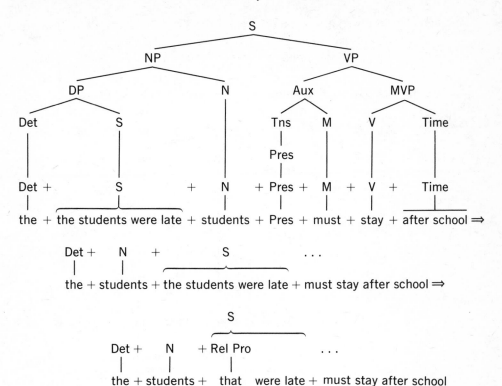

3. That brilliant star is Venus.

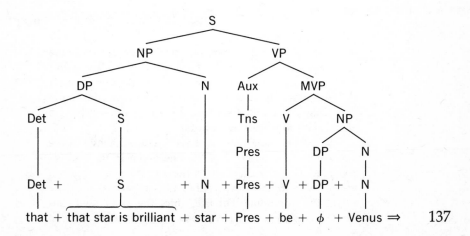

137

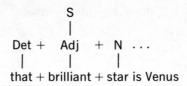

4. The girl that has measles missed the party.

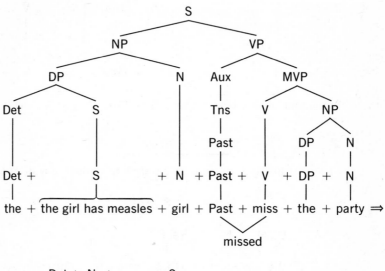

In preparation for this exercise, students should study the paragraphs and particularly the diagram preceding it and use the diagram for a model. Their work could be checked and discussed in class by having various students put their diagrams on the board and by asking other members of the class to correct any errors.

Note: The diagrams we have included above in the key are more detailed than the one given in the student text preceding the exercise. In none of the sentences is it necessary to break down either the embedded *S* or the *VP* of the dominant sentence, since the embedded sentence occurs in the *NP*. We have included more detailed

138

diagrams simply for your information in case you wish
to have your students break down the *VP*'s for practice.

REVIEW — *page L79 (a written assignment)*

> **PURPOSE:** To provide a guide for reviewing the main
> concepts of the chapter.

1. What is meant by *closely related sentences*?   **Sentences that have
   the same deep structure.**

2. Why are the following sentences closely related?

   > The wicked bishop died in the tower.
   > The bishop that was wicked died in the tower.

   They have the same deep structure.

3. How does knowing how to describe the deep structure of one
   of the sentences above help you to describe the other?   **Since
   they have the same deep structure, the same rules can be used
   to describe the deep structure of each.**

4. If the sentences in question 2 have the same deep structure, why
   do they have different surface structures?   **Different transformations have changed the deep structure to the surface structure.**

5. Where are relative clauses found in the deep structure?   **In the
   deep structure, relative clauses are found embedded between
   the determiner and the noun of a noun phrase.**

6. Where are they found in the surface structure?   **Following the
   noun which they preceded in the deep structure.**

7. What does a relative pronoun replace?   **A noun phrase that is
   identical to the noun phrase in which the relative clause was
   embedded.**

8. What is the difference between the underlined words in the
   following sentences?

   > The exhibit <u>that</u> won was very interesting.   **Here, *that* is a relative
   > pronoun.**
   > <u>That</u> exhibit should win.   **Here, *that* is a determiner.**

   **Some of the questions are more suited to extended dis-
   cussion than to written answers, but asking students to
   write the answers should ensure that each member of the**

class gives some thought to them. In the follow-up discussion you might ask the students to furnish examples of closely related sentences, or of sentences with relative clauses, etc.

Note: The most important thing for students to have learned in this chapter, in addition to their skill in recognizing relative clauses, is that such constructions can be represented as sentences within other sentences. The ability to recognize relative clauses and to understand their relation to another part in the sentence will be useful to both students and teachers in discussing sentence construction in writing assignments. This familiarity with relative clauses is also important for the language curriculum in understanding a fundamental relationship in language.

Chapter **5**

What's in a Word?

PERFORMANCE OBJECTIVES

Students should be able to

1. Explain what is meant by a grammatical feature.

2. Explain what is meant by a semantic feature.

3. Make clear (a.) how nouns with the plural number feature differ from nouns that lack the feature; (b.) how the number feature of a noun affects the form of the verb or auxiliary that follows; and (c.) how it affects the determiners that can occur with it.

4. Explain how nouns with each of the following features can be distinguished from nouns that lack the feature: count, animate, proper, feminine, human.

5. Discuss how features of verbs are identified and give examples of some verb features.

6. Use the proper notation for indicating what features a noun or verb has or lacks.

7. Identify the noun features that are shared by a given group of nouns.

8. Identify the verb features that are shared by a given group of verbs.

9. Explain what is meant by *synonymous* in terms of feature.

10. Identify some grammatical and semantic features that coincide.

141

SYNOPSIS

The chapter consists of the following sections:

1. The introductory section (pages L81–82) introduces the notion that every word consists of a whole set of different phonological, syntactic, and semantic features which we are unconsciously aware of when we know a word. We know, that is, how to pronounce the word, what it means, and where it fits in the structure of a sentence.

2. What Are Some Grammatical Features of Nouns? (pages L82–87) is concerned with identifying some of the features that characterize the class of words we call nouns. The following are identified:

> **a.** The **number feature,** which distinguishes plural nouns from singular nouns.
>
> **b.** The **count feature,** which distinguishes count nouns such as *boy* or *tree* from mass nouns such as *water* or *magic*.
>
> **c.** The feature **proper,** which distinguishes nouns like *boy* from nouns like *Bill*.
>
> **d.** The feature **animate,** which distinguishes nouns that can be replaced by *he* and *she* from nouns that can be replaced only by *it*.
>
> **e.** The feature **feminine,** which distinguishes nouns that in the singular can be replaced only by *she* or *her*.

> The chapter also discusses, and shows students how to indicate by the use of a plus or minus sign, the difference between a noun that has a certain feature and one that lacks it. For example, the noun *cars* has the feature [+*plur*]; the noun *car* lacks this feature and is marked [−*plur*].

3. Another Grammatical Feature of Nouns (pages L87–90) identifies the feature human and shows how to distinguish between nouns that have the feature and those that lack it by the kind of pronouns they can be replaced by.

4. Features of Verbs (pages L90–97) identifes the main features that distinguish one verb from another, determined by what the verb can occur with. Those that are discussed are verbs that may, must, or cannot be followed by noun phrases, verbs followed by predicates, verbs that occur with manner adverbials, verbs that can occur with directional adverbials, and verbs that occur with indirect objects.

5. Semantic Features (pages L98–100) distinguishes between grammatical and semantic features and illustrates what is meant by semantic features and how they can be indicated.

6. The Relationship Between Semantic and Grammatical Features (pages L100–05) is concerned with certain semantic and grammatical features that coincide (*e.g.,* a noun may have the semantic feature *human* as well as the grammatical feature *human*).

7. Review (pages L105–06) provides some questions to test the students' understanding of the chapter and to guide review.

TEACHING THE CHAPTER

1. Features of words are discussed briefly in the "Teacher's Introduction" (page 50). In preparation for teaching the chapter, you should read that material as well as the background information that is included for your information at the end of this section. You will, ahead of time, want to work through the chapter in the student text with the key to the exercises in hand, which key includes some specific suggestions about particular exercises.

2. For students who have studied in the previous texts in this series, the material at the beginning of the chapter through Exercise 3, and the section on Verb Features through Exercise 7, will be a review. For students without this background, you may want to supplement some of the exercises with additional items. If you do so, think them through ahead of time to make sure that they don't present any unexpected problems. You will note that we provide some additional exercises in the note in the key to Exercise 2.

3. It is important to discuss the expository sections that occur before and after the exercises.

4. The chapter lends itself to inductive teaching because in talking about words we are dealing quite directly with what each individual knows (unconsciously for the most part) about his own use of language. The approach should be to try to help students sort out what they know about words by examining their own use of them. In most exercises you will be able to ask students to supply additional examples to reinforce the point being made. Such an approach will make the subject matter more relevant to the student, since it will be based on what he actually does rather than what someone says he should do.

5. You should bear in mind that there are variations at times in how two speakers of a language use a given word and how they understand it. You should be prepared, therefore, to accept some individual variations in the answers to some of the questions in the exercises. We have tried to note in the key where some of these differences may occur. When they do occur, you will have an opportunity to discuss the normal variations that occur within any language.

Background Information for the Teacher

The characteristics that distinguish one word from another are called **features** of the word. Each word consists of a complex set of features and, in fact, the total configuration of features that a word has is what makes it unique. No matter how many features two words may share, if they are two distinct words there must be at least one feature in which they differ.

Words have three basic kinds of features—**phonological, syntactic,** and **semantic.** In identifying the phonological features of words, we must identify the features of the individual sounds and the way the sounds are combined. For example, the word *bat* and the word *bad* are distinguished phonologically by a feature called *voiced.* The sound spelled *d* in *bad* has the feature; the sound spelled *t* in *bat* lacks it. Phonological features are not dealt with in this text.

Syntactic features are those that determine where a word fits in the structure of a sentence and what must, can, and cannot occur with it. The features of nouns are intrinsic characteristics that determine the kinds of elements that occur with nouns or that can replace nouns. For instance, nouns with the feature mass normally occur in the singular with the null determiner or *some,* but not with *a (rice, some rice).* Nouns with the feature human are replaced by *who* and *he* or *she,* but not by *it.* Nouns with the feature singular affect the form of present tense verbs following them. Features of nouns, then, are determined by how they affect what occurs with them.

Features of verbs, on the other hand, are determined by what they may occur with. For instance, a very small class of verbs, of which *be* is the chief representative, occurs before either a noun phrase, an adjective, or a place adverbial:

The bird is a robin.
The bird is beautiful.
The bird is in the birdbath.

These three parts—adjective, noun phrase, or place adverbial—are called **predicates** when they can all follow the same verb. Another characteristic of some verbs is their ability or inability to occur with a noun phrase following. For instance, a verb like *fix* must have a noun phrase following it. A verb like *eat* may or may not be followed

144

by a noun phrase. A verb like *sleep* does not occur with a noun phrase following immediately.

Traditionally, verbs with noun phrases following immediately have been called **transitive verbs** and the noun phrase following is known as the **direct object.** Those verbs appearing without a noun phrase have been called **intransitive.** Attempts to classify verbs into either one or the other of these two categories, however, often entail problems when the same verb may or may not be followed by a noun phrase:

> He eats oysters.
> He eats rapidly.

Simply recognizing that such verbs have the characteristic of being able to appear with or without a noun phrase solves the problem.

Verbs also differ in their ability to occur with manner adverbials. Verbs which appear without a following *NP* may appear with a manner adverbial, and most verbs which can appear with an *NP* immediately following can also appear with manner adverbials. A few, however, cannot. The simplest way to explain the difference is to say that such verbs share the feature of a following *NP* but differ in their ability to appear with the manner adverbial. In reality, verbs, like nouns, consist of a group of features and two verbs may share some of the same features while they differ in others.

Semantic features are related to what a word means, that is, to how we interpret it. Each word has a whole set of semantic features, and words often share some semantic features while differing in others. Semantic features are introduced very briefly in this chapter, for they are very difficult to identify. Although we may know what a word means, we often have trouble pinpointing the meaning. There is a slight difference, for example, between the meaning of the words *boy* and *lad* and between *small* and *tiny*. But the difference is hard to define. Some syntactic and semantic features coincide. For example, there is a syntactic feature called **human** which causes us to use *who* rather than *which* when we replace a noun like *man* with a relative pronoun. There is also a semantic feature called **human** which distinguishes the word *child* from the word *puppy*. The word *child* has both the semantic feature human and the syntactic feature human.

An important relationship exists between our knowledge of the features of words, which is largely unconscious, and the structure of sentences. As you know, syntactic rules describe the possible structures of the sentences of a language. There are a limited number of basic kinds of parts and a limited number of possible basic structures made up of these parts. The basic structures, of course, can be combined in a variety of ways to produce an unlimited number of sentences. The following diagram represents one possible structure in English:

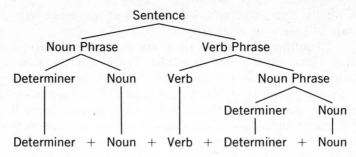

The above is the structure of a sentence like *The blast shattered the windows.* You can think of many other examples of sentences with this structure. Within this kind of structure, there are certain places where words we call *nouns* can appear. Any word that could fit in that part of the structure we have labeled *Noun* has the characteristic of being a noun. In the same way, a word that would fit into the part of the structure labeled *Verb* has the characteristic of being a verb. Although a noun can occur in the part of the structure labeled *Noun* and a verb in the part labeled *Verb*, not every noun and every verb can occur together in the same structure. This is where features come in. The syntactic features of the nouns and verbs determine whether they can occur together in a given example of that kind of structure. For instance, in a sentence in which the place of the first noun is filled with the word *flood*, the place of the verb could not ordinarily be filled with the verb *thinks*, because the verb *think* has a feature that requires it to follow animate nouns. In a sentence in which the first noun is *gamewarden* and the second is *gun*, the place of the verb could not ordinarily be filled by the verb *surprise*, which requires an animate noun following it. Our internalized knowledge of the features of these words determines how we put them together within the possible structures of the language.

Features are indicated by a special notation. In order to refer easily to the various features that distinguish a word, we use a system of symbols, including + and −[1]. When a word is distinguished by having a feature, the feature is marked + for that word. If a word is distinguished by lacking the feature, it is marked − for that word. The syntactic features of nouns are put in square brackets. For instance, if we wanted to show that the word *man* has the feature human, we would mark it *man* [+ *hum*]. *Dog* which lacks the feature human would be marked *dog* [− *hum*]. Some features can be either present or absent in the same word. The number feature is such a feature. Most nouns can appear in either a plural or singular form.

[1] This is the first text in the series that makes use of the plus and minus signs in marking features. In the previous texts, the lack of a feature was given a name. We referred, for example, to the plural feature and to the singular feature. It is actually more economical, however, to identify a feature which characterizes certain nouns and then to indicate by a minus sign that other nouns lack the feature. This cuts the number of features in half, but, more important, it immediately indicates the difference between a noun that has a feature and one that lacks it.

Therefore, in the lexicon they are marked [± *plur*]. In an actual sentence, a noun will be either [+ *plur*] or [− *plur*], since it can appear in only one of these two forms at a time.

Features of verbs are determined by the environment in which they can occur. Verbs that must be followed by noun phrases, for instance, are marked [+ ___*NP*]. The blank shows where the verb goes in relation to the *NP*. This is just an abbreviated way of saying that the verb must be followed by a noun phrase.

Semantic features are marked with pluses and minuses, but are put in angular brackets to distinguish them from the syntactic features. For instance, the noun *man,* which has the semantic feature human, would be marked *man* ⟨+ *hum*⟩.

KEY TO THE EXERCISES

EXERCISE 1 — *page L83 (for discussion)*

PURPOSE: To make students aware of the few nouns which have only a plural or only a singular form.

Some nouns in English appear only in the plural form, and some only in the singular. Can you think of examples of each?   **Plural: *trousers, pants, scissors;* singular: *jewelry, physics.*   How would the number feature of such nouns be indicated?   Those which appear only in the plural would always be marked [+ *plur*]; those which appear only in the singular would be always marked [− *plur*].**

Use as part of the general discussion of the section "What Are Some Grammatical Features of Nouns?" Before going on to the part of the section following this exercise, students should have a good understanding of:

1. What is meant by a class of words (words that share the same grammatical feature, determined by where they occur in the basic structure of the sentence).

2. How the grammatical feature of a noun can be indicated, and why it is more economical to use a plus or minus than to use two terms in indicating whether a word has or lacks a certain feature.

147

EXERCISE 2—*page L86 (a written assignment)*

> PURPOSE: **To provide practice in identifying certain features of nouns.**

Review what you know about features of nouns by listing the nouns in the following sentences together with their grammatical features. For example:

The neighbors came from Buffalo.

neighbors $\begin{bmatrix} +\text{N} \\ +\text{plur} \\ +\text{count} \\ -\text{prop} \\ +\text{an} \\ -\text{fem} \end{bmatrix}$

Buffalo $\begin{bmatrix} +\text{N} \\ -\text{plur} \\ +\text{count} \\ +\text{prop} \\ -\text{an} \\ -\text{fem} \end{bmatrix}$

1. Joe eats butter on cookies.

Joe $\begin{bmatrix} +\text{N} \\ -\text{plur} \\ +\text{count} \\ +\text{prop} \\ +\text{an} \\ -\text{fem} \end{bmatrix}$
butter $\begin{bmatrix} +\text{N} \\ -\text{plur} \\ -\text{count} \\ -\text{prop} \\ -\text{an} \\ -\text{fem} \end{bmatrix}$
cookies $\begin{bmatrix} +\text{N} \\ +\text{plur} \\ +\text{count} \\ -\text{prop} \\ -\text{an} \\ -\text{fem} \end{bmatrix}$

2. A truck was hauling sand.

truck $\begin{bmatrix} +\text{N} \\ -\text{plur} \\ +\text{count} \\ -\text{prop} \\ -\text{an} \\ -\text{fem} \end{bmatrix}$
sand $\begin{bmatrix} +\text{N} \\ -\text{plur} \\ -\text{count} \\ -\text{prop} \\ -\text{an} \\ -\text{fem} \end{bmatrix}$

3. The captain found gravel in his fish pond.

captain $\begin{bmatrix} +\text{N} \\ -\text{plur} \\ +\text{count} \\ -\text{prop} \\ +\text{an} \\ -\text{fem} \end{bmatrix}$
gravel $\begin{bmatrix} +\text{N} \\ -\text{plur} \\ -\text{count} \\ -\text{prop} \\ -\text{an} \\ -\text{fem} \end{bmatrix}$
pond $\begin{bmatrix} +\text{N} \\ -\text{plur} \\ +\text{count} \\ -\text{prop} \\ -\text{an} \\ -\text{fem} \end{bmatrix}$

Note: **Allow the students to list either** *pond* **or** *fish pond.* **Fish in this sentence is a derived modifier, but the students won't know how to describe it and may think of** *fish pond* **as a single unit.**

4. The Pettifogs spent the summer on the islands.

Pettifogs
$$\begin{bmatrix} + \text{N} \\ + \text{plur} \\ + \text{count} \\ + \text{prop} \\ + \text{an} \\ - \text{fem} \end{bmatrix}$$
summer
$$\begin{bmatrix} + \text{N} \\ - \text{plur} \\ + \text{count} \\ - \text{prop} \\ - \text{an} \\ - \text{fem} \end{bmatrix}$$
islands
$$\begin{bmatrix} + \text{N} \\ + \text{plur} \\ + \text{count} \\ - \text{prop} \\ - \text{an} \\ - \text{fem} \end{bmatrix}$$

5. The children from camp rode on the ferry.

children
$$\begin{bmatrix} + \text{N} \\ + \text{plur} \\ + \text{count} \\ - \text{prop} \\ + \text{an} \\ - \text{fem} \end{bmatrix}$$
camp
$$\begin{bmatrix} + \text{N} \\ - \text{plur} \\ + \text{count} \\ - \text{prop} \\ - \text{an} \\ - \text{fem} \end{bmatrix}$$
ferry
$$\begin{bmatrix} + \text{N} \\ - \text{plur} \\ + \text{count} \\ - \text{prop} \\ - \text{an} \\ - \text{fem} \end{bmatrix}$$

6. Down the road came the gamewarden.

road
$$\begin{bmatrix} + \text{N} \\ - \text{plur} \\ + \text{count} \\ - \text{prop} \\ - \text{an} \\ - \text{fem} \end{bmatrix}$$
gamewarden
$$\begin{bmatrix} + \text{N} \\ - \text{plur} \\ + \text{count} \\ - \text{prop} \\ + \text{an} \\ - \text{fem} \end{bmatrix}$$

7. Some of the dogs had found a raccoon.

dogs
$$\begin{bmatrix} + \text{N} \\ + \text{plur} \\ + \text{count} \\ - \text{prop} \\ + \text{an} \\ - \text{fem} \end{bmatrix}$$
raccoon
$$\begin{bmatrix} + \text{N} \\ - \text{plur} \\ + \text{count} \\ - \text{prop} \\ + \text{an} \\ - \text{fem} \end{bmatrix}$$

8. Jeff was throwing rocks at the bottles.

Jeff
$$\begin{bmatrix} + \text{N} \\ - \text{plur} \\ + \text{count} \\ + \text{prop} \\ + \text{an} \\ - \text{fem} \end{bmatrix}$$
rocks
$$\begin{bmatrix} + \text{N} \\ + \text{plur} \\ + \text{count} \\ - \text{prop} \\ - \text{an} \\ - \text{fem} \end{bmatrix}$$
bottles
$$\begin{bmatrix} + \text{N} \\ + \text{plur} \\ + \text{count} \\ - \text{prop} \\ - \text{an} \\ - \text{fem} \end{bmatrix}$$

149

9. Mary made a delicious cake.

Mary $\begin{bmatrix} +\text{N} \\ -\text{plur} \\ +\text{count} \\ +\text{prop} \\ +\text{an} \\ +\text{fem} \end{bmatrix}$ cake $\begin{bmatrix} +\text{N} \\ -\text{plur} \\ +\text{count} \\ -\text{prop} \\ -\text{an} \\ -\text{fem} \end{bmatrix}$

10. The giraffe was invisible in the tall grass.

giraffe $\begin{bmatrix} +\text{N} \\ -\text{plur} \\ +\text{count} \\ -\text{prop} \\ -\text{an} \\ -\text{fem} \end{bmatrix}$ grass $\begin{bmatrix} +\text{N} \\ -\text{plur} \\ -\text{count} \\ -\text{prop} \\ -\text{an} \\ -\text{fem} \end{bmatrix}$

The features that students are asked to identify in this exercise are those introduced in the previous text. The exercise, therefore, will be a review for those students who may have studied in that text. For others, it will provide necessary practice in characterizing nouns according to the various features they may have or may lack. And for all, the exercise will provide practice in using the plus and minus system of notation.

Note: Assign the exercise only after careful discussion of the various features described in the section preceding the exercise. The features identified are the number feature and the features count, proper, animate, and feminine. As you discuss each one, ask students to think of examples of words that have the feature and some that lack it. If you feel that supplementary exercises are needed for any students, you may find the following useful. Answers are included.

Supplementary Material

An exercise to reinforce the number feature:

Write the form of the noun indicated by the given feature. For example:

rock [+ plur]: rocks

1. mouse [− plur]: **mouse**
2. tree   [+ plur]: **trees**
3. boot   [− plur]: **boot**
4. foot   [+ plur]: **feet**
5. house   [− plur]: **house**

6. child   [+ plur]: **children**
7. tooth   [+ plur]: **teeth**
8. plane   [− plur]: **plane**
9. goose   [+ plur]: **geese**
10. peach   [+ plur]: **peaches**

An exercise for teaching the count feature:

A. List the nouns in the following sentences before which you
    you could use *a* (or *an*).

    1. _____ rat sat on _____ woodpile.   **rat, woodpile**
    2. _____ boy kicked _____ football.   **boy, football**
    3. _____ water clogged _____ street.   **street**
    4. _____ cement was poured on _____ field.   **field**
    5. _____ farmer raises _____ wheat.   **farmer**
    6. _____ milk is sour.
    7. _____ gasoline dripped from _____ tank.   **tank**

    Note: The rest of the nouns could be used with *a* or *an* too, but
    only with a special meaning.

B. List in a column the nouns in section A before which you
    could not use *a (an)*.

    water
    cement
    wheat
    milk
    gasoline

C. Which of the nouns in section A could you use with the null
    determiner? **All those listed for section B.** Which nouns
    require a visible determiner? **All those listed for section A.**

D. Which of the nouns in section A would fit in the blank in the
    following sentence?

        How much _____ is there?

All those listed for section B.

E. Change the nouns in the sentences in section A to their plural
    forms and decide which ones have an added meaning when
    they are used in the plural. **The plural forms are *rats, wood-
    piles, boys, footballs, waters, streets, cements, fields, farmers,
    wheats, milks, gasolines, tanks*. The following have an added**   151

meaning in the plural: *waters, cements, wheats, milks, gaso-lines.*   What meaning is it necessary to add?   "Kinds of."

An exercise to use in teaching the feature proper:

In which of the blanks in the following sentences must there be a visible determiner?   **In 1, 3, 5, and 6.**

1. _____ dog sat on the end of the dock.
2. _____ Rover sat on the end of the dock.
3. _____ Rover that belongs to the Mitchells sat on the end of the dock.
4. _____ Chicago is different now.
5. _____ city is different now.
6. _____ Chicago that I visited is different now.

An exercise to use in teaching the feature animate:

Which of the nouns in the following sentences can be replaced by *he* or *she*? *Boy, hunter, dogcatcher, Georgeanne, seamstress, sailor.* Which could be replaced only by *it*? *Turtle, water, coral, reefs* **(only in singular form could *reefs* be replaced by *it*),** *cougar, shadow, community, boat, harbor, shore.*

1. A turtle swam just below the water.
2. The boy found coral on the reefs.
3. The hunter saw the cougar in the shadow.
4. The community elected a dogcatcher.
5. Georgeanne is a good seamstress.
6. The boat collapsed in the harbor.
7. A sailor swam to shore.

An exercise to use in teaching the feature feminine:

Which of the nouns in the following sentences can be replaced by *he* or *she*? *Teacher, captain, singer, doctor.* Which can be replaced only by *she*? *Lioness, woman, queen, girl.*

1. The lioness abandoned the cubs.
2. George has talked to the teacher.
3. The woman is waiting for a bus.
4. The captain eased the ferry into the dock.
5. They are expecting a singer.
6. The queen is making an appearance.
7. He is looking for his girl.
8. The doctor is on call.

EXERCISE 3 — *page L87 (a written assignment)*

> PURPOSE: To test students' understanding of various noun features.

1. What effect does the feature [− *plur*] have on the form of the verb or auxiliary that follows? **It will end in a sound that is spelled -*s* or -*es* if it is in the present tense.**

2. What effect does it have on the preceding determiner?

    Note: **The answer to this question is closely related to the answers to questions 3 and 5.**

    In many cases the effect of [− *plur*] depends on whether the noun has the feature [+ *count*] or [− *count*]. Nouns with the features [+ *count*] and [− *plur*] ordinarily occur with *a/an*, rather than with *some*. They do not occur with the null determiner unless they also have the feature [+ *prop*]. Nouns with the feature [− *plur*] occur with *this* and *that*, rather than with *these* or *those*.

3. What effect do the features [+ *count*] and [− *count*] have on the preceding determiners? **Nouns with the feature [+ *count*], if they are singular and not proper, occur freely with *a/an*. However, nouns with the feature [− *count*] will occur with *a/an* in the singular only if the meaning "a kind of" or "a type of" is included. Singular nouns with the feature [+ *count*], if they are not proper, must occur with a visible determiner, whereas nouns with the feature [− *count*] occur with the null determiner.**

4. What effect does the feature [+ *an*] have on the choice of pronouns? **Nouns with the feature [+ *an*] can be replaced by *he* or *she* as well as by *it*, but nouns with the feature [− *an*] can only be replaced by *it*.**

5. What effect does the feature [+ *prop*] have on the preceding determiner? **If the noun is also [− *plur*], it will be preceded by the null determiner, unless followed by a relative clause** *(the Smith who lives on Main Street)*, **or by a related modifier** *(the famous Goethe).*

6. What effect does the feature [+ *fem*] have on the choice of pronouns? **Singular nouns with the feature [+ *fem*] are replaced by *she*.**

> **This exercise should be discussed after it has been done individually by students. Ask them to supply examples to support their answers.**

153

EXERCISE 4—*pages L87–88 (a written assignment)*

> PURPOSE: To enable students to identify the syntactic feature human.

A. Fill in the blanks in the following sentences with the relative pronouns *who* or *which*.

1. The cat __which__ scratched you is a coward.
2. The man __who__ brings the mail is always cheerful.
3. One of the boys __who__ were running around the track is here.
4. The chrysanthemum __which__ you put on the patio froze last night.
5. The lady __who__ made the cookies is my grandmother.
6. The season __which__ I hate is winter.

B. List the relative pronouns you selected, and after each, list the *NP* in the deep structure that it has replaced.

which — the cat
who — the man
who — the boys
which — the chrysanthemum
who — lady
which — the season

What is the difference between the *NP*'s replaced by *who* and those replaced by *which*? **Those replaced by *who* refer to humans.**

C. Were there any *NP*'s that could be replaced by either *which* or *who*? **Not normally.** If so, which ones?

Note: **Since children often think of certain animals as having human characteristics, some students may possibly say that** *the cat* **could be replaced by either** *which* **or** *who*. **To do so, however, means giving** *cat* **an interpretation it does not normally have.**

D. Were there any *NP*'s that could not be replaced by *who*? **Yes.** If so, which ones? *The chrysanthemum* **and** *the season* **and for most people** *the cat*.

EXERCISE 5—*pages L88–89 (a written assignment)*

> PURPOSE: To help students identify the personal pronouns that have the feature human.

A. What personal pronouns would you use to replace the italicized words in the following sentences? Are there any that could be replaced by more than one pronoun?

1. *The cat* scratches you. *He, she,* **or** *it.*
2. *The man* brings the mail. *He.*
3. *The boy* was running around the track. *He.*
4. You put *the chrysanthemum* on the patio. *It.*
5. *The lady* made the cookies. *She.*
6. I hate *the season*. *It.*

B. Compare the pronouns you chose to replace the *NP*'s in these sentences with the relative pronouns you chose to replace the *NP*'s in Exercise 4. It will help if you list the *NP*'s first and then, following them, the relative pronouns and the personal pronouns with which they can be replaced. For example:

the girl   who   she

1.	the cat	which	it, she, or he
2.	the man	who	he
3.	the boy	who	he
4.	the chrysanthemum	which	it
5.	the lady	who	she
6.	the season	which	it

The pronouns *he* and *she* **replace the same** *NP* **that is replaced by** *who*. **The pronoun** *it* **replaces the same** *NP* **that is replaced by** *which*.

C. What personal pronouns can replace the *NP*'s that could also be replaced by *who*? *He* **or** *she*. What personal pronouns did you use to replace the *NP*'s that could also be replaced by *which*? *It.*

D. Notice the *NP*'s replaced by *who*. Could you use *it* to replace any of them? **No.** Are there any *NP*'s that would never be replaced by *it*? If so, which ones? *The girl, the man, the boy, the lady.*

E. Make a statement about which personal pronouns are related to the feature [+ *hum*] and which are related to the feature [− *hum*]. *He* **and** *she* **are related to the feature** [+ *hum*]. *It* **is related to the feature** [− *hum*].

You can have students write the answers individually or you may use the exercise for oral response. The important thing is for them to have time to consider their answers and to draw their conclusions on the basis of these answers.

155

EXERCISE 6—*pages L89–90 (an activity to be used to fit the needs of your class)*

PURPOSE: To provide practice in identifying the features that characterize various nouns.

List the nouns in the following sentences and indicate with a plus (+) or a minus (−) what features each one has and what each one lacks. For example:

The canary lost his feathers.

canary
$$\begin{bmatrix} +\,N \\ -\,plur \\ +\,count \\ -\,prop \\ -\,hum \\ +\,an \\ -\,fem \end{bmatrix}$$
feathers
$$\begin{bmatrix} +\,N \\ +\,plur \\ +\,count \\ -\,prop \\ -\,hum \\ -\,an \\ -\,fem \end{bmatrix}$$

1. The small sailboat sank out of sight in the west.

sailboat
$$\begin{bmatrix} +\,N \\ -\,plur \\ +\,count \\ -\,prop \\ -\,hum \\ -\,an \\ -\,fem \end{bmatrix}$$
sight
$$\begin{bmatrix} +\,N \\ -\,plur \\ -\,count \\ -\,prop \\ -\,hum \\ -\,an \\ -\,fem \end{bmatrix}$$
west
$$\begin{bmatrix} +\,N \\ -\,plur \\ -\,count \\ +\,prop \\ -\,hum \\ -\,an \\ -\,fem \end{bmatrix}$$

2. Wheat was turning yellow on the rolling hills.

wheat
$$\begin{bmatrix} +\,N \\ -\,plur \\ -\,count \\ -\,prop \\ -\,hum \\ -\,an \\ -\,fem \end{bmatrix}$$
hills
$$\begin{bmatrix} +\,N \\ +\,plur \\ +\,count \\ -\,prop \\ -\,hum \\ -\,an \\ -\,fem \end{bmatrix}$$

3. A badger stuck his head out of a hole and looked around.

badger
$$\begin{bmatrix} +\,N \\ -\,plur \\ +\,count \\ -\,prop \\ -\,hum \\ +\,an \\ -\,fem \end{bmatrix}$$
head
$$\begin{bmatrix} +\,N \\ -\,plur \\ +\,count \\ -\,prop \\ -\,hum \\ -\,an \\ -\,fem \end{bmatrix}$$
hole
$$\begin{bmatrix} +\,N \\ -\,plur \\ +\,count \\ -\,prop \\ -\,hum \\ -\,an \\ -\,fem \end{bmatrix}$$

4. Timothy ran down the road toward the creek.

Timothy $\begin{bmatrix} +\text{N} \\ -\text{plur} \\ +\text{count} \\ +\text{prop} \\ +\text{hum} \\ -\text{an} \\ -\text{fem} \end{bmatrix}$ road $\begin{bmatrix} +\text{N} \\ -\text{plur} \\ +\text{count} \\ -\text{prop} \\ -\text{hum} \\ -\text{an} \\ -\text{fem} \end{bmatrix}$ creek $\begin{bmatrix} +\text{N} \\ -\text{plur} \\ +\text{count} \\ -\text{prop} \\ -\text{hum} \\ -\text{an} \\ -\text{fem} \end{bmatrix}$

5. A rooster crowed shrilly somewhere in the distance.

rooster $\begin{bmatrix} +\text{N} \\ -\text{plur} \\ +\text{count} \\ -\text{prop} \\ -\text{hum} \\ +\text{an} \\ -\text{fem} \end{bmatrix}$ distance $\begin{bmatrix} +\text{N} \\ -\text{plur} \\ +\text{count} \\ -\text{prop} \\ -\text{hum} \\ -\text{an} \\ -\text{fem} \end{bmatrix}$

6. Wallabies are natives of Australia.

wallabies $\begin{bmatrix} +\text{N} \\ +\text{plur} \\ +\text{count} \\ -\text{prop} \\ -\text{hum} \\ +\text{an} \\ -\text{fem} \end{bmatrix}$ natives $\begin{bmatrix} +\text{N} \\ +\text{plur} \\ +\text{count} \\ -\text{prop} \\ -\text{hum} \\ +\text{an} \\ -\text{fem} \end{bmatrix}$ Australia $\begin{bmatrix} +\text{N} \\ -\text{plur} \\ +\text{count} \\ +\text{prop} \\ -\text{hum} \\ -\text{an} \\ -\text{fem} \end{bmatrix}$

7. The Cherokees and the settlers were not very friendly.

Cherokees $\begin{bmatrix} +\text{N} \\ +\text{plur} \\ +\text{count} \\ +\text{prop} \\ +\text{hum} \\ -\text{fem} \end{bmatrix}$ settlers $\begin{bmatrix} +\text{N} \\ +\text{plur} \\ +\text{count} \\ -\text{prop} \\ +\text{hum} \\ +\text{an} \\ -\text{fem} \end{bmatrix}$

8. A burglar took the jewelry from the safe but left the money.

burglar $\begin{bmatrix} +\text{N} \\ -\text{plur} \\ +\text{count} \\ -\text{prop} \\ +\text{hum} \\ +\text{an} \\ -\text{fem} \end{bmatrix}$ jewelry $\begin{bmatrix} +\text{N} \\ -\text{plur} \\ -\text{count} \\ -\text{prop} \\ -\text{hum} \\ -\text{an} \\ -\text{fem} \end{bmatrix}$

safe $\begin{bmatrix} +\text{N} \\ -\text{plur} \\ +\text{count} \\ -\text{prop} \\ -\text{hum} \\ -\text{an} \\ -\text{fem} \end{bmatrix}$
money $\begin{bmatrix} +\text{N} \\ -\text{plur} \\ -\text{count} \\ -\text{prop} \\ -\text{hum} \\ -\text{an} \\ -\text{fem} \end{bmatrix}$

9. The sound of a trumpet pierced the air.

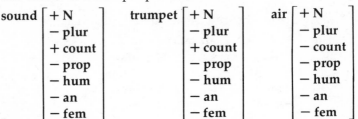

sound $\begin{bmatrix} +\text{N} \\ -\text{plur} \\ +\text{count} \\ -\text{prop} \\ -\text{hum} \\ -\text{an} \\ -\text{fem} \end{bmatrix}$
trumpet $\begin{bmatrix} +\text{N} \\ -\text{plur} \\ +\text{count} \\ -\text{prop} \\ -\text{hum} \\ -\text{an} \\ -\text{fem} \end{bmatrix}$
air $\begin{bmatrix} +\text{N} \\ -\text{plur} \\ -\text{count} \\ -\text{prop} \\ -\text{hum} \\ -\text{an} \\ -\text{fem} \end{bmatrix}$

10. The women with petitions gathered on the grass in the park.

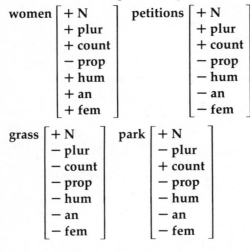

women $\begin{bmatrix} +\text{N} \\ +\text{plur} \\ +\text{count} \\ -\text{prop} \\ +\text{hum} \\ +\text{an} \\ +\text{fem} \end{bmatrix}$
petitions $\begin{bmatrix} +\text{N} \\ +\text{plur} \\ +\text{count} \\ -\text{prop} \\ -\text{hum} \\ -\text{an} \\ -\text{fem} \end{bmatrix}$

grass $\begin{bmatrix} +\text{N} \\ -\text{plur} \\ -\text{count} \\ -\text{prop} \\ -\text{hum} \\ -\text{an} \\ -\text{fem} \end{bmatrix}$
park $\begin{bmatrix} +\text{N} \\ -\text{plur} \\ +\text{count} \\ -\text{prop} \\ -\text{hum} \\ -\text{an} \\ -\text{fem} \end{bmatrix}$

If you feel your students need the practice, you can use this exercise for an individual written assignment; or you may want to assign only selected sentences; or you can do the exercise in class, putting the answers on the board as students give them to you.

Note: Students may not agree about every feature. For example, *west* in sentence 1 may seem like a proper noun to some. They may notice that, like mass nouns, *west* doesn't appear easily with *a* or in the plural. Some

158

students may mark *Timothy* [+ *hum*] and others may mark it [− *hum*] because it can be replaced by *which* as well as by *who* (*The dog Timothy, which bites mailmen, ...*). Some may mark *native* in sentence 6 [+ *hum*] while others may realize that there is nothing in the word itself to indicate that it should be considered a human noun, and indeed it too can be replaced by *which* (*The wallaby, which comes from Australia, ...*).

It is not necessary for students to agree about every noun. Encourage discussion and ask only that they defend their opinions. Some words do not fit easily into some of the categories we have discussed because they have features that we have not yet identified. The important thing is to help students understand that each word has a set of features peculiar to it, that there are some individual differences, and that grammatical (syntactic) features are determined not by what a word happens to refer to but by where it goes in a sentence and how it relates to other parts of the sentence.

EXERCISE 7 — *pages L92–93 (a written assignment)*

PURPOSE: To provide practice in identifying the features that characterize verbs.

List the verbs in the following sentences and mark the grammatical features of each one. For example:

The orange cat snored quietly in the sun.

$$\text{snore} \begin{bmatrix} + \text{V} \\ - \_\_\text{NP} \\ - \_\_\text{Pr} \\ + \_\_(\text{Man}) \end{bmatrix}$$

1. Her old car had a flat tire.

$$\text{have} \begin{bmatrix} + \text{V} \\ + \_\_\text{NP} \\ - \_\_\text{Pr} \\ - \_\_\text{Man} \end{bmatrix}$$

2. The campers listened apprehensively.

$$\text{listen} \begin{bmatrix} + \text{V} \\ - \_\_\text{NP} \\ - \_\_\text{Pr} \\ + \_\_(\text{Man}) \end{bmatrix}$$

159

3. Suddenly a bear appeared.

appear^1
$$\begin{bmatrix} +\text{ V} \\ -\underline{\quad}\text{NP} \\ -\underline{\quad}\text{Pr} \\ +\underline{\quad}\text{(Man)} \end{bmatrix}$$

4. The plumber will fix the bathtub.

fix
$$\begin{bmatrix} +\text{ V} \\ +\underline{\quad}\text{NP} \\ -\underline{\quad}\text{Pr} \\ +\underline{\quad}\text{(Man)} \end{bmatrix}$$

5. The boat is an outrigger.

be
$$\begin{bmatrix} +\text{ V} \\ -\underline{\quad}\text{NP} \\ +\underline{\quad}\text{Pr} \\ -\underline{\quad}\text{Man} \end{bmatrix}$$

6. Jack became a scuba diver.

become
$$\begin{bmatrix} +\text{ V} \\ -\underline{\quad}\text{NP} \\ +\underline{\quad}\text{Pr, except for Place} \\ +\underline{\quad}\text{(Man)} \end{bmatrix}$$

7. The ferries have been late all week.

be
$$\begin{bmatrix} +\text{ V} \\ -\underline{\quad}\text{NP} \\ +\underline{\quad}\text{Pr} \\ -\underline{\quad}\text{Man} \end{bmatrix}$$

8. George will accept the position.

accept
$$\begin{bmatrix} +\text{ V} \\ +\underline{\quad}\text{(NP)} \\ -\underline{\quad}\text{Pr} \\ +\underline{\quad}\text{(Man)} \end{bmatrix}$$

[1] There may be a difference of opinion about the verb *appear*. Actually, there are two verbs *appear*, which are pronounced the same way but have different semantic and syntactic features. The *appear* in sentence 3 means "come into view." It belongs to the class of verbs that are not followed by NP's. The other *appear* means "seems to be" and requires a predicate. This sentence should give you a chance to talk about words that are pronounced the same but that are really different words because they differ in some features. In this connection, the students might suggest that the verb *land* in sentence 10 is different from the verb *land* in *The pilot landed the plane,* in which *land* is followed by a direct object and seems to require an animate subject. For now, accept this interpretation. *Land* in *The pilot landed the plane* is probably another of those verbs that are derived from a sentence with *cause: The pilot caused the plane to land,* but you won't want to go into this now.

9. Mr. Whiteoaks is filling the truck with gravel.

fill $\begin{bmatrix} + \text{V} \\ + \underline{\quad}\text{NP} \\ - \underline{\quad}\text{Pr} \\ + \underline{\quad}\text{(Man)} \end{bmatrix}$

10. The planes landed in an empty field.

land $\begin{bmatrix} + \text{V} \\ - \underline{\quad}\text{NP} \\ - \underline{\quad}\text{Pr} \\ + \underline{\quad}\text{(Man)} \end{bmatrix}$

11. Some of the barbers are going to the convention.

go $\begin{bmatrix} + \text{V} \\ - \underline{\quad}\text{NP} \\ - \underline{\quad}\text{Pr} \\ + \underline{\quad}\text{(Man)} \end{bmatrix}$

12. Most of the gear has arrived.

arrive $\begin{bmatrix} + \text{V} \\ - \underline{\quad}\text{NP} \\ - \underline{\quad}\text{Pr} \\ + \underline{\quad}\text{(Man)} \end{bmatrix}$

This exercise should be assigned only after careful discussion of the preceding material in "Features of Verbs." As you discuss each feature, have students suggest examples of verbs that have the feature. To test their examples, they should use them in a sentence.

Students should understand:

1. How features of verbs are marked and why.
2. The terms *transitive, intransitive, predicate, manner adverbial*, and *mid verb*.

EXERCISE 8 — *page L93 (the basis for a discussion)*

PURPOSE: To identify a subclass of verbs that occur with directional adverbials.

A. Study the following pairs of sentences and try to describe the feature that is shared by the verbs in the first sentence of each pair but not by those in the second sentence.

1. He drove the car into the garage.
   *He left the car into the garage.

2. He sent the package to Chicago.
   *He bought the package to Chicago.

161

3. They rode mules into Death Valley.
*They needed mules into Death Valley.

4. Joe went to the store.
*Joe studied to the store.

The verbs in the first sentence of each pair can be followed by an adverbial of direction. The verbs in the second sentence of each pair are not grammatical when followed by an adverbial of direction.

Note: **The students will probably use some other term than "adverbial of direction" in trying to describe these sentences.**

B. How would you describe the phrases *into the garage, to Chicago, into Death Valley,* and *to the store*?   **They all indicate a direction toward which something is going.**

C. What is the relationship between such phrases and the verbs in the first sentence of each pair? Is there, that is, a restriction on the kind of verbs with which such phrases can occur?   **Only certain verbs can be followed by phrases of this kind. Some verbs, like those in the first sentence of each pair, are grammatical with such phrases, and some, like those in the second sentence of each pair, aren't.**

> Students should understand that not all verbs can occur with directional adverbials and they should, of course, read and discuss the paragraph following the exercise.
>   *Note:* Since directional adverbials occur only with certain verbs, they in a sense categorize those verbs and are therefore considered part of the same constituent (the *MVP*) as the verb, branching off from the *MVP* in a diagram:

EXERCISE 9 — *page L94 (the basis for a discussion)*

> PURPOSE: To specify the restrictions on the occurrence of directional adverbials.

A. What are some other verbs with the feature [+ ___(*NP*)] (in addition to those in Exercise 8) that can occur with adverbials of direction?   **Answers will vary. Some possibilities are** *fly (fly the plane to Chicago); mail (mail the story to the paper);*

carry (carry supplies to the camp).   What are some that cannot?
Answers will vary. Some possibilities are *bake, eat, draw, lock,*
prepare.

B. What are some other verbs with the feature [− ___*NP*] that can
occur with adverbials of direction?   **Answers will vary. Possi-**
bilities are *walk (walk to school); run (run to the base); crawl*
(crawl to the door).   What are some that cannot?   **Answers**
will vary. Possibilities are *think, sleep, laugh, imagine.*

C. Would you say that the verb *drive* must occur with a direction
adverbial or that it may occur with one?   **May.**   Which of the
following symbols would best describe this feature of the
verb *drive?*   [− ___*Dir*], [+ ___*Dir*], [+ ___*(Dir)*]

D. Which of the symbols above indicates a feature of the verb
buy?   [− ___**Dir**]

> *Note:* Directional adverbials should be distinguished
> from place adverbials, though they both answer the
> question *Where?* Directional adverbials are more properly
> related to the question *To what place?* and place ad-
> verbials to *In what place?*

EXERCISE 10 — *page L95 (the basis for a discussion)*

> **PURPOSE: To identify indirect objects and the verbs**
> **that may occur with them.**

A. Look at the following pairs of sentences and try to describe how
they are related.
   1. He gave a book to Henry.
      He gave Henry a book.
   2. Mrs. Palmerlee offered her cottage to us.
      Mrs. Palmerlee offered us her cottage.
   3. She made a cake for us.
      She made us a cake.
   4. He told a story to the children.
      He told the children a story.
   5. The mailman left a package for you.
      The mailman left you a package.
   6. Pete brought some fish to us.
      Pete brought us some fish.

The sentences of each pair say the same thing, but in the first   163 sentence of each pair, the *NP* that tells to whom or for whom something is done is the object in a prepositional phrase that follows the direct object. In the second, this *NP* follows the verb immediately.

B. What kind of verb do you find in the first sentence in each pair? In other words, what feature do the verbs all share? **They are all followed by noun phrases so they have the feature [+ ___ *(NP)*] or [+ ___ *NP*].**

All of the sentences in section A have direct objects, that is, they have noun phrases immediately following the verbs. What follows the direct objects in the first sentence of each pair? **A preposition plus a noun phrase.**

C. Now describe how the second sentence in each pair differs from the first. **The preposition has been dropped and the object of the preposition has been moved ahead of the direct object.**

> This exercise should be discussed together with the paragraphs that follow it. Students should understand:
>
> 1. The difference between a direct and an indirect object.
> 2. How to recognize an indirect object.
> 3. How to represent the deep structure of an indirect object and to transform it to the surface structure in which the indirect object precedes the direct object.
>
> See page 27 in the "Teacher's Introduction" for further discussion of the indirect object.

EXERCISE 11 — *page L97 (a written assignment)*

> PURPOSE: To provide practice in identifying indirect objects.

A. In each of the following sentences, find the *NP* that could also occur as an indirect object immediately after the verb. Then rewrite the sentences, placing the indirect objects in that position.

1. The superintendent awarded a trophy to **the team.**
   The superintendent awarded the team a trophy.

2. The waiter made a milkshake for **Sophie.**
   The waiter made Sophie a milkshake.

3. The company will send a bonus to **George.**
   The company will send George a bonus.

4. Clarice gave soup to **the invalid.**
   Clarice gave the invalid soup.

5. She told a story to **the child.**
She told the child a story.

B. Find the indirect object in each of the following sentences. Then write the related sentence in which the indirect object follows a preposition.

1. The ambassador bought **the interpreter** a dictionary.
The ambassador bought a dictionary for the interpreter.

2. The government sold **Japan** the minerals.
The government sold the minerals to Japan.

3. Isabella gave **Columbus** the ships.
Isabella gave the ships to Columbus.

4. Few politicians have offered **the people** a choice.
Few politicians have offered a choice to the people.

5. The banker made **Jim** an offer.
The banker made an offer to Jim.

EXERCISE 12 — *page L97 (a written assignment)*

> PURPOSE: To provide practice in distinguishing indirect objects from directional and place adverbials.

Which of the verbs in the following sentences occur with indirect objects? Which occur with direction adverbials? Which occur with place adverbials?

1. Mary Jane will be going to the fair.   *Dir.*
2. Mr. Isaacson is giving his fortune to the city.   IO.
3. Pauline left the kitten on the porch.   *Place.*
4. Pauline left the kitten for her nephew.   IO.
5. The plane is standing in the hangar.   *Place.*
6. The plane is coasting into the hangar.   *Dir.*
7. The carpenter built a garage for us.   IO.
8. The explorer told a fascinating story to the club.   IO.

> Since indirect objects can occur with prepositions, they appear to have, on the surface, the same structure as directional and place adverbials — a prepositional phrase following the direct object. Students will have to apply the test for the indirect object and also will have to ask themselves if the prepositional phrase is related to *In what place?* or *To what place?*

165

EXERCISE 13 — *page L98 (the basis for a discussion)*

> **PURPOSE:**   To pinpoint differences based on the meaning (semantic interpretation) of a word.

A. In the following sentences, do *man* and *boy* differ in any of the grammatical features you have learned about?   **No.**

> The man caught three fish.
> The boy caught three fish.

B. If not, how would you account for the fact that these two sentences mean different things?   *Man* **and** *boy* **mean different things.**

C. In what way is the meaning of the word *man* like that of the word *boy*?   **Part of the meaning of both is "male human being."**   In what way are they both different from the word *girl*?   **Part of the meaning of** *girl* **is "female human being."**

> This exercise should be used to introduce the discussion of the section "Semantic Features," which deals with the third component of grammar, the semantic component. It offers opportunity for lively class discussion and relies largely on the students' intuitive knowledge of his language and of his own use of and interpretation of words.

EXERCISE 14 — *page L100 (a class exercise)*

> **PURPOSE:**   To demonstrate that the meaning of a word consists of several semantic features.

Make a table like the following one and fill it in with pluses and minuses to show the features found in the meanings of the words listed. The first one has been done for you.

	parent	offspring	sibling	feminine
father	+	−	−	−
mother	+	−	−	+
son	−	+	−	−
daughter	−	+	−	+

	parent	offspring	sibling	feminine
sister	−	−	+	+
brother	−	−	+	−

Have students put the table on the board and discuss their answers. Point out how each word has a different configuration of semantic features.

EXERCISE 15 — *page L102 (a written assignment)*

PURPOSE: To provide an opportunity for students to interpret lines of poetry in which restrictions have been broken and to try to identify the restrictions that have thus been broken.

A. Study the following lines of poetry and discuss any kinds of semantic or grammatical restrictions you think have been broken in each instance. Explain how you interpret what the poet means.

Notice that the footnote numbers here and in the student book begin at 2 in the exercise, because of a prior poetic reference (numbered 1) in the preceding paragraph of the text.

In all of the following, answers will vary, for those given are only suggestions. This exercise should stimulate thoughtful discussion because so many possibilities for interpretation exist.

1. The moon is able to command the valley tonight[2]   A grammatical restriction is broken. *Command* usually requires an animate subject, but in this sentence its subject is the usually inanimate noun *moon*. The poet probably means that no clouds are blocking the moonlight from the valley.

2. Bring me the sunset in a cup[3]   The meaning of *sunset* is not compatible with the meaning of "being in a cup." Some semantic restrictions are broken. The poet may mean that the sunset is so lovely she would like to be able to capture it and perhaps drink it, or that she'd like someone to capture the loveliness for her and confine it.

3. The years ride out from the world[4]   A grammatical restriction has been broken. *Years* is treated as an animate

[2] Carl Sandburg, "Moist Moon People."
[3] Emily Dickinson, "Bring Me the Sunset in a Cup."
[4] Stephen Vincent Benét, "Song of the Riders."

noun, since it is the subject of *ride*, which ordinarily takes an animate subject. The poet is probably alluding to the fact that the years lived are gone and cannot be relived.

4. In a grove of clean sun interwoven with swallows[5]   Semantic restrictions are broken. Sunlight and swallows are described as if they were threads which could be woven. Also, a grove ordinarily consists of trees, not of sun and swallows. Sun is not usually considered clean or dirty. The poet is creating a picture composed of forest, sunlight, and birds, which owes much of its beauty to the suggestion that these elements can be woven together.

5. To bathe their hearts in moonlight[6]   Hearts are usually encased in bodies, and moonlight is not water. The poet, in creating this romantic illusion, is breaking some semantic restrictions.

6. Truly the spouting fountains of light . . . sing one song but they think silence[7]   *Fountains* is treated as an animate noun, subject of *sing* and *think*. *Silence* as a direct object is not compatible with *think*. Fountains are usually composed of water, not light. Both syntactic and semantic restrictions are broken. The author may be expressing the idea that a display of moving lights gives him the impression of a unified chorus of song although not a sound can be heard.

7. I poked him with an angry stick[8]   *Angry* ordinarily modifies animate nouns, and *stick* is inanimate. Here, grammatical and semantic restrictions are broken. We understand the poet to mean that he himself, the "I" of the sentence, was angry, and showed it by the way he poked "him" with the stick.

   Note that, in some instances, breaking a grammatical rule may also involve breaking a semantic rule, as in the case of using inanimate nouns with verbs usually requiring animate nouns. It is sometimes difficult to determine whether the rule that was broken was grammatical or semantic or whether both kinds of rules were broken.

B. If you are taking any literature courses or if you like to read poetry, look for some other examples of places where a poet has broken semantic or grammatical restrictions.

---

[5] Louis Untermeyer, "Archibald MacLeish/Suspends the Five Little Pigs."
[6] Wallace Stevens, "Homunculus et La Belle Étoile."
[7] Robinson Jeffers, "Night."
[8] Richard Eberhart, "The Groundhog."

EXERCISE 16—*page L103 (a written assignment)*

> **PURPOSE: To provide practice in trying to identify the kinds of semantic features that a group of words may share while differing in others.**

A. Try to describe the semantic feature (or features) shared by all the words in each of the following groups.

1.	water	2.	Coke	3.	wheat

1. water
   tea
   coffee
   root beer
   milk
   ⟨+ liquid
   + beverage⟩

2. Coke
   7-Up
   soda pop
   root beer
   ⟨+ liquid
   + beverage
   + carbonated⟩

3. wheat
   oats
   barley
   ⟨+ grain⟩

4. trees
   shrubs
   grass
   vines
   ⟨+ plant⟩

5. kitten
   puppy
   calf
   child
   ⟨− mature⟩

6. cement
   brick
   wood
   stone
   ⟨+ building materials⟩

7. ant
   bee
   cricket
   earwig
   roach
   ⟨+ insect⟩

8. run
   crawl
   skip
   gallop
   ⟨+ locomotion⟩

B. List the grammatical features shared by the words in each group.

1. [+ N
− plur
− count
− hum
− prop
− fem
− an]

2. [+ N
− plur
− hum
− fem
− an]

3. [+ N
− plur
− count
− prop
− hum
− fem
− an]

4. [+ N
− hum
− prop
− fem
− an]

5. [+ N
− plur
+ count
− prop
+ an
− fem]

6. [+ N
− plur
− prop
− hum
− an
− fem]

169

7. $\begin{bmatrix} + \text{N} \\ - \text{plur} \\ + \text{count} \\ - \text{prop} \\ - \text{hum} \\ + \text{an} \\ - \text{fem} \end{bmatrix}$ 8. $\begin{bmatrix} + \text{V} \\ - \underline{\quad}\text{NP} \\ - \underline{\quad}\text{Pr} \\ + \underline{\quad}(\text{Man}) \\ + \underline{\quad}(\text{Dir}) \end{bmatrix}$

Some students may list [− *count*] in item 6. *Brick* can occur either as a count or as a mass noun, and it would be normal for some to interpret it as a mass noun here. You may need to point out that a word is characterized by a minus feature as much as by a plus feature.

C. Try to think of some other groups of words that share semantic features, that is, that share some meaning.

Answers will vary. A few possibilities are listed here.

1. apples	2. throw	3. bed
oranges	toss	cot
lemons	hurl	hammock
prunes	cast	couch

There may be some variation in the way students identify the semantic features in section A. Encourage discussion and do not insist on a given answer. Simply ask students to defend their answers.

EXERCISE 17 — *page L104 (a written assignment)*

PURPOSE: To provide practice in identifying semantic similarities and also to demonstrate that synonymous words can vary in degree of semantic similarity.

Place each of the following groups of words into one of these categories: (a) words that are very closely related in semantic features, (b) words that share most of the same semantic features but differ in a few, and (c) words that seem to share no semantic features.

1. brook	2. car	3. road	4. rich
creek	train	highway	wealthy
stream	boat	path	
(a)	(b)	(b)	(a)

5. sofa	6. cloudy	7. physician	8. man
davenport	foggy	doctor	job
(a)	rainy	(a)	idea
	(b)		(c)

9. construct	10. wind	11. totally	12. slowly
build	wave	completely	carefully
(a)	**(c)**	**(a)**	**(c)**

Be sure to ask students to defend their answers during class discussion.

REVIEW — *pages L105–06 (an activity to fit the needs of your class)*

PURPOSE: To provide a guide for reviewing and reinforcing the concepts of the chapter.

1. What is the difference between a grammatical feature and a semantic feature?   **A grammatical feature is related to how a word fits into the structure of a sentence; a semantic feature is related to what a word means.**

2. What grammatical feature do all nouns share?   **All nouns share the grammatical feature [+ N] and almost all nouns share the feature [± *plur*].**

3. What grammatical features do the nouns in each of the following groups share?

   man, boys, dog   [+ N]; [+ *an*]; [− *fem*]; [− *prop*]; [+ *count*]

   pencil, record, buttons   [+ N]; [− *an*]; [− *hum*]; [− *prop*]; [+ *count*]; [− *fem*]

   Bill, wheat, bird   [+ N]; [− *fem*]; [− *plur*]

   George, girls, child   [+ N]; [+ *hum*]; [+ *count*]; [+ *an*]

   rice, snow, paint   [+ N]; [− *prop*]; [− *plur*]; [− *count*]; [− *hum*]; [− *an*]; [− *fem*]

   Henry, Idaho, Russia   [+ N]; [− *plur*]; [+ *prop*]; [+ *count*]; [− *fem*]

4. What grammatical features do the verbs in each of the following groups share?

   come, go, proceed [+ V]; [− ___ NP]; [+ ___ (*Man*)]; [+ ___ (*Dir*)]

   stay, remain, be   [+ V]; [+ ___ Pr]

   drive, send, ride   [+ V]; [+ ___ (*Man*)]; [+ ___ (*Dir*)]

   give, tell, send   [+ V]; [+ ___ NP (+ prep + NP)]; [+ ___ (*Man*)]

   fix, find, make   [+ V]; [+ ___ NP]; [+ ___ (*Man*)]

171

5. Find the word in each of the following groups that differs in grammatical features from the other words in the group. Name the feature that is different.

boat, water, rudder   [− *count*]

paint, bucket, turpentine   [+ *count*]

tree, bird, worm   [− *an*]

child, kitten, puppy   [+ *hum*]

man, woman, child   [+ *fem*]

rise, raise, sit   [+ ___*NP*]

eat, send, fix   [+ ___*(NP)*]

have, carry, cost   *Carry* differs both in [+ ___*(Dir)*] and [+ ___*(Man)*]

become, be, build   [+ ___*NP*]

6. What is the difference between the way we distinguish the grammatical features of nouns and the way we distinguish the grammatical features of verbs? **We distinguish the grammatical features of nouns by what can occur with them or replace them; we distinguish the grammatical features of verbs by restrictions as to what they can or must occur with.**

7. What are some grammatical features of adjectives?

The students should be able to name one: [+ *Adj*]. Some members of the class might mention also that where adjectives can occur, *NP*'s and place adverbials also can occur.

8. How would you define *synonymous* in terms of features? **Words that are synonymous have approximately the same semantic and syntactic features.**

9. What are some semantic features that coincide with grammatical features? **Human, feminine, plural, animate.**

10. List some words that have the same grammatical features but different semantic features.

Answers will vary. A few possibilities are listed here.

a.	man	b.	water	c.	pictures	d.	Fred Astaire
	boy		snow		walls		John Doe
	brother		paint		desks		Ivan Ivanov
	son		gas		chairs		Jack Robinson

The semantic features of proper nouns are few, hardly including more than a distinction between feminine and nonfeminine.

These review questions ask students to draw conclusions on the basis of what they have learned in the chapter, rather than simply to repeat factual information. If students can draw the proper conclusions, it can be assumed that they have understood the important concepts of the chapter. You will probably want them to work out the answers individually, in writing for the most part, before beginning to discuss them.

Chapter 6

Family Ties: More Relative Clauses

PERFORMANCE OBJECTIVES

The student should be able to

1. Identify relative clauses occurring anywhere in a sentence.

2. Identify the deep structure underlying a sentence with a relative clause and illustrate such deep structure both in a sentence string and on a branching diagram.

3. Recognize the noun phrase that has been replaced by a relative pronoun.

4. Describe the transformations that are needed to change the deep structure of a sentence with a relative clause to the surface structure.

5. Make clear the meaning of *recursiveness* and also why it is possible to produce an infinite number of sentences.

6. Explain why the rules used to describe the deep structure of basic sentences can also be used to describe the deep structure of sentences with relative clauses.

7. Account for relative pronouns always occurring at the beginning of the relative clause.

8. Explain what restriction there is on the basic sentence that underlies a relative clause.

9. Demonstrate various ways in which basic sentences can be combined.

SYNOPSIS

The chapter consists of the following sections:

1. The introductory section (pages L107–12) consists primarily of six exercises which first help students review what they know about relative clauses that include the verb *be* plus an adjective, and then demonstrate that any basic sentence can be embedded as a relative clause in another sentence as long as the two sentences have a noun phrase in common. The relative clause, of course, is embedded in the common noun phrase in the dominant sentence.

2. Where Do Relative Clauses Occur? (pages L112–13) shows that relative clauses can occur in any noun phrase in a sentence, no matter where that noun phrase may be.

3. What *NP*'s Can Be Replaced by Relative Pronouns? (pages L114–17) demonstrates that any noun phrase in the embedded sentence — subject, object, object of preposition, or predicate noun phrase — may be the one replaced by a relative pronoun as long as it is identical to the noun phrase in which it is embedded.

4. The Transformations That Describe Relative Clauses (pages L117–21) helps students describe the three transformations that are needed to change the deep structure description of a sentence with a relative clause to the surface structure: the transformation that moves the embedded sentence to a position following the noun that it modifies; the transformation that replaces the common noun phrase in the embedded sentence with a relative pronoun; and the transformation that moves the relative pronoun to the beginning of its clause if it does not already occur there. These transformations are also expressed symbolically.

5. Recursiveness (pages L121–27) is concerned with the characteristic of human language that makes it possible to produce an infinite number of sentences. That one basic sentence can be embedded in another, and a third in the second, and a fourth in the third, indefinitely, is what makes this production possible. A basic sentence structure, in other words, can recur an infinite number of times. And when we know how to produce basic sentences and how to embed them in other basic sentences, we then know how to produce an infinite number of sentences. You will find that   175 the section provides considerable practice in embedding one sentence in another.

6. Review (page L127) provides questions to help students consolidate and review the basic concepts of the chapter.

TEACHING THE CHAPTER

1. In preparation for teaching the chapter, you should study carefully pages 42–48 in the "Teacher's Introduction." Ahead of time, you will, of course, want to work through the chapter in the student's text and also the key to the exercises in this guide, which key includes additional information.

2. The chapter is a long one because it has been designed for inductive teaching. Its many exercises should lead students step by step to some important generalizations about the deep structure of all relative clauses and the transformations that change the deep structure to surface structure. These generalizations account not only for most noun modifiers but also for the recursive nature of language—that one basic sentence structure can be embedded in another and a third in the second and so on indefinitely. Because these concepts, though quite simple in themselves, are important to an understanding of the structure and derivation of many of the sentences of the language, students will use them over and over again. It will pay, therefore, to proceed slowly enough to make sure that all members of the class have a good understanding of them.

3. You will notice that, as in previous chapters, many exercises are designed simply to serve as guides to discussion; others are designed as class exercises to be done in class and discussed; and still others are intended for reinforcement and practice.

4. Extensive use is made of branching diagrams and underlying sentence strings, to help students visualize the deep structure of sentences with relative clauses and the steps needed to change the deep structure to surface structure. May we suggest that, in addition to having students construct the diagrams themselves, you make frequent use of the board or overhead. You could, for example, have the students take turns putting the diagrams and sentence strings on the board and these could be used as the basis for discussing particular sentences.

5. Remember, however, that diagrams and sentence strings are only visual aids to understanding and not ends in themselves. They do not have to be any more complex than is necessary to illustrate the particular structure involved. The diagrams we have provided in the key do not break down the embedded sentences, for example, though students should realize that such embedded sentences could be broken down into their various parts in exactly the same way that the dominant sentences are broken down.

KEY TO THE EXERCISES

EXERCISE 1—*pages L107–08 (a class exercise)*

> PURPOSE: To help students review what they have learned previously about the deep structure of sentences with relative clauses and prenominal adjectives and about the transformations that change the deep structure to surface structure.

A. Make a diagram that can represent the deep structure of either of the sentences below:

The shaggy dog slept on the steps.
The dog that was shaggy slept on the steps.

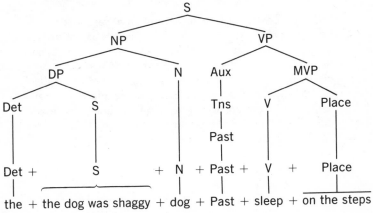

B. Show how the sentence string at the bottom of your diagram can be changed to become *The shaggy dog slept on the steps.*

Det +   S   + N
  | ‾‾‾‾‾‾‾‾‾‾‾‾‾‾‾‾‾‾ |
the + the dog was shaggy + dog + Past + sleep on the steps ⟹

                    S
                    |
        Det +   Adj   + N
          | | |
        the + shaggy + dog + Past + sleep on the steps
                                  ＼＿／
                                  slept

177

C. Show how the same string can be changed to become *The dog that was shaggy slept on the steps.*

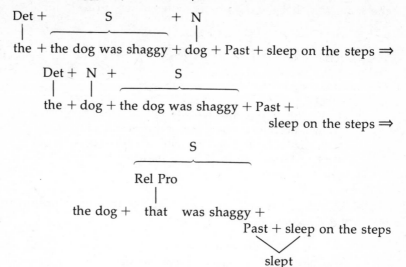

Det +   S   + N

the + the dog was shaggy + dog + Past + sleep on the steps ⟹

Det + N +   S

the + dog + the dog was shaggy + Past +

sleep on the steps ⟹

S

Rel Pro

the dog +   that   was shaggy +

Past + sleep on the steps

slept

This exercise could be worked out in a class discussion, but you may want to ask each student to construct the diagram individually and then have someone put it on the board. Using two colors of chalk is a good way to distinguish between the two sentences found in the deep structure. You could point out that the place adverbial consists of a preposition plus a noun phrase. Have students explain what the transformations are or have them do them for themselves; then have someone put them on the board as a basis for discussion.

EXERCISE 2 — *page L108 (a class exercise)*

PURPOSE: To identify a relative clause that does not include the verb *be* plus an adjective.

A. Study the following sentence and answer the questions that follow:

The raccoon that steals the garbage hid.

1. How many *S*'s are there in the deep structure of this sentence? **Two.** What are they? *The raccoon hid* **and** *The raccoon steals the garbage.*

2. Does this sentence contain a relative clause? **Yes. If so, what is it? That steals the garbage.** How did you identify it? **Answers may vary. Some students may identify it by the relative pronoun; some because it follows the noun** *raccoon,* **which they will intuitively know it modifies.**

3. Where do you think the relative clause would be located in the deep structure? (Remember where other relative clauses you know about have been located in the deep structure.) **By analogy with other relative clauses, it is assumed, students will locate it as part of the determiner phrase in** *the raccoon* **of the sentence** *The raccoon hid.*

4. The relative clause *that was shaggy* in *the dog that was shaggy* tells *which* dog. What answers this same question about *raccoon* in *the raccoon that steals the garbage*? **That steals the garbage.**

B. Construct a branching diagram showing the deep structure of *The raccoon that steals the garbage hid.*

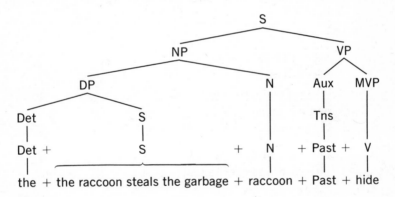

What students should assume is that any relative clause can be described as deriving from a basic sentence embedded in the noun phrase of another sentence.

Note: Since the relative clause in this sentence is part of the subject *NP*, it would not be necessary to break the verb phrase down. It could simply be brought down as a unit in the sentence string:

179

However, in this diagram, and in diagrams in subsequent exercises, we do indicate what the various parts are. How much detail you require will depend on your class and on whether you think the students' understanding of sentence structure will benefit by constructing detailed diagrams.

EXERCISE 3—*page L109 (a written assignment to be done individually)*

PURPOSE: To provide practice in identifying the deep structure of sentences with relative clauses and in identifying the noun phrase that the relative clause has in common with the sentence in which it is embedded.

A. List the basic sentences in the deep structure of each of the following sentences. Underline the deep structure sentence that appears as the relative clause in the surface structure. List the part each pair of deep structure sentences has in common. For example:

The cat that caught the bird ran away.

deep structure sentences:
the cat ran away
the cat caught the bird

part in common: the cat

1. The vase that was on the table broke.

    The vase broke.
    The vase was on the table.
    the vase

2. The girl that won the contest will appear here tomorrow.

    The girl will appear here tomorrow.
    The girl won the contest.
    the girl

3. The carpenter that built the house has returned.

    The carpenter has returned.
    The carpenter built the house.
    the carpenter

4. The woman that drove the bus is a housewife.

    The woman is a housewife.
    The woman drove the bus.
    the woman

5. The package that arrived was on the porch.

    The package was on the porch.
    The package arrived.
    the package

B. Construct branching diagrams showing the deep structure of sentences 1 and 3.

1. The vase that was on the table broke.

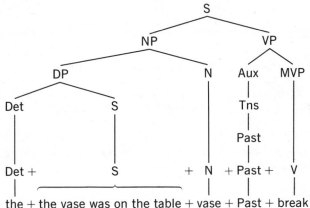

the + the vase was on the table + vase + Past + break

3. The carpenter that built the house has returned.

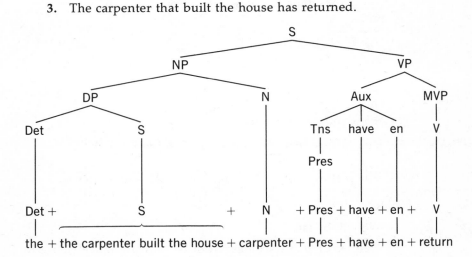

the + the carpenter built the house + carpenter + Pres + have + en + return

> **This exercise should be discussed in class before you ask students to work on it at home. If they need a sample diagram to follow for section B, you could have them help you put the following on the board, using two colors of chalk:**
>
> **The cat that caught the bird ran away.**

181

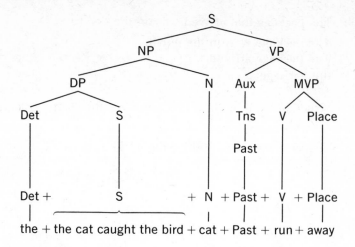

the + the cat caught the bird + cat + Past + run + away

EXERCISE 4 – *pages L109–10 (a written assignment)*

> **PURPOSE: To emphasize that there must be a common *NP* if a sentence is to become a relative clause in another sentence.**

A. For each of the following pairs of sentences, write a related sentence in which one sentence of the pair becomes a relative clause in the other sentence. Underline the relative clause. For example:

> The girl lives in Columbus.
> The girl won the contest.
> The girl that won the contest lives in Columbus.

1. The picture is hanging in the hall.
    The picture won a prize.

    The picture that won a prize is hanging in the hall.
    or
    The picture that is hanging in the hall won a prize.

2. The car has stalled.
    We will be late.

    Neither of these sentences can become a relative clause in the other because the sentences don't have a common *NP*.

3. The students will be punished.
    The students cheat.

    The students that (who) cheat will be punished.
    or
    The students that (who) will be punished cheat.

182

4. The buses are late.
    The buses come this way.

    The buses <u>that (which) are late</u> come this way.
    or
    The buses <u>that (which) come this way</u> are late.

5. The sky is blue.
    The storm is over.

    Neither of these sentences can become a relative clause in the other because the sentences don't have a common *NP*.

6. The church burned down.
    The church was a landmark.

    The church <u>that (which) was a landmark</u> burned down.
    or
    The church <u>that (which) burned down</u> was a landmark.

7. A horsefly bit me.
    Horseflies are pests.

    Neither of these sentences can become a relative clause in the other because the sentences don't have a common *NP*. The subject *NP*'s differ in number.

8. The boat stops here.
    The boat runs to the islands.

    The boat <u>that (which) runs to the islands</u> stops here.
    or
    The boat <u>that (which) stops here</u> runs to the islands.

B. Were there any pairs of sentences that couldn't be combined to make a related sentence containing a relative clause? **Yes, 2, 5, and 7.** If so, how are these pairs different from the sentences that could be combined in this way? **They do not have a common *NP*.** Can you explain what conditions are necessary for one sentence to be embedded as a relative clause in another? **They must have a common *NP*.**

> **Use section B to guide discussion.**
>
> *Note:* Some students will make one sentence of a pair the relative clause while others will make the alternate the relative clause. Both are correct. In anticipation of the next exercise, ask students why it is possible to make either sentence a relative clause in the other. Usually the only restriction is that the two have a common noun phrase. In some cases, however, one of the two constructions may seem unusual. In sentence 3, for example, the sentence *The students that will be punished*

183

cheat is a little strange. The strangeness is related to the cause-and-effect relationship between the two parts. This points up that there are many kinds of restrictions which we automatically follow in producing sentences.

Some students may use *who* or *which* instead of *that*. These are, of course, acceptable and will give you an opportunity to discuss why we use *who* in some instances and *which* in others.

EXERCISE 5 *– pages L110–11 (a class exercise)*

PURPOSE: To demonstrate that any sentence can be a relative clause in another sentence if such sentences have a noun phrase in common.

A. Study the following pair of sentences and try to explain in what way the sentences are alike and in what way they are different.

The girl that works in the office takes tickets.
The girl that takes tickets works in the office.

The sentences are alike in containing the same information and the same basic sentences in their deep structure. They differ in the way the basic sentences are combined and, as a result, the emphasis is different. In each case the emphasis is on the sentence that is dominant, whereas the embedded sentence has a subordinate role and serves only to modify the noun in the noun phrase in which it is embedded.

1. What basic sentences are found in the deep structure of each? *The girl takes tickets* **and** *The girl works in the office.*

2. In the first sentence in section A, which basic sentence is the embedded sentence in the deep structure? *The girl works in the office.*

3. In the second sentence in section A, which basic sentence is the embedded sentence in the deep structure? *The girl takes tickets.*

B. Construct diagrams to represent the deep structure of each of the two sentences in section A. Explain how they are different.

The diagrams are different because the embedded sentence in one is the dominant sentence in the other and vice versa.

The girl that works in the office takes tickets.

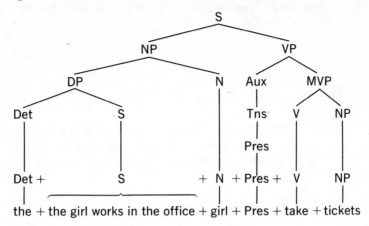

the + the girl works in the office + girl + Pres + take + tickets

The girl that takes tickets works in the office.

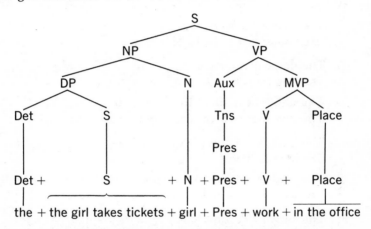

the + the girl takes tickets + girl + Pres + work + in the office

C. When two sentences have a noun phrase in common, which sentence can become a relative clause embedded in the other? **Either can.**

> Sections A and C could be used for discussion only, but section B should, of course, be written, probably right in class, after which the diagrams could be put on the board to form the basis of discussion.
>
> *Note:* As you proceed through the chapters, it is desirable occasionally to point out that whatever conclusions are drawn are drawn on the basis of the evidence presented. It is possible that additional evidence or other circumstances might cause the conclusions to be modified. For example, the answer to section C should probably be "Usually either can." And there might be some sentences with noun phrases in common, such as the two in item 3

185

of Exercise 4, that could be combined in only one way
because of other restrictions having to do with the sentences' content.

EXERCISE 6—*page L111 (a written assignment)*

> PURPOSE: To provide practice in embedding basic sen-
> tences in other sentences as relative clauses; to explore
> the possibilities for combining sentences in this way.

A. For each of the following pairs of sentences, make two related
   sentences containing relative clauses. For example:

   The runner won the race.
   The runner is tired.

   The runner that won the race is tired.
   The runner that is tired won the race.

   1. The dog eats pretzels.
      The dog lives here.

      The dog that (which) lives here eats pretzels.
      The dog that (which) eats pretzels lives here.

   2. The bird is circling over the valley.
      The bird is black.

      The bird that (which) is black is circling over the valley.
      The bird that (which) is circling over the valley is black.

   3. The singer has long hair.
      The singer is practicing.

      The singer that (who) is practicing has long hair.
      The singer that (who) has long hair is practicing.

   4. The plane crashed in the fog.
      The plane was flying too low.

      The plane that (which) was flying too low crashed in the fog.
      The plane that (which) crashed in the fog was flying too low.

   5. One painting cost $200,000.
      One painting disappeared.

      One painting that (which) disappeared cost $200,000.
      One painting that (which) cost $200,000 disappeared.

B. Make branching diagrams to represent the first two sentences
   containing relative clauses that you wrote in section A.

The dog that lives here eats pretzels.

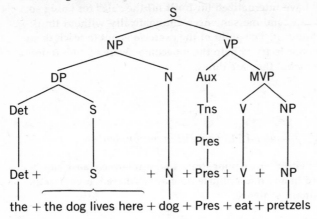

The dog that eats pretzels lives here.

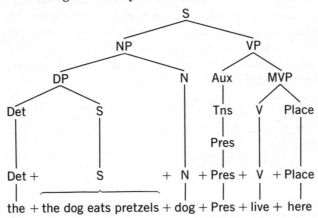

In making these diagrams, does it help you to know how to diagram the original sentences in the pair? **Yes.** If so, why? **The diagrams of the basic sentences in each pair are the same whether one is embedded in the other or not.** Does knowing how to make basic sentences help you make sentences with relative clauses? **Yes. If so, why? Because sentences with relative clauses are made by combining two basic sentences.**

The questions in section B are related to one of the major points of the grammar: that knowing how to describe basic sentences enables us to describe more complex sentences which include the basic sentences in their deep structure. This helps to explain why humans are able to make an infinite number of sentences. In discussing the exercise, you should take the opportunity to point out that students

187

have no trouble combining the sentences. This is because they have internalized (or built in) the rules for doing so, and can combine sentences automatically without thinking about it. The point of the exercise is not to teach them how, but to try to help them become aware of and understand what they are doing.

EXERCISE 7 — *page L113 (a written assignment)*

> PURPOSE: To demonstrate that a relative clause can be found in any noun phrase no matter where it occurs in the dominant sentence.

A. The following sentences contain relative clauses. Copy each one and underline the relative clause in it. List the basic sentences found in the deep structure of each and underline the one that becomes a relative clause. In the other deep structure sentence, draw a circle around the noun phrase in which the relative clause will be embedded. List the part the two deep structure sentences have in common. For example:

> I saw the man that brought the paper.
>
> **deep structure sentences:**
> I saw (the man)
> the man brought the paper
>
> **part in common:** the man

1. Ellen found the book that gives the answers.

    deep structure sentences:
    Ellen found (the book).
    The book gives the answers.

    part in common: the book

2. The book that gives the answers is on the desk.

    deep structure sentences:
    (The book) is on the desk.
    The book gives the answers.

    part in common: the book.

3. The dog that has only three legs was in the circus.

    deep structure sentences:
    (The dog) was in the circus.
    The dog has only three legs.

    part in common: the dog

188

4. We saw the dog that has only three legs.

   deep structure sentences:
   We saw (the dog).
   The dog has only three legs.

   part in common: the dog

5. Jerry was in the bus that slid off the road.

   deep structure sentences:
   Jerry was in (the bus).
   The bus slid off the road.

   part in common: the bus.

6. Our class listened to the man that came from Turkey.

   deep structure sentences:
   Our class listened to (the man).
   The man came from Turkey.

   part in common: the man.

7. The police caught the tiger that escaped.

   deep structure sentences:
   The police caught (the tiger).
   The tiger escaped.

   part in common: the tiger.

B. Notice where the *NP*'s containing relative clauses occur in the sentences in section A. Decide if a relative clause can occur in a noun phrase in any part of a sentence. **As students should have discovered from doing section A, a relative clause can occur in any noun phrase no matter where that noun phrase may occur.** What must a relative clause have in its deep structure in order to be embedded in a noun phrase in another *S*? **It must have a noun phrase identical to the noun phrase in which it is embedded.**

C. Do we need a new transformation to account for relative clauses embedded in noun phrases following the verb? **No.** Why or why not? **Every embedded sentence underlying a relative clause is embedded before the noun in the noun phrase, whether the noun phrase occurs before the verb or after it. And in each case the same changes, or transformations, must be made to change the deep structure to surface structure: move the embedded sentence to follow the noun; replace the common noun phrase in the embedded sentence with a relative pronoun; and if it isn't already at the beginning of the clause move it there.**   189

You will probably want to go over the example in class to make sure students know what they are asked to do. When you discuss the sentences, emphasize that in each case the relative clause occurs in an *NP* that follows the verb. Use sections B and C to guide your discussion of section A. As a result of this exercise students should begin to see that all relative clauses have the same relationship to the noun phrases in which they occur, no matter where the *NP* may be in the sentence.

EXERCISE 8 – *page L114 (for discussion)*

> PURPOSE: To suggest that the noun phrase that is replaced by a relative pronoun may not always occur at the beginning of its own basic sentence structure and thus to supply motivation for the next two exercises.

A. Look at the relative clauses in the sentences in Exercise 7. Where does the relative pronoun occur in each relative clause?   **At the beginning.**

B. The deep structure of *The tiger that escaped was tame* contains the sentences *the tiger was tame* and *the tiger escaped.* Which is the embedded sentence?   **The tiger escaped.**

C. What part of this embedded sentence is replaced by the relative pronoun *that*?   **The subject *NP*.**   Can you think of any sentences in which the *NP* replaced by a relative pronoun is not the subject *NP*?

   Answers will vary. Students may or may not come up with examples. The following could be suggested: *The book that I lost was Mary's* (from *the + I lost the book + book was Mary's*); *The boy that you saw is my brother* (from *the + you saw the boy + boy is my brother*).

EXERCISE 9 – *pages L114–15 (a class exercise)*

> PURPOSE: To demonstrate that a noun phrase that follows the verb can be replaced by a relative pronoun in the relative clause.

A. Find the relative clause in the following sentence and list the sentences in its deep structure.

   The record that I bought sounds great.

The record sounds great and I bought the record.

B. Construct a diagram representing the deep structure of the sentence in section A. Underline the part in the sentence string that represents the embedded sentence.

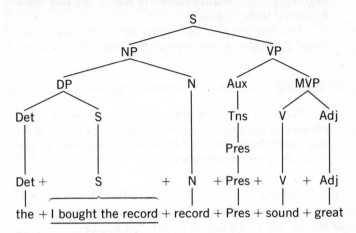

C. What is the first transformation that must take place in changing a deep structure of this kind to a sentence containing a relative clause? **The embedded sentence must be moved to a position beyond the noun.** Rewrite the sentence string, making this change.

$$\text{Det} + \quad S \quad + \quad N \quad + \text{Pres} + \quad V \quad + \text{Adj}$$
the + I bought the record + record + Pres + sound + great ⟹

$$\text{Det} + \quad N \quad + \quad S \quad + \text{Pres} + \quad V \quad + \text{Adj}$$
the + record + I bought the record + Pres + sound + great

D. What noun phrase in the embedded sentence must be replaced with *that*? **The record.** What part of the sentence is this noun phrase? **The direct object *NP*. It is part of the *MVP*.**

E. Does the string now represent a grammatical sentence? **No.** If not, what other change is necessary? **The relative pronoun must be moved to the beginning of the relative clause.** Why? **All relative pronouns in relative clauses occur at the beginning of the clause.** Rewrite the string, making this change.

$$S$$
$$\text{Det} + \quad N \quad + \textbf{Rel Pro} \quad + \text{Pres} + \quad V \quad + \text{Adj}$$
the + record + **that** I bought + Pres + sound + great

191

This exercise can be taught inductively. The questions are designed to lead the students to the realization that sometimes relative pronouns replace *NP's* that aren't at the beginning of the relative clause, in which case they must be moved to the beginning.

The diagram and the strings should be put on the board by students and used as the basis of discussion.

EXERCISE 10 — *page L116 (a written assignment)*

PURPOSE: To provide practice in identifying the noun phrase that has been replaced by a relative pronoun when that noun phrase does not occur at the beginning of the clause in the deep structure.

Copy the following sentences and underline the relative clause in each. Write down the deep structure sentence that has become the relative clause and underline the part that has been replaced by the relative pronoun. For example:

The house that Jack built was large.
Jack built the house.

1. The movie that we saw lasted three hours.
    We saw the movie.

2. Some of the girls found the money that you lost.
    You lost the money.

3. Sue is wearing the dress that her mother made.
    Her mother made the dress.

4. The violin that the movers broke came from Italy.
    The movers broke the violin.

5. The manager served the dinner that we had ordered.
    We had ordered the dinner.

This exercise should be discussed just before you assign Exercise 11. Point out that in the embedded sentence of the example, the noun phrase that will be replaced by the relative pronoun follows the verb.

EXERCISE 11 — *pages L116–17 (a written assignment)*

PURPOSE: To provide practice in identifying the deep structure of sentences with relative clauses and in showing the steps in changing their deep structure to surface structure.

For each sentence in Exercise 10, write the deep structure sentences in a string, with one embedded in the other. Then show how this deep structure string becomes the surface structure. Attach the symbols *Det, N, S,* and *Rel Pro* to the parts involved in the transformations. Also use the symbol *NP* to label the part that will be replaced by a relative pronoun. For example:

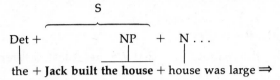

S

Det +   NP   +   N . . .

the + **Jack built the house** + house was large ⟹

moving the embedded S:

S

Det +   N   +   NP . . .

the + house + **Jack built the house** + was large ⟹

replacing the NP with a relative pronoun:

S

Det +   N   +   **Rel Pro . . .**

the + house + **Jack built that** + was large ⟹

moving the relative pronoun:

S

Det +   N   + **Rel Pro**   . . .

the + house + **that Jack built** + was large

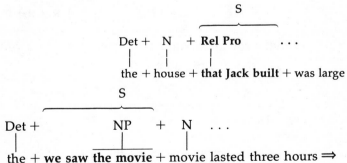

S

Det +   NP   +   N   . . .

1.   the + **we saw the movie** + movie lasted three hours ⟹

S

Det +   N   +   NP   . . .

the + movie + **we saw the movie** + lasted three hours ⟹   193

S

Det + N + **Rel Pro** . . .

the + movie + **we saw that** + lasted three hours ⟹

S

Det + N + **Rel Pro** . . .

the + movie + **that we saw** + lasted three hours

S

. . . Det + NP + N

2.   some of the girls found the + **you lost the money** + money ⟹

S

. . . Det + N + NP

some of the girls found the + money + **you lost the money** ⟹

S

. . . Det + N + **Rel Pro**

some of the girls found the + money + **you lost that** ⟹

S

. . . Det + N + **Rel Pro**

some of the girls found the + money + **that you lost**

S

. . . Det + NP + N

3.   Sue is wearing the+ **her mother made the dress** + dress ⟹

S

. . . Det + N + NP

Sue is wearing the+ dress + **her mother made the dress** ⟹

194

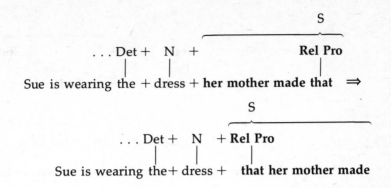

```
                                                              S
                                       ┌────────────────────────┐
          ... Det +   N   +                         Rel Pro
               │      │                               │
        Sue is wearing the + dress + her mother made that   ⟹

                                              S
                                   ┌──────────────────────┐
              ... Det +   N   + Rel Pro
                    │     │       │
           Sue is wearing the + dress +   that her mother made
```

```
                                     S
               ┌──────────────────────────────┐
      Det +                          NP      +  N   ...
       │                             │          │
4.    the + the movers broke the violin + violin came from Italy ⟹

                                              S
                          ┌────────────────────────────┐
      Det +  N   +                         NP       ...
       │     │                             │
      the + violin + the movers broke the violin + came from Italy ⟹

                                            S
                        ┌──────────────────────────┐
      Det +   N   +                    Rel Pro   ...
       │      │                          │
      the + violin + the movers broke that + came from Italy ⟹

                                     S
                    ┌───────────────────────────────┐
      Det +   N   + Rel Pro                        ...
       │      │      │
      the + violin +   that the movers broke + came from Italy
```

```
                                              S
                          ┌────────────────────────────┐
          ... Det +                   NP      +  N
                │                     │          │
5.    the manager served the + we had ordered the dinner + dinner ⟹

                                                    S
                            ┌────────────────────────────────┐
          ... Det +    N   +                     NP
                │      │                         │
      the manager served the + dinner + we had ordered the dinner ⟹
```

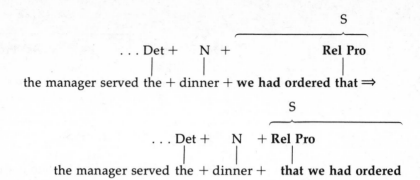

the manager served the + dinner + we had ordered that ⟹

the manager served the + dinner +   that we had ordered

Go over the example carefully to make sure that students understand what they are asked to do. Point out again that the brace under S is used to make it easy to identify the embedded S. Point out also that only the parts of the sentence involved in the transformations need to be labeled. The rest can be shown by ellipses.

EXERCISE 12 — *pages 117–18 (a written assignment)*

PURPOSE: To help students consolidate their understanding of the transformations that change the deep structure of a sentence with a relative clause to the surface structure.

A. In the deep structure of a sentence with a relative clause, one *S* is embedded between a determiner and a noun in another *S*. Write a statement that explains how the position of the embedded *S* is changed. Illustrate your statement by using the following sentence: *The cat that ate the bird looked guilty.*

Answers will vary. The student's statement should include the following information: A sentence embedded between a determiner and a noun in another *S* is moved to a position following the noun. In *The cat that ate the bird looked guilty*, for example, *the cat ate the bird* is embedded between *the* and *cat: the + the cat ate the bird + cat looked guilty.* It must, therefore, be moved to a position after *cat: the cat + the cat ate the bird + looked guilty.*

B. An embedded sentence that becomes a relative clause includes an *NP* that is identical to the *NP* in which it is embedded. For example, in the deep structure of *The house that Jack built was large*, both the embedded *S* and the dominant *S* include the *NP the house*. What happens to the identical *NP* in the embedded sentence when it becomes a relative clause? Write a statement

196

that describes this change. Show how it applies in deriving *The cat that ate the bird looked guilty.*

Answers will vary. The student's statement, however, should include the following information: When a noun phrase in an embedded sentence is identical to a noun phrase in which it is embedded, the identical noun phrase in the embedded sentence is replaced by a relative pronoun. In *the cat + the cat ate the bird + looked guilty,* for example, *the cat* is the identical noun phrase and it is replaced by *that: the cat + that ate the bird + looked guilty.*

C. Where does the relative pronoun occur in all relative clauses? If the noun phrase that is replaced by a relative pronoun doesn't happen to be at the beginning of the embedded sentence, what transformation must take place? Write a statement that describes this transformation. Explain why this transformation would be needed in deriving the following sentence: *The bird that the cat ate was delicious.*

Answers will vary. The student's statement should include the following information: If the noun phrase replaced by the relative pronoun isn't at the beginning of the embedded sentence, the relative pronoun must be moved to the beginning. For example, in the deep structure of *The bird that the cat ate was delicious,* the embedded sentence is *the cat ate the bird.* The noun phrase that is replaced is *the bird.* It occurs after the verb in the embedded sentence and therefore must be moved to the beginning of the embedded sentence.

the bird + the cat ate the bird + was delicious ⇒

the bird + the cat ate <u>that</u> + was delicious ⇒

the bird + <u>that</u> the cat ate + was delicious

The discussion of this exercise should continue into a careful discussion of the section that follows, a section in which the transformations the students have described in words are translated into symbolic statements. You will probably want to put these on the board and illustrate them with sentences. Students should begin to understand that the rules they have described can be used to explain how any relative clause is derived. They should see that this relatively simple set of rules can account for an infinite number of sentences.

Note: Up until this time, the symbol *Rel Pro* has been used to label relative pronouns. Now the symbol *Wh-word* is used to make the transformation more general, that is, any *Wh-word* will move to the beginning of the

197

clause in which it occurs. **This is the same transformation that moves the *Wh-words* in questions to the beginning, and students will eventually discover that the same transformation applies to words like *where* and *when* in deriving adverbial clauses. (See pages 45–46 in the "Teacher's Introduction.")**

EXERCISE 13 — *pages L120–21 (a written assignment)*

PURPOSE: To provide practice in identifying the deep structure of sentences with relative clauses and in showing how the deep structure can be transformed to surface structure by the transformations that have been identified.

List the basic sentences found in the deep structure of each of the following sentences. Then write the deep structure sentence string for that part of the deep structure that contains the embedded sentence. Use the symbols *Det, S,* and *N* to label the parts involved. Use *NP* to label the part that will be replaced by a relative pronoun. Finally, show the transformations that change the deep structure to the surface structure. For example:

The candy that the class is selling came from Pittsburgh.

deep structure sentences:
the candy came from Pittsburgh
the class is selling the candy

deep structure string:

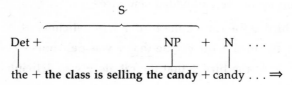

$T_{repos\ S}$:

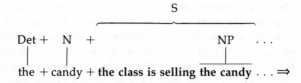

$T_{Wh-word}$:

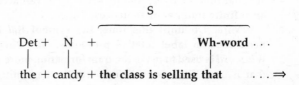

T$_{repos}$ Wh-word:

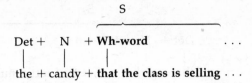

S

Det + N + **Wh-word** . . .
| | |
the + candy + **that the class is selling** . . .

1. The books that are on reserve should help you.

    deep structure sentences:
    The books should help you.
    The books are on reserve.

    deep structure string:

    Det + S + N . . .
    |
    the + **the books are on reserve** + books . . . ⟹

    T$_{repos}$ S:

    Det + N + S . . .
    | |
    the + books + **the books are on reserve** . . . ⟹

    T$_{Wh-word}$:

    S

    Det + N + **Wh-word** . . .
    | |
    the + books + **that are on reserve** . . .

2. Joe called the girl that had left a number.

    deep structure sentences:
    Joe called the girl.
    The girl had left a number.

    deep structure string:

    . . . Det + S + N
    |
    . . . the + **the girl had left a number** + girl ⟹

    T$_{repos}$ S:

    . . . Det + N + S
    | |
    . . . the + girl + **the girl had left a number** ⟹

199

T_{Wh-word}:

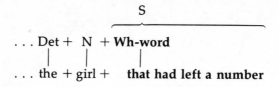

... Det + N + **Wh-word**
     | | |
... the + girl +   **that had left a number**

3. The man that called you is coming today.
    The man is coming today.
    The man called you.

    deep structure string:

Det +   S   + N ...
 |
the + **the man called you** + man ... ⟹

T_{repos S}:

Det + N   S   ...
 | |
the + man + **the man called you** ... ⟹

T_{Wh-word}:

             S
Det + N + **Wh-word**   ...
 | | |
the + man +   **that called you** ...

4. The specimen that we examined today was a cobra.
    deep structure sentences:
    The specimen was a cobra.
    We examined the specimen today.

    deep structure string:

Det +   S   + N   ...
 |
the + **we examined the specimen today** + specimen ... ⟹

T_{repos S}:

Det + N   +   S   ...
 | |
the + specimen + **we examined the specimen today** ... ⟹

T_{Wh-word}:

$$S$$

Det +   N   +   **Wh-word**   . . .
| | |
the + specimen + **we examined that today** . . . ⟹

T_{repos Wh-word} :

$$S$$

Det +   N   + **Wh-word**   . . .
| | |
the + specimen +   **that we examined today** . . .

5. The police recovered the money that the thief had taken.

   deep structure sentences:
   The police recovered the money.
   The thief had taken the money.

   deep structure string:

   . . . Det +   S   +   N
   | |
   . . . the + **the thief had taken the money** + money ⟹

T_{repos S}:

   . . . Det +   N   +   S
   | |
   . . . the + money + **the thief had taken the money** ⟹

T_{Wh-word}:

$$S$$

   . . . Det +   N   +   **Wh-word**
   | | |
   . . . the + money + **the thief had taken that**   ⟹

T_{repos Wh-word} :

$$S$$

   . . . Det +   N   + **Wh-word**
   | | |
   . . . the + money +   **that the thief had taken**   201

Point out, in making the assignment and in looking at the example with your students, that only the part of the sentence involved in the transformation need be listed. The rest can be indicated by ellipses.

Note: Students may need help in determining that in sentences 2 and 5 the ellipses occur at the beginning because the relative clause occurs in a noun phrase at the end of the sentence.

EXERCISE 14—*pages L123–24 (a written assignment)*

PURPOSE: To provide practice in embedding one sentence in another and in exploring the number of possible sentences that can be produced in this way.

A. Each of the following pairs consists of two basic sentences. For each pair, write a deep structure sentence string, embedding the second sentence in the first. Then write the surface structure sentence that would result from applying transformations to produce either relative clauses or adjectives before nouns. If two surface structures are possible, write them both. For example:

> Robin looked at the vase.
> The vase was gold.
>
> deep structure sentence string:
> Robin looked at the + the vase was gold + vase ⟹
>
> > Robin looked at the vase that was gold.
> > Robin looked at the gold vase.

1. The turkey strutted alongside the fence.
    The turkey was angry.

    deep structure sentence string:
    the + the turkey was angry +
    > **turkey strutted alongside the fence ⟹**

    > **the turkey that was angry strutted alongside the fence**
    > **the angry turkey strutted alongside the fence**

2. The picture hangs in the hall.
    Anthony painted the picture.

    deep structure sentence string:
    the + Anthony painted the picture +
    > **picture hangs in the hall ⟹**

    > **the picture that Anthony painted hangs in the hall**

3. The butterfly emerged from the cocoon.
    The butterfly was beautiful.

deep structure sentence string:
the + the butterfly was beautiful +
                    butterfly emerged from the cocoon ⟹

the butterfly that was beautiful emerged from the
                                        cocoon
the beautiful butterfly emerged from the cocoon

4. All of the family watched the program.
    The program lasted three hours.

    deep structure sentence string:
    all of the family watched the +
                the program lasted three hours + program ⟹

    all of the family watched the program that lasted
                                        three hours

5. The astronauts are young.
    The astronauts are going to the moon.

    deep structure sentence string:
    the + the astronauts are going to the moon +
                            astronauts are young ⟹

    the astronauts that are going to the moon are young

6. The dog sleeps all day.
    The dog howls all night.

    deep structure sentence string:
    the + the dog howls all night + dog sleeps all day ⟹

    the dog that howls all night sleeps all day

7. I saw the whale.
    The whale was lying on the horizon.

    deep structure sentence string:
    I saw the + the whale was lying on the horizon + whale ⟹

    I saw the whale that was lying on the horizon

8. The ferry goes to Sidney.
    The ferry is late.

    deep structure sentence string:
    the + the ferry is late + ferry goes to Sidney ⟹

        the ferry that is late goes to Sidney
        the late ferry goes to Sidney

B. Now write the sentences that would result if the first sentence
    in each pair were embedded in the second. In each case, explain
    how the effect is different from that of the sentences you wrote
    in section A.

1. The turkey that strutted alongside the fence was angry.

   In the sentence in section A the emphasis is on the turkey's strutting alongside the fence. Here it is on the turkey's being angry.

2. Anthony painted the picture that hangs in the hall.

   In the sentence in section A the emphasis is on where the picture that Anthony painted is hanging, that is, in the hall. Here the emphasis is on Anthony's having painted the picture.

3. The butterfly that emerged from the cocoon was beautiful.

   In the sentence in section A the emphasis is on the butterfly's emergence from the cocoon. Here it is on the butterfly's being beautiful.

4. The program that all of the family watched lasted three hours.

   In the sentence in section A the emphasis is on the family's watching the program. Here it is on how long the program lasted.

5. The astronauts that are young are going to the moon.
   or
   The young astronauts are going to the moon.

   In the sentence in section A the emphasis is on the astronauts' being young. Here it is on their going to the moon.

6. The dog that sleeps all day howls all night.

   In the sentence in section A the emphasis is on the dog's sleeping all day. Here it is on his howling all night.

7. The whale that I saw was lying on the horizon.

   In the sentence in section A the emphasis is on seeing the whale. Here it is on the whale's lying on the horizon.

8. The ferry that goes to Sidney is late.

   In the sentence in section A the emphasis is on the ferry's going to Sidney. Here it is on the ferry's being late.

Students should have little trouble in combining the sentences and in doing so will recognize that they have an intuitive ability to form sentences of this kind. They will also see that being able to combine sentences in this way increases the number of sentences that can be produced. The exercise also illustrates how a change in emphasis takes place, depending on which one of the sentences to be combined is dominant and which one is subordinate.

Note: Before assigning the exercise, be sure to discuss the preceding section on *Recursiveness*.

EXERCISE 15 — *pages L125–26 (a written exercise)*

> **PURPOSE:** To provide practice in combining sentences
> and to explore how many possibilities there are.

A. In each of the following sets, there are three basic sentences. For
each set, (1) write the surface structure sentence that would
result if sentence c were embedded in sentence b and became a
relative clause. Then (2) take the sentence you just wrote and try
to embed it in sentence a. Apply the transformations necessary
to produce grammatical sentences. For example:

> **a.** We found the dog.
> **b.** The dog bit the girl.
> **c.** The girl was visiting.
>
> **(1)** The dog bit the girl that was visiting.
> **(2)** We found the dog that bit the girl that was visiting.

1. **a.** We met the girl.
   b. The girl knows the boy.
   c. The boy is from Norway.

   (1) The girl knows the boy that is from Norway.
   (2) We met the girl that knows the boy that is from Norway.

2. **a.** The boy caught the fish.
   b. The fish swallowed the fly.
   c. The boy had made the fly.

   (1) The fish swallowed the fly that the boy had made.
   **(2) The boy caught the fish that swallowed the fly that the
   boy had made.**

3. **a.** The class liked the rat.
   b. The rat ate the cheese.
   c. Mary brought the cheese.

   (1) The rat ate the cheese that Mary brought.
   **(2) The class liked the rat that ate the cheese that Mary
   brought.**

4. **a.** George is the lifeguard.
   b. The lifeguard rescued the boy.
   c. The boy was little.

   **(1) The lifeguard rescued the boy that was little (or *the
   little boy*).**
   **(2) George is the lifeguard that rescued the boy that was
   little (or *the little boy*).**

5. **a.** We camped in a park.
   b. A park has a lake.
   c. A lake is beautiful.

205

    (1)   A park has a lake that is beautiful (or *a beautiful lake*).

    (2)   We camped in a park that has a lake that is beautiful (or *a beautiful lake*).

B. Make as many other sentences as you can by combining the sentences in each set in different ways.

Answers will vary. The following are some possibilities:

1. The girl that we met knows the boy from Norway.
The boy that the girl that we met knows is from Norway.
We met the girl and the girl knows the boy and the boy is from Norway.

2. The boy had made the fly that the fish that the boy caught swallowed.
The fish that the boy caught swallowed the fly that the boy had made.
The boy had made the fly and caught the fish that swallowed the fly.

3. Mary brought the cheese that the rat that the class liked ate.
The rat that the class liked ate the cheese that Mary brought.
The class liked the rat and the rat ate the cheese and Mary brought the cheese.

4. The lifeguard George rescued the little boy.
The boy that the lifeguard George rescued was little.
George is the lifeguard and the lifeguard rescued the little boy.

5. A park that we camped in has a beautiful lake.
A lake that a park that we camped in has is beautiful.
We camped in a park that has a lake and a lake is beautiful.

The exercise provides opportunity to talk about the great variety that is possible because we can both combine and transform basic structures in various ways. You might also want to talk about how some combinations that can be made are more difficult to follow and to understand than others. See, for example, the second sentence in item B-5 above.

EXERCISE 16 — *page L126 (a written assignment)*

PURPOSE: To provide practice in identifying the deep structure in which one basic sentence is embedded in another which in turn is embedded in another.

For each of the following sentences, list the sentences that are found in the deep structure. Underline the dominant sentence. Then try to write a deep structure sentence string showing how the subordinate sentences are embedded in the dominant sentence.

1. The class that won the gold trophy worked hard.

   S¹ <u>The class worked hard.</u>
   S² The class won the trophy.
   S³ The trophy was gold.

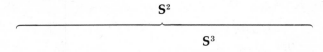

   the + the class won the + the trophy was gold + trophy +
   class worked hard

2. The boy that played the part that you wanted is a sophomore.

   S¹ <u>The boy is a sophomore.</u>
   S² The boy played the part.
   S³ You wanted the part.

   S²
   ———————————————————
   S³
   —————————

   the + the boy played the + you wanted the part + part +
   boy is a sophomore

3. This is the rat that ate the malt that lay in the house that Jack built.

   S¹ <u>This is the rat.</u>
   S² The rat ate the malt.
   S³ The malt lay in the house.
   S⁴ Jack built the house.

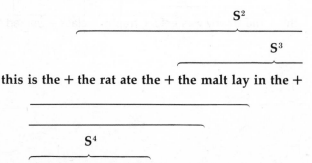

   this is the + the rat ate the + the malt lay in the +

   S⁴

   Jack built the house + house + malt + rat

207

Supplementary Material

Your superior students might enjoy trying to diagram these sentences; thus the following are included in case you wish to use them. If nothing more, students might find it interesting to see the complex arrangement of parts involved in a sentence that sounds relatively simple and to realize that they are able to put such a set of parts together without thinking about it whenever they use language. Point out that each sentence consists of several basic structures one within another.

1. The class that won the gold trophy worked hard.

2. This is the rat that ate the malt that lay in the house that Jack built.

3. The boy that played the part that you wanted is a sophomore.

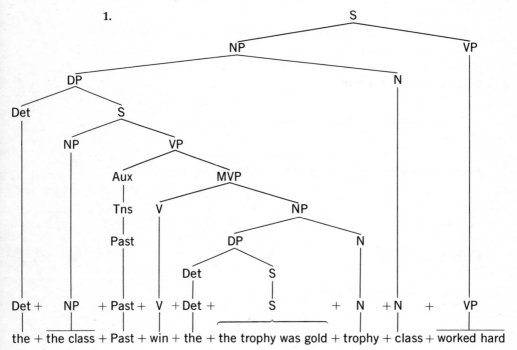

2.

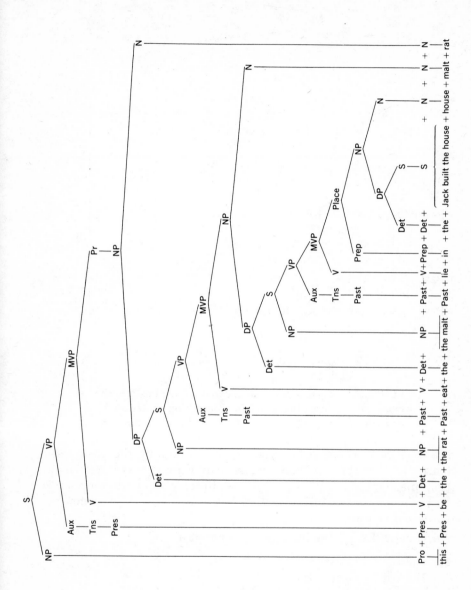

3.

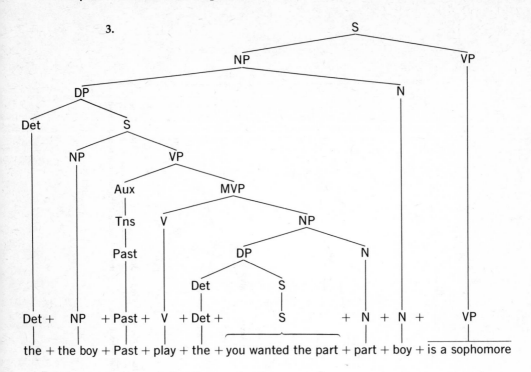

EXERCISE 17 — *pages L126–27 (a written assignment)*

PURPOSE: To provide practice and to demonstrate the many possibilities that exist for combining sentences by embedding one in another and a third in the second, etc.

Make as many sentences as you can by combining the basic sentences in each of the following sets in various ways. You may combine them in compound sentences, in sentences with compound parts, in sentences with adjectives before nouns, and in sentences with relative clauses.

Answers will vary. We include some possibilities.

1. The whale was shiny.
    The whale was sleek.
    The whale jumped into the air.
    We watched the whale.
    The whale caught a fish.

    We watched the shiny sleek whale that jumped into the air and caught a fish.
    The whale which we watched was shiny and sleek.
    The whale which jumped into the air and caught the fish was shiny and sleek.

210

2. The girls bought a kite.
The kite went very high.
The kite is stuck in a tree.
The tree is tall.
The girls went to the field.

The girls that went to the field bought a kite that went very high and stuck in a tall tree.
The kite which the girls that went to the field bought went very high and is stuck in a tall tree.
The girls that bought a kite that went very high and is stuck in a tall tree went to the field.

3. The pigeon walked on the curb.
The pigeon pecked at the crumbs.
The crumbs were in the gutter.
The boys saw the pigeon.
The boys caught the pigeon.

The pigeon that the boys saw and caught walked on the curb and pecked at the crumbs that were in the gutter.
The boys saw the pigeon that pecked at the crumbs in the gutter and caught the pigeon that walked on the curb.
The pigeon walked on the curb and pecked at the crumbs in the gutter, and the boys saw and caught the pigeon.

4. The cat watched the woman.
The woman put wood on the fire.
The woman needed the cat.
The cat was sly.
The fire burned brightly.

The sly cat watched the woman who needed the cat and who put wood on the fire that burned brightly.
The sly cat watched the woman who needed the cat while the woman put wood on the fire which burned brightly.
The woman who needed the sly cat put wood on the fire which burned brightly and the cat watched the woman.

REVIEW—*page L127 (a take-home assignment)*

PURPOSE: To serve as a guide for reviewing the chapter.

1. Do all relative clauses contain adjectives? **No, any kind of sentence can be a relative clause.**

211

2. What must a basic sentence have in order to be embedded as a relative clause in another sentence?   **It must have an *NP* like the *NP* in which it is embedded.**

3. Where can relative clauses occur in sentences?   **Relative clauses can occur in any noun phrase in a sentence; they follow the noun in the noun phrase.**

4. What *NP* in a relative clause is replaced by a relative pronoun?   **The *NP* that is like the *NP* in which the clause is embedded.**

5. Where does the relative pronoun occur in a relative clause?   **At the beginning.**

6. In what way are relative pronouns and the *Wh*-words in questions alike?   **They both occur at the beginning of their own sentence structure.**

7. Describe the transformations that change a deep structure to a surface structure sentence with a relative clause.   **In the deep structure the relative clause is part of a determiner phrase in some noun phrase. In the deep structure sentence string, it is between the determiner and the noun. The first transformation moves it out so that it follows the noun. Another transformation substitutes a relative pronoun for the *NP* in the relative clause that is like the *NP* in which it was embedded. If that relative pronoun isn't at the beginning of the clause, it must then be moved there.**

8. At least how many *S*'s must there be in the deep structure of a sentence with a relative clause?   **At least two: the sentence that becomes a relative clause and the sentence in which it is embedded.**

9. How many embedded *S*'s may there be in a sentence?   **An infinite number.**

10. What do we mean when we say that grammar rules are recursive?   **Grammar rules can be used over and over again in describing a sentence, because some parts can occur over and over again.**

11. Why are transformations, as well as phrase structure rules, needed to show how sentences are derived?   **Phrase structure rules can show all that we understand in the deep structure, but what they describe isn't like a sentence we hear or speak.**

212

It takes transformations to show how the deep structure can become the surface structure. Otherwise we would be describing only what we understand but not what we hear.

Many of the questions are more suited for oral discussion than for written answers, but students should study them ahead of time and be prepared to go over them in class. You may want to have sample sentences with relative clauses available to serve as illustrations for the various points, or you may wish to ask students to provide examples to support their answers.

All in the Family: Place Adverbials and Appositives

PERFORMANCE OBJECTIVES

The students should be able to

1.   Identify place adverbials modifying nouns and indicate what their deep structure is and how their surface structure can be derived.

2.   Produce, when given a sentence with a place adverbial modifying a noun, the related sentence with a relative clause, and explain how we know that the two are related.

3.   Make clear what the difference in function is between a place adverbial modifying a noun (that is, a place adverbial within a noun phrase) and a place adverbial that is part of the verb phrase.

4.   Identify appositives and indicate what their deep structure is and the transformations needed to derive their surface structure.

5.   Produce, when given a sentence with an appositive, the related sentence with a relative clause, and explain how we know they are related.

6.   Explain in what way the deep structure of sentences with prenominal adjectives, appositives, and place adverbials modifying nouns are alike.

7. Explain what parts have been deleted from the deep structure of sentences with prenominal adjectives, place adverbials modifying nouns, and appositives, and why it is possible to delete them.

8. Make clear what the *be*-deletion transformation does and why it is needed in deriving prenominal adjectives, place adverbials modifying nouns, and appositives.

9. Explain what the sentence repositioning transformation does and why it is needed in deriving relative clauses, appositives, and place adverbials modifying nouns.

SYNOPSIS

The chapter consists of the following sections:

1. The introductory section (pages L129–31) reviews the difference between deep and surface structure; how related sentences can be used in determining the deep structure of a given sentence; and the two basic ways in which basic sentence structures are combined (either coordinately or with one embedded in the other).

2. Accounting for Another Sentence Part (pages L131–37) is concerned first with identifying place adverbial modifiers of nouns and then with determining through a series of exercises that their deep structure, like that of prenominal adjectives and relative clauses, consists of one basic sentence embedded in a determiner phrase of another. In this case the embedded sentence includes the verb *be* plus a place adverbial. As in sentences with prenominal adjectives, everything up through the verb *be* can be deleted from the embedded sentence, and as in sentences with relative clauses, the embedded sentence (in this case only what is left after the deletion) is moved to a position following the noun.

3. Other Sentences Containing Place Adverbials (pages L137–39) distinguishes between place adverbials modifying nouns (which, because they are really part of the determiner phrase, are related to the question *Which?*) and place adverbials following verbs (which are related to the question *Where?*)

4. Using a Noun Phrase to Single Out Another Noun Phrase (pages L139–45) is concerned with identifying appositives (a noun phrase following another noun phrase and used to modify the

215

first noun phrase by telling *Which one?* about it) and with showing that their deep structure, like that of prenominal adjectives, relative clauses, and place adverbial modifiers of nouns, consists of a sentence embedded in a determiner phrase of another sentence. In this case the embedded sentence includes the verb *be* plus a noun phrase. The transformations needed to change this deep structure to surface structure are the same transformations that are needed to change the deep structure of a place adverbial modifier of a noun to surface structure: deleting everything from the embedded sentence except the part following *be*, then moving that part to a position following the noun it modifies.

5. **Deleting Sentence Parts** (pages L145–46) again points up that parts are deleted from the deep structure only when speakers of English know intuitively what has been deleted. For example, when the embedded sentence includes the verb *be* plus a noun phrase, everything except the noun phrase following *be* can be deleted because all speakers of English understand what embedded sentence the noun phrase has derived from.

6. **Appositives, Place Adverbials, and Adjectives Before Nouns** (pages L146–49) shows that prenominal adjectives, place adverbial modifiers of nouns, and appositives are all predicates following the verb *be* in the embedded sentence from which they derive. The transformation that deletes everything in the embedded sentence except the part following *be* can therefore be stated in very general terms. Instead of describing three different transformations, it can be shown that when a sentence which consists of the subject *NP* plus the verb *be* plus a predicate is embedded between a determiner and a noun of another sentence, everything but the predicate can be deleted. (Incidentally, this is an even more general transformation than is indicated in this chapter. Students will eventually learn that it applies to any embedded sentence that includes *be*, whether *be* is the main verb or an auxiliary verb, and whether the part following is a predicate, a possessive noun, or one of the forms of a verb that may follow the auxiliary *be*. Refer to pages 42–45 in the "Teacher's Introduction" for further discussion.) This section not only describes this deletion transformation in terms of symbols but also describes the transformation that moves the embedded *S*, or whatever is left of it after deletion, to a position following the noun. The statement of the transformation includes the information that when only an adjective is left in the embedded sentence, the adjective is not moved.

7. **Review** (page L150) provides questions to help students consolidate and review the major points of the chapter.

TEACHING THE CHAPTER

1. In preparation for teaching the chapter, review pages 41–49 in the "Teacher's Introduction." Also look back over Chapters 3, 4, and 6, which include related material on which you can build, and work through the chapter in the student text with the key to the exercises in hand.

2. The chapter can be taught inductively, though you should use it in any way that works best for you. Most of it consists of exercises interspersed with explanatory material. The majority of the exercises includes data for the students to examine, as well as questions to guide them both in analyzing the data so as to form conclusions about place adverbial noun modifiers and in generalizing about how all the kinds of noun modifiers are related. It is expected that the students will draw on what they have learned previously, insuring that the chapter will go fairly rapidly.

3. You will find that the exercises can be grouped into convenient teaching units. For example, Exercises 2–9 deal with place adverbial noun modifiers. Within that group, Exercises 2–6 — class exercises which can probably be worked through at one time — will help students to recognize place adverbial modifiers, to identify their deep structure, and to determine how the deep structure can be changed to surface structure. Exercises 7–9 provide practice and reinforcement. A second unit can be built around Exercises 10–15, which deal with appositives, beginning with class exercises to identify appositives and to determine their deep structure and continuing with the transformations that will change deep to surface structure. Exercises to provide practice and reinforcement follow. Exercise 16 leads students to generalize about how prenominal adjectives, place adverbial noun modifiers, and appositives are alike, and Exercise 17 provides reinforcement.

4. It is important, of course, for students to discuss and to understand the explanatory material which reinforces and sometimes elaborates on the concepts developed in the exercises.

KEY TO THE EXERCISES

EXERCISE 1 — *page L131 (a written assignment)*

PURPOSE: To help students review what they know about the deep structure and derivation of prenominal adjectives and relative clauses.

217

A. In order to review what you know about embedded sentences, make a branching diagram representing the deep structure of each of the following sentences.

1. The black dog stole a bone.

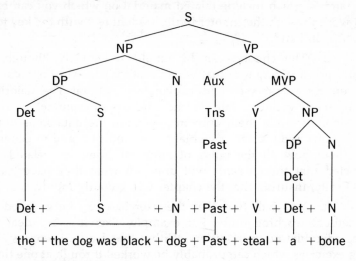

the + the dog was black + dog + Past + steal + a + bone

2. The dog that was black stole a bone.

    Note: **The diagram for sentence 2 is the same as for sentence 1.**

3. The dog that stole the bone ran away.

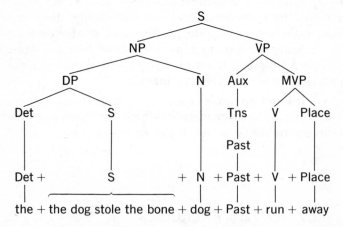

the + the dog stole the bone + dog + Past + run + away

B. Explain why the deep and surface structures of these sentences are different. **The deep structures show everything we understand in the sentence. Because of the relationship between the noun modifiers and the nouns modified, we describe the deep structures with the sentences from which the modifiers are derived as embedded in the determiner phrase of the dominant**

218

sentence. The surface structure of each sentence, however, is different because different transformations have been used. In the first, all the parts of the embedded sentence but the adjective have been deleted. In sentences 2 and 3, the embedded sentences have moved to a position following, rather than preceding, the nouns they modify, and a noun phrase in each of the embedded sentences has been replaced by a relative pronoun.

> Use this exercise as a follow-up to the discussion of the introductory paragraphs. Have the diagrams put on the board so that you can talk about them, compare them, and discuss how the deep structure should be changed to surface structure.

EXERCISE 2 — *page L131 (a class exercise)*

> PURPOSE: To help students identify place adverbials modifying nouns and to suggest what the deep structure of such modifiers might be.

A. Look at the following sentences and list the parts in each one that you would have trouble placing on a branching diagram.

1. The house **on the hill** burned down.
2. The store **across the street** sells dill pickles.
3. The sign **in the window** was dusty.
4. The boats **in the harbor** looked empty.
5. The man **on the corner** is waving a flag.
6. The books **on the floor** arrived recently.
7. The road **at the top of the mountain** is narrow.
8. The dishes **in the sink** will wait.
9. All of the students **in that class** were late.
10. Two of the elephants **in the zoo** had escaped.

B. Have you found parts like the ones you listed in section A in other sentences?

> Students should realize that these parts are place adverbials, since they are related to the question "In what place?" They should also remember that in basic sentence structures, place adverbials normally occur in the verb phrase.

If so, give some examples.

> Answers will vary. The following are possibilities:
> He keeps rabbits <u>in the garage</u>.
> They built their <u>house on the hill</u>.
> The cat sleeps <u>under the table</u>.

Where did they occur?   **In the verb phrase.**   What kind of sentence part are they?   **Place adverbials.**

219

C. Describe where all of these parts occur in the sentences above. **As part of the subject** *NP.* What do you think the deep structure of the parts might be?

Answers will vary. If students are able to relate these modifiers to the prenominal adjectives and relative clauses they have already described, they may suggest that the modifiers derive from a sentence embedded in the determiner phrase of the dominant sentence. You might want to remind them of how the deep structures of other modifiers have been described and also ask them what they understand the relationship to be between the place adverbial and the noun it follows.

You may wish to have students do section A individually and then talk about their answers. Section B, of course, is a discussion question. Again, remind students that they have found that other closely related sentences are derived from the same deep structure.

EXERCISE 3 — *pages L132–33 (a class assignment)*

PURPOSE: To help students discover that a noun phrase with a place adverbial modifier is related to a noun phrase modified by a relative clause with the same place adverbial.

A. Match each sentence in column I with the sentence most closely related to it in column II.

I	II
1. The house on the hill burned down. **d.**	a. The man that is on the corner is waving a flag.
2. The store across the street sells dill pickles. **i.**	b. Two of the elephants broke out of their cage.
3. The sign in the window was dusty. **c.**	c. The sign that was in the window was dusty.
4. The boats in the harbor looked empty. **j.**	d. The house that was on the hill burned down.
5. The man on the corner is waving a flag. **a.**	e. Nobody lives in the boats in the harbor.
6. The books on the floor arrived recently. **l.**	f. Two of the elephants that were in the zoo had escaped.
7. The road at the top of the mountain is narrow. **g.**	g. The road that is at the top of the mountain is narrow.
8. The dishes in the sink will wait. **m.**	h. The books on the floor

9. All of the students in that class were late.   **k.**
10. Two of the elephants in the zoo had escaped.   **f.**

    were delivered today.

i. The store that is across the street sells dill pickles.

j. The boats that were in the harbor looked empty.

k. All of the students that were in that class were late.

l. The books that were on the floor arrived recently.

m. The dishes that are in the sink will wait.

B. Can you think of a way to show that the sentences you matched are closely related?

Answers will depend on whether students perceive, on the basis of experience with other related sentences, that the close relationship can be demonstrated by showing that the related sentences derive from the same deep structure.

EXERCISE 4 — *page L133 (a class exercise)*

> **PURPOSE:** To help students realize that a sentence with a place adverbial noun modifier can be derived from the same deep structure as a related sentence with a relative clause.

A. Look again at two of the related sentences from Exercise 3.

    1. The house on the hill burned down.

    d. The house that was on the hill burned down.

Construct a branching diagram to illustrate the deep structure of sentence d.

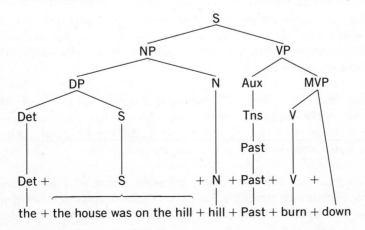

221

Note: **Students will probably have trouble identifying "down."
They should simply include it in the sentence string with a line
leading to** *MVP,* **since it is part of the main verb phrase. Actually, "burn down" is an English idiom, that is, a special construction with a unique interpretation not commonly associated
with the words used separately. It can, in effect, be considered
a verb.**

B. In what way are sentences 1 and d in section A related?   **They
    mean the same thing and have most of the same parts.**   What
    do you think the deep structure of sentence 1 might be?   **Answers will depend on whether students generalize, on the basis
    of previous experience, that sentence 1 probably has the same
    deep structure as sentence d.**

C. If two sentences have the same deep structure, how is it possible
    for their surface structures to be different?   **They have been
    derived by different transformations.**

> **You will probably want to have students do section A
> individually and then put the diagram on the board.
> Sections B and C can be used to guide discussion. Encourage students to offer their own suggestions as to what
> the deep structure might be. Leave the diagram on the
> board for use in Exercise 5. The paragraphs following the
> exercise should be discussed at the same time as is the
> exercise.**

EXERCISE 5 — *page L134 (a class assignment)*

> **PURPOSE: To help students identify the specific steps
> involved in transforming to surface structure the deep
> structure of a sentence with a place adverbial modifying
> a noun.**

A. Write the sentence string that represents the deep structure of
    The house that is on the hill burned down, showing that one sentence is embedded in the other.   **the + the house was on the hill
    + house burned down**

B. What sentence string will represent the deep structure of *The
    house on the hill burned down,* if we assume that it has the same
    deep structure as *The house that is on the hill burned down?*   **the +
    the house was on the hill + house burned down**

C. In the sentence *The house on the hill burned down,* what is missing
    from the surface structure that exists in the deep structure string
    that you wrote in section B?   ***The house was*** **in the embedded**

222

sentence. Try deleting these parts from the deep structure. **the + on the hill + house burned down** Have you used a transformation like this before? **Yes.** If so, for what kind of sentence? **A sentence with a prenominal adjective.**

D. What must you still do in order to change the deep structure of this sentence to the surface structure? **Move what is left of the embedded sentence to a position following** *house.* In what way is this transformation like one used in producing relative clauses? **It is like the transformation that moves the embedded sentence to a position following the noun it is to modify.**

> Have students start with the sentence string at the bottom of the diagram they constructed for Exercise 4. Point out that they can either combine *Past* and *burn* and *Past* and *be* as *was* and *burned* or list them as they are in the string at the bottom of the diagram.
>
> *Note:* The order in which the two transformations are applied is important in deriving a sentence with a place adverbial. Deleting the subject and the verb *be* from the embedded sentence before moving what is left makes it possible to use the same transformations that are used in deriving sentences with prenominal adjectives and sentences with relative clauses ($T_{delete\ be}$ and $T_{repos\ s}$). It is not necessary to formulate any new transformations. This shows that the transformations are very general ones, and this will be demonstrated again and again as new kinds of noun modifiers are described. On the other hand, to move the embedded sentence first and then to delete the subject and verb would make it necessary to describe one kind of transformation applying to sentences with adjectives before the noun and another kind for sentences with place adverbials and noun phrases following the noun. That the same process is involved in each case would thus be lost.

EXERCISE 6 — *page L134 (a class exercise)*

> **PURPOSE:** To reinforce the understanding of how the deep structure of a sentence with a place adverbial noun modifier is changed to surface structure.

In three or four sentences, explain what changes had to be made in the deep structure of *The house on the hill burned down* to change it to the surface structure. In your explanation include the following information.

223

1. What the embedded sentence was.   *The house was on the hill.*
2. Where it was embedded.   **In the** *NP the house.*
3. What parts were deleted.   *The house was.*
4. What kind of part was left.   *On the hill* — the place adverbial.
5. What other change had to be made.   *On the hill* was moved to a position following *house.*

> You might have students write their explanations individually and then have some of these read aloud to be used as the basis of discussion. Though the wording will vary, the explanations should include the information indicated above.

EXERCISE 7 — *pages L134–35 (a written assignment)*

> PURPOSE: To provide practice and reinforcement in identifying the deep structure of sentences with place adverbial noun modifiers and in showing the steps by which their surface structures are derived.

A. For each of the following, list the basic sentences found in the deep structure. Then write sentence strings to represent the deep structure of each, showing how one basic sentence is embedded in the other. Finally, show how each deep structure becomes surface structure, first by deleting the parts not found in the surface structure, second by moving the part of the embedded sentence that is left. Label the parts involved in the transformations as in the following example:

The building on the corner needs paint.

deep structure sentences:
the building needs paint
the building is on the corr.er

deep structure string:

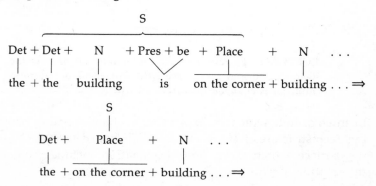

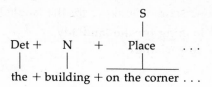

S
|
Det +   N   +   Place   . . .
| | |_____|
the + building + on the corner . . .

1. The room above this one has two windows.

    The room has two windows.
    The room is above this one.

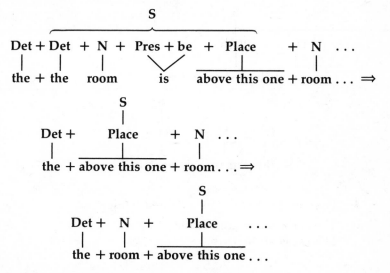

S
|
Det + Det + N + Pres + be + Place   + N . . .
 | | | ___/ |_____| |
the + the   room   is   above this one + room . . . ⟹

S
|
Det +   Place   + N . . .
 | |_____| |
the + above this one + room . . . ⟹

S
|
Det + N +   Place   . . .
 | | |_____|
the + room + above this one . . .

2. The farm on the river belongs to the Edgewaters.

    The farm belongs to the Edgewaters.
    The farm is on the river.

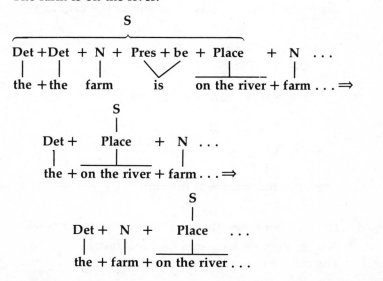

S
|
Det + Det + N + Pres + be + Place   + N . . .
 | | | ___/ |_____| |
the + the   farm   is   on the river + farm . . . ⟹

S
|
Det +   Place   + N . . .
 | |_____| |
the + on the river + farm . . . ⟹

S
|
Det + N +   Place   . . .
 | | |_____|
the + farm + on the river . . .

225

3. The man downstairs is looking for the landlady.

   The man is looking for the landlady.
   The man is downstairs.

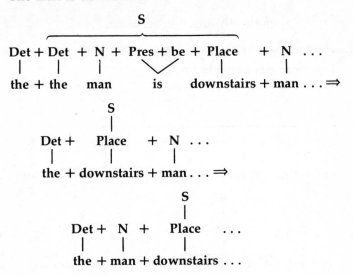

4. The car at the curb has a dented fender.

   The car has a dented fender.
   The car is at the curb.

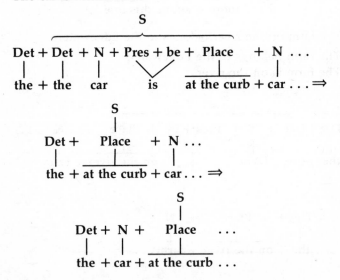

5. The children across the street eat ice cream for breakfast.

   The children eat ice cream for breakfast.
   The children are across the street.

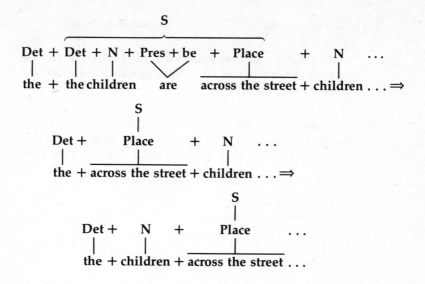

B. In deriving each of the sentences in section A from its deep structure, what kind of part was left in the embedded sentence after some parts had been deleted?   **A place adverbial.**   In each of the sentences, where did this part have to be moved to? **Following the noun.**

> Go over the example with your students before they do the exercise. Point out that they need not label all the parts of the dominant sentence with symbols—only those involved in the transformations. Also point out that after the deletion transformation only the place adverbial is left in the embedded sentence.
> If you prefer, you can have students simply list all of the embedded sentences under *S* without indicating what each of the parts is. For instance, for the example sentence they might use one of the following strings:

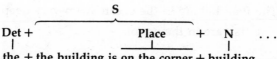

> or

S
Det +   Place   + N   ...
the + the building is on the corner + building ...

> This will depend on how much practice you feel students need.

227

EXERCISE 8 — *pages L136–37 (a written assignment)*

> **PURPOSE:**   To demonstrate that the subject *NP* and the verb can be deleted from the embedded sentence only when the verb is *be*.

A. The following sentences have relative clauses containing place adverbials. For each one, write the embedded sentence that the relative clause has been derived from. For example:

> The robin that was in the yard found a worm.
>
> **embedded sentence:**
> the robin was in the yard

1. The boy that was on the bus had a water pistol.
   The boy was on the bus.

2. The people that keep dogs in the doghouse are nuisances.
   The people keep dogs in the doghouse.

3. The people that are on the corner are waving their arms.
   The people are on the corner.

4. The tree that was in the shade grew crooked.
   The tree was in the shade.

5. The children that are playing in the corner are twins.
   The children are playing in the corner.

6. People that buy groceries in the supermarket get many bargains.
   People buy groceries in the supermarket.

7. I know the man that is working in the yard.
   The man is working in the yard.

8. The cable cars that are in San Francisco are unique.
   The cable cars are in San Francisco.

9. The men that fish in the ocean start at dawn.
   The men fish in the ocean.

10. The fish that are in the ocean swim very deep.
    The fish are in the ocean.

B. From which of these embedded sentences can parts be deleted to form new surface structure sentences with the same meaning? Write the sentences that would result if these parts were deleted.

For example:

The robin that was in the yard found a worm.

sentence with parts deleted:
The robin in the yard found a worm.

Parts can be deleted from 1, 3, 4, 7, 8, and 10. The sentences with the parts deleted are:

1. The boy on the bus had a water pistol.
3. The people on the corner are waving their arms.
4. The tree in the shade grew crooked.
7. I know the man working in the yard.
8. The cable cars in San Francisco are unique.
10. The fish in the ocean swim very deep.

Note: Sentences 2, 5, 6, and 9 can also have parts deleted and still remain grammatical, but they will be sentences with a different meaning. For example, we can delete parts from sentence 2 to produce *The people in the doghouse are nuisances,* which is grammatical, but we assume that such a sentence is related to *The people that are in the doghouse are nuisances* rather than to *The people that keep dogs in the doghouse are nuisances.*

Note: Be in sentence 7 is the auxiliary verb *be* rather than the main verb. You need not mention this unless students notice it. If they do you can point out that it doesn't matter whether *be* is the auxiliary or the main verb, as this sentence demonstrates. In either case it can be deleted from the embedded sentence, leaving what follows.

C. In the sentences in section A, how are the embedded sentences from which parts can be deleted different from those from which parts cannot be deleted? **The sentences from which parts can be deleted with no change in meaning include the verb *be*. The others do not.** What do the embedded sentences from which parts can be deleted have in common? **They all include the verb *be* plus a place adverbial.** Write a symbol string that will represent the deep structure of each of the embedded sentences from which parts can be deleted. (Since they have the same verb, you can simply name the verb.) *NP + Tns + be + Place*

Note: **Since the tense can be either *Past* or *Pres*, the particular tense is not indicated.**

D. How is this symbol string similar to the one representing an embedded sentence from which we get an adjective modifying a noun? **It is like the symbol string representing the embedded**   229 sentence underlying an adjective modifier except for what follows the verb *be*.

E. When adjectives modify nouns, where are they located?   **Just before the noun.**   When place adverbials modify nouns, where are they located?   **Just after the noun.**

Note: **As students may discover later, adjectives precede the nouns they modify only when they are not followed by other parts, for example,** *The children, happy with their toys, were playing quietly* **rather than** *The happy with their toys children were playing quietly.*

You may wish to have students write out only sections A and B and use C, D, and E as the basis of discussion.

EXERCISE 9 — *pages L137–38 (a written assignment)*

PURPOSE: **To provide practice in identifying the deep structure of sentences with place adverbials and to distinguish between place adverbials when they function as noun modifiers and when they occur in the verb phrase of basic sentences.**

A. Find the place adverbials in the following sentences. Describe their position in the sentence. Are they related to the question *Where?* or the question *Which?*   Draw diagrams illustrating the deep structure of each.

1. The seals **in the water** swim well.

The place adverbial follows the noun. Actually it is part of the noun phrase and tells *which.*

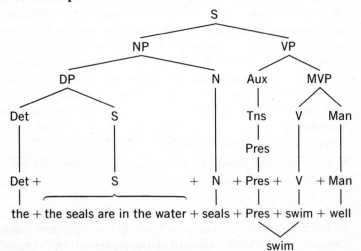

2. The seals play **in the water.**

   The place adverbial is part of the verb phrase and tells *where.*

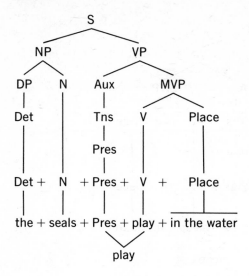

3. The birds **in the trees** sing heartily.

   The place adverbial is part of the noun phrase and tells *which.*

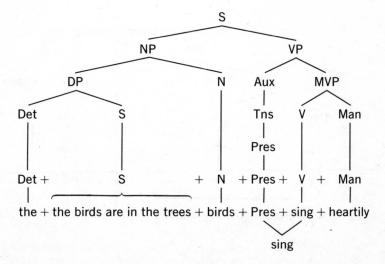

231

4. The birds sleep **in the trees.**

    The place adverbial is part of the verb phrase and tells *where.*

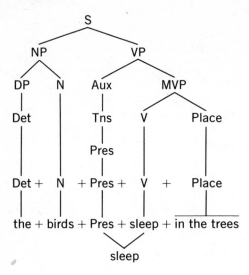

5. The children **upstairs** are noisy.

    The place adverbial is part of the noun phrase and tells *which.*

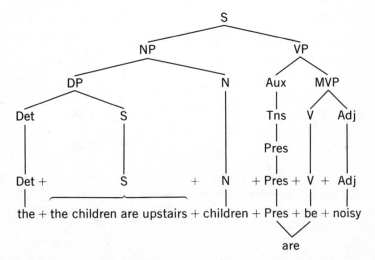

6. The children play **upstairs.**

   The place adverbial is in the verb phrase and tells *where.*

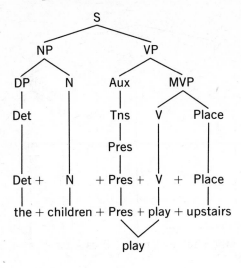

7. The man eats **in the kitchen.**

   The place adverbial is in the verb phrase and tells *where.*

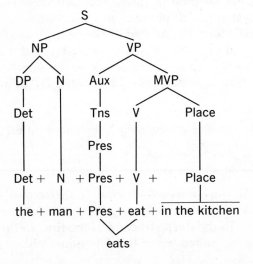

233

8. The man **in the kitchen** is a boarder.

The place adverbial is part of the subject *NP* and tells *which*.

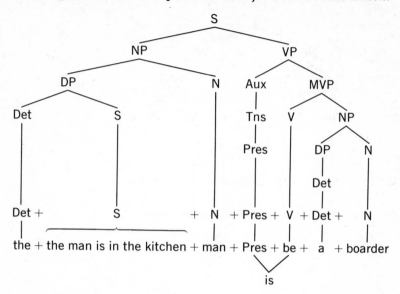

B. On the basis of your diagrams, explain how the deep structure of place adverbials that answer the question *Which?* differs from the deep structure of place adverbials that answer just the question *Where?*   **In the deep structure, place adverbials that answer the question *Which?* are predicates in sentences embedded in the determiner phrase of another sentence, and in their derivation all but the place adverbials are deleted from the embedded sentences. Place adverbials that answer the question *Where?* derive from sentences in which they are part of the verb phrase and they retain that position in the surface structure. They can be found in almost any verb phrase.**   In basic sentences, where are place adverbials found?   **As part of the verb phrase following almost any kind of verb.**   When a place adverbial modifies a noun, what kind of deep structure does it derive from?   **It is a *Pr* following *be* in a sentence embedded in the *DP* of another sentence.**

C. How does the meaning of the following sentences differ?

The man in the store raises dogs.
The man raises dogs in the store.

In the first, *in the store* tells *which* man. In the second, *in the store* tells *where* the man raises dogs.   How do their deep structures differ?   **In the deep structure of the first, *in the store* is a *Pr* in a sentence embedded in the determiner phrase of *the***

man. **In the deep structure of the second, a basic sentence,** *in the store* **is a place adverbial in the verb phrase.**

EXERCISE 10 — *page L139 (for class discussion)*

> **PURPOSE:** **To make students aware of appositives and to stimulate them to think about how such appositives might be described.**

A. Are the following sentences like the sentences you have already learned to analyze? If not, in what way are they different?

1. Frank the astronaut walked on the moon.
2. Gloria the baby-sitter lives next door.
3. Mr. Pemberton the principal rides a bicycle.
4. George the mayor raises petunias.
5. Simpson the painter moved into a new studio.

Students have not yet analyzed sentences in which two noun phrases occur together, one after the other.

B. List the parts that you wouldn't know where to put in a diagram. **The astronaut, the baby-sitter, the principal, the mayor, and the painter.**

C. How might you find out what the deep structure of these sentences is? **On the basis of their experience with other sentences, students might suggest that they think of some related sentences which they already know how to describe.**

> **Use this exercise simply to introduce the section on appositives.**

EXERCISE 11 — *page L140 (a class exercise)*

> **PURPOSE:** **To identify sentences with relative clauses related to sentences with appositives.**

A. In what way are the following two sentences related?

> Frank the astronaut walked on the moon.
> The Frank that is the astronaut walked on the moon.

They have the same meaning and in general have the same parts.

B. Complete the following chart by writing sentences that are related to those in column I in the same way that the first pair are related.

235

	I	II
1.	Frank the astronaut walked on the moon.	**The Frank that is the astronaut walked on the moon.**
2.	Gloria the baby-sitter lives next door.	**The Gloria that is the baby-sitter lives next door.**
3.	Mr. Pemberton the principal rides a bicycle.	**The Mr. Pemberton that is the principal rides a bicycle.**
4.	George the mayor raises petunias.	**The George that is the mayor raises petunias.**
5.	Simpson the painter moved into a new studio.	**The Simpson that is the painter moved into a new studio.**

C. What do the sentences you wrote in column II have in common? **They all include relative clauses and their subject *NP*'s include proper nouns preceded by the determiner *the*.**   Is the structure of these sentences familiar to you? **Sentences with relative clauses are familiar to the students, but the proper noun preceded by a determiner may not be.**   Can you think of occasions when you might use such sentences? If so, when? **Such sentences are used to point out *which one* about a proper noun.**

> **Discuss section A, then have students do section B individually, and finally use the questions in C to guide discussion. The exercise should lead into an introduction of the material that follows, where the use of a visible determiner with a proper noun when it also occurs with a relative clause is presented. A distinction is made between restrictive appositives—those that identify the noun being modified—and nonrestrictive appositives—those that simply add some information. The purpose of the discussion is to explain why we assume that in the deep structure of a proper noun followed by an appositive, the proper noun is preceded by *the*.**

EXERCISE 12 — *page L142 (a class assignment)*

> **PURPOSE: To identify the deep structure of a sentence with an appositive by comparing it to a related sentence with a relative clause.**

A. What are the two sentences in the deep structure of *The Frank that is the astronaut walked on the moon*? (Remember that a relative pronoun replaces an *NP* just like one in the dominant sentence.)

The Frank walked on the moon.
The Frank is the astronaut.

236

B. Construct a branching diagram to show how these sentences are related in the deep structure. What is the sentence string that represents the deep structure?

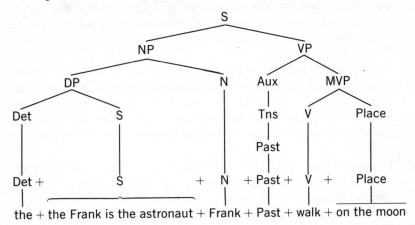

the + the Frank is the astronaut + Frank + Past + walk + on the moon

the + the Frank is the astronaut + Frank walked on the moon

C. What transformations are needed to change this string to the surface structure sentence *The Frank that is the astronaut walked on the moon?* **The embedded sentence must be moved to a position following the noun** *Frank* **and** *the Frank* **in the embedded sentence must be replaced by** *that.* What transformations describe these changes? *T*repos s **describes the first and** *T*wh-word **describes the second.**

> Have this exercise prepared in class so that you can help students think it through. They should understand that because *the* precedes *Frank* in the surface structure it must have been there in the deep structure. You will need to point out (as is reiterated in the paragraphs that follow the exercise) that deep structure is often different from surface structure, and often ungrammatical as far as the sentences we actually use go. Have the diagram put on the board and use it as the basis of discussion. Then save it for use in Exercise 13.

EXERCISE 13 – *page L143 (a guide to discussion)*

> PURPOSE: To identify the transformations needed to change the deep structure of an appositive to surface structure.

A. Look once more at the diagram you constructed in Exercise 12 and copy the sentence string that represents the deep structure   237 of *The Frank that is the astronaut walked on the moon.* Remember that closely related sentences with the same meaning have the same deep structure. We will assume, therefore, that this string also represents the deep structure of *Frank the astronaut walks on the moon.*   **the + Frank is the astronaut + Frank walked on the moon**

B. Decide what transformations are needed to change the sentence string that represents the deep structure of *The Frank that is the astronaut walked on the moon* to *Frank the astronaut walked on the moon.* **Everything but *the astronaut* must be deleted from the embedded sentence and *the* before *Frank* must be deleted.**

C. Have you used any of these transformations before? If so, which ones? **Yes, the transformation that deletes everything up through the verb *be* in the embedded sentence.** Did you make any changes that you have not used before? If so, which ones? **The deletion of *the* before *Frank* is a transformation not used before.**

> **Use the diagram constructed for Exercise 12 as the basis of discussion for this exercise.**

EXERCISE 14 — *page L144 (a written assignment)*

> **PURPOSE: To provide practice in identifying the deep structure of sentences with appositives and in showing how their surface structure is derived.**

A. List the appositives in each of the following sentences. Then list the basic sentences in the deep structure of each. Show how one S is embedded in the other in the deep structure by writing a deep structure sentence string. Finally, show how the deep structure becomes surface structure. For example:

> Joe the carpenter builds windmills.
>
> **appositive:** the carpenter
>
> **basic sentences in the deep structure:**
> the Joe builds windmills
> the Joe is the carpenter
>
> **sentence string:**
> **the + the Joe is the carpenter + Joe builds windmills ⟹**
>   **the + the carpenter + Joe builds windmills ⟹**
>   the Joe + **the carpenter +** builds windmills ⟹
>   Joe + **the carpenter +** builds windmills

1. Betsy our cousin came to visit us.

    appositive: **our cousin**

    basic sentences in the deep structure:
    the Betsy came to visit us
    the Betsy is our cousin

    sentence string:
    the + the Betsy is our cousin + Betsy came to visit us ⟹
        the + our cousin + Betsy came to visit us ⟹
            the Betsy + our cousin + came to visit us ⟹
                Betsy + our cousin + came to visit us

2. Rover the sheepdog saved the lambs.

    appositive: **the sheepdog**

    basic sentences in the deep structure:
    the Rover saved the lambs
    the Rover was the sheepdog

    sentence string:
    the + the Rover was the sheepdog + Rover saved the lambs ⟹
        the + the sheepdog + Rover saved the lambs ⟹
            the Rover + the sheepdog + saved the lambs ⟹
                Rover + the sheepdog + saved the lambs

3. Grover the boxer became champion.

    appositive: **the boxer**

    basic sentences in the deep structure:
    the Grover became champion
    the Grover was the boxer

    sentence string:
    the + the Grover was the boxer + Grover became champion ⟹
        the + the boxer + Grover became champion ⟹
            the Grover + the boxer + became champion ⟹
                Grover + the boxer + became champion

4. Katy Larson the singer always stays at the hotel.

    appositive: **the singer**

    basic sentences in the deep structure:
    the Katy Larson always stays at the hotel
    the Katy Larson is the singer

    sentence string:
    the + the Katy Larson is the singer + Katy Larson always stays at the hotel ⟹
        the + the singer + Katy Larson always stays at the hotel ⟹
            the Katy Larson + the singer + always stays at the hotel ⟹
                Katy Larson + the singer + always stays at the hotel

5. Crampton the elf lived in a matchbox.

    appositive: **the elf**

    basic sentences in the deep structure:
    the Crampton lived in a matchbox
    the Crampton was the elf

    sentence string:
    the + the Crampton was the elf + Crampton lived in a matchbox ⟹
    the + the elf + Crampton lived in a matchbox ⟹
    the Crampton + the elf + lived in a matchbox ⟹
    Crampton + the elf + lived in a matchbox

6. William the Conqueror won at Hastings.

    appositive: **the Conqueror**

    basic sentences in the deep structure:
    the William won at Hastings
    the William was the Conqueror

    sentence string:
    the + the William was the Conqueror + William won at Hastings ⟹
    the + the Conqueror + William won at Hastings ⟹
    the William + the Conqueror + won at Hastings ⟹
    William + the Conqueror + won at Hastings

B. What does each of the embedded sentences in the sentences in section A share with the sentence in which it is embedded?   **A noun phrase.**

> It may take students a little while to get used to the word *the* before the proper noun. Emphasize that deep structure is only a way of describing what we understand, not what we say.
>
> You might wish to discuss how each of the embedded sentences is alike (they all have the verb *be* followed by a noun phrase), and how the transformations used in deriving each sentence are alike (in each all but the part following the verb *be* is deleted from the embedded sentence, then what is left moves to a position following the noun and the *the* in the dominant sentence is deleted). This regularity is what enables us to identify the deep structure and show how that deep structure is changed to surface structure.

EXERCISE 15 — *pages L145–46 (a written assignment)*

PURPOSE: To distinguish the embedded sentence underlying an appositive (from which parts can be

deleted) from embedded sentences from which parts
cannot be deleted.

A. The following sentences all have relative clauses. For each one,
    write the embedded sentence that has been changed into a
    relative clause. For example:

    The girl that painted the picture lives on an island.
    embedded sentence:
    the girl painted the picture

1. The Frank that is the astronaut walked on the moon.
    the Frank is the astronaut

2. The Frank that builds boats gives advice.
    the Frank builds boats

3. The Gloria that is the baby-sitter lives next door.
    the Gloria is the baby-sitter

4. The Gloria that raises bloodhounds visited Aunt Emma.
    the Gloria raises bloodhounds

5. The Mr. Pemberton that is the principal rides a bicycle.
    the Mr. Pemberton is the principal

6. The Mr. Pemberton that sells brooms rides a bicycle.
    the Mr. Pemberton sells brooms

7. The George that is the mayor raises petunias.
    the George is the mayor

8. The George that works for the city raises petunias.
    the George works for the city

9. The Simpson that is the painter moved into a new studio.
    the Simpson is the painter

10. The Simpson that inherited a fortune moved into a new
    studio.
    the Simpson inherited a fortune

B. From which of these embedded sentences can parts be deleted
    to form appositives? **1, 3, 5, 7, and 9.** What do they all have
    in common? **The verb *be* followed by a noun phrase.**

C. How do the embedded sentences from which parts can be
    deleted differ from the embedded sentences from which parts   241

cannot be deleted? **They include the verb** *be* **plus a noun phrase. The other sentences contain various other verbs and various other parts.**

D. Write a symbol string that will represent each of the embedded sentences from which parts can be deleted. (If the same verb appears in all of the sentences, name it in your string of symbols, rather than using the symbol *V*.)   *NP + Tns + be + NP*

E. Is the symbol string you wrote in section D like the symbol strings that represent the deep structure of adjective and place adverbial modifiers? If so, in what way?   **Yes, it is like the symbol string representing the deep structure of sentences with adjective or place adverbial modifiers in that it includes the verb** *be*. **The only way that it differs is in what follows** *be*.

EXERCISE 16 — *pages L146–47 (a written assignment)*

> **PURPOSE: To provide practice in identifying the deep structure of noun modifiers and to demonstrate the similarity in the deep structure and in the derivation of prenominal adjectives, place adverbial noun modifiers, and appositives.**

A. List the sentences in the deep structure of each of the following. Then mark the place where one of the deep structure sentences is embedded in the other. For example:

The house on the hill burned down.

deep structure sentences:
the ✕ house burned down
the house was on the hill

1. A pale light was shining.

   deep structure sentences:
   a ✕ light was shining
   a light was pale

2. The boy on the ladder held a hammer.

   deep structure sentences:
   the ✕ boy held a hammer
   the boy was on the ladder

3. The nervous milkmaid dropped the bucket.

   deep structure sentences:
   the ✕ milkmaid dropped the bucket
   the milkmaid was nervous

4. My cousin the banker carries an umbrella.

   deep structure sentences:
   my ✕ cousin carries an umbrella
   my cousin is the banker

5. The people downstairs have been waiting all day.

   deep structure sentences:
   the ✕ people have been waiting all day
   the people are downstairs

6. A scarlet bird flew through the window.

   deep structure sentences:
   a ✕ bird flew through the window
   a bird was scarlet

7. An official letter was lying on the desk.

   deep structure sentences:
   a ✕ letter was lying on the desk
   a letter was official

8. The building on the corner is a landmark.

   deep structure sentences:
   the ✕ building is a landmark
   the building is on the corner

9. Mr. James the driver was late this morning.

   deep structure sentences:
   the ✕ Mr. James was late this morning
   the Mr. James was the driver

10. Sarah the violinist practices constantly.

    deep structure sentences:
    the ✕ Sarah practices constantly
    the Sarah is the violinist

B. The embedded sentences all contain forms of the same verb. What is the verb?   *Be.*   What kinds of parts follow the verb in the embedded sentences?   **Adjectives, noun phrases, or place adverbials.**   What are these parts called when they follow the verb *be*?   **Predicates.**

C. What is deleted from each of the embedded sentences?   **The subject *NP*, tense, and the verb *be*.**   In each, what is left of the embedded sentences in the surface structure?   **The predicate, the part that follows *be*.**   What generalization can you make about what can be deleted from a deep structure sentence embedded in a *DP*?   **When the embedded sentence includes the**   243

verb *be* plus a predicate, everything but the predicate can be
deleted.

D. Write the sentence strings that represent the deep structure for
sentences 3, 8, and 9 of section A. Then show what transformations are necessary to change each of these deep structure strings
to surface structure sentences. Mark the parts involved in the
transformations with *Det, S,* and *N.* Label the part left after
deletion with *NP, Adj,* or *Place.* For example:

The house on the hill burned down.

Det +   S   + N
| _____ |
the + the house was on the hill + house burned down ⟹

                    S
                    |
        Det +   Place   + N
        | _____ |
        the + on the hill + house burned down ⟹

                            S
                            |
            Det + N +   Place
            | | _____
            the + house + on the hill + burned down

3. The nervous milkmaid dropped the bucket.

    the + the milkmaid was nervous +
                                milkmaid dropped the bucket

    Det +   S   +   N   . . .
    | _____ |
    the + the milkmaid was nervous + milkmaid . . . ⟹

                    S
                    |
        Det +   Adj   +   N   . . .
        | | |
        the + nervous + milkmaid . . .

8. The building on the corner is a landmark.

    the + the building is on the corner + building is a landmark

    Det +   S   +   N   . . .
    | _____ |

the + the building is on the corner + building . . . ⟹

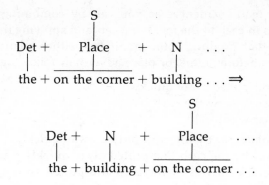

S
|
Det +   Place   +   N   . . .
 | | |
the + on the corner + building . . . ⟹

                            S
                            |
        Det +   N   +   Place   . . .
         | | |
        the + building + on the corner . . .

9. Mr. James the driver was late this morning.
    the + the Mr. James was the driver +
                        Mr. James was late this morning

Det +   S   +   N   . . .
 | |
the + the Mr. James was the driver + Mr. James . . . ⟹

              S
              |
    Det +   NP   +   N   . . .
     | | |
    the + the driver + Mr. James . . . ⟹

                    S
                    |
      Det +   N   +   NP   . . .
       | | |
      the + Mr. James + the driver . . . ⟹

            Mr. James + the driver . . .

E. Do all three of the sentences you examined in section D undergo
    the same transformations? If not, which transformations are the
    same and which are different? **They all undergo the same
    deletion transformation, but in sentences 8 and 9 the parts of the
    embedded sentences left after deletion are moved to a position
    following the nouns they modify. The adjective in sentence 3 is
    not moved.**

EXERCISE 17 — *page L149 (a written assignment)*

> **PURPOSE: To provide practice in consciously com-
> bining basic sentences in various ways to produce a
> variety of sentences and thus demonstrate the recursive
> nature of language.**

245

A. Make as many sentences as you can by combining the basic sentences in each of the following sets and applying the transformations that produce noun modifiers—either relative clauses, adjectives before nouns, or place adverbials following nouns.

1. The car pulled away quickly.
    The car was by the curb.
    The car was black.

    The black car by the curb pulled away quickly.
    The car by the curb that pulled away quickly was black.
    The black car was by the curb and pulled away quickly.

2. That package belongs to the boy.
    That package is on the table.
    The boy has the poodle.
    The poodle is nervous.

    That package on the table belongs to the boy that has the
      nervous poodle.
    That package that belongs to the boy that has the nervous
      poodle is on the table.
    That package is on the table and belongs to the boy that has
      the nervous poodle.

3. A dog sat in the shade.
    A dog was bedraggled.
    The shade was under the tree.

    A bedraggled dog sat in the shade under the tree.
    A dog that sat in the shade under the tree was bedraggled.
    A dog that was bedraggled sat in the shade that was under
      the tree.

4. The moon rose early tonight.
    The moon is under a cloud.
    The cloud is dark.

    The moon that rose early tonight is under a dark cloud.
    The moon that is under a dark cloud rose early tonight.
    The moon rose early tonight and is under a dark cloud.

5. The starfish is a specimen.
    The specimen is rare.
    The starfish is on the rock.
    The rock juts out.

    The starfish that is a rare specimen is on the rock that juts
      out.
    The starfish that is on the rock that juts out is a rare
      specimen.
    The starfish is a rare specimen and it is on the rock that
      juts out.

246

B. Think of five sentences with appositives in which the appositives answer the question *Which?*

Answers will vary. The following are possibilities:

Mary the tennis player came from Gary.
Baron the Great Dane was a nuisance.
Jack the giantkiller climbed the beanpole.
Bartholomen the king's page returned to the castle.
Penelope the sorceress wove a magic spell.

> The point of this exercise is not to teach students how to combine basic sentences. They already know how to do that and will no doubt make various new sentences out of the basic sentences automatically, with no trouble at all. The important thing is for them to become conscious of the process that they are using. They embed one sentence in another and perform the necessary transformations that produce the surface structure without giving it any thought.

REVIEW — *page L150 (an exercise to fit the needs of your class.)*

> PURPOSE: To provide a guide for students in reviewing the chapter.

1. Where can a sentence containing a place adverbial be embedded in another sentence? **Between the determiner and noun of some noun phrase.**

2. What is the difference between the deep structure of a place adverbial that answers the question *Which?* and the deep structure of a place adverbial that answers just the question *Where?* **A place adverbial that answers the question *Which?* is part of a sentence embedded in a noun phrase of another sentence (between the determiner and the noun). A place adverbial that answers the question *Where?* is not part of an embedded sentence; it is part of a verb phrase.**

3. What transformations are needed to change the deep structure of *The house that was on the hill burned down* to *The house on the hill burned down*? **The first transformation deletes the subject NP and verb of the embedded sentence; the second moves what is left out beyond the noun.**

4. When a place adverbial follows a noun in the surface structure of a sentence, what verb is in the embedded sentence in the deep structure? **A form of the verb *be.***

247

5. What is an appositive? **A noun phrase following immediately another *NP*.** Where is it found in the deep structure? **As part of a sentence embedded between a *Det* and a noun.**

6. What do the subject *NP*'s in the following three sentences have in common?

   > Frank the barber lives next door.
   > A strange cloud hovered overhead.
   > The park across the street is closed today.

   Each of the sentences has a part that is derived from a sentence embedded in the subject *NP*. In each, the part derived from the embedded sentence is a noun modifier.

7. In what ways are the deep structures of the three sentences in question 6 alike? **In each there is an embedded sentence which includes the verb *be* plus a predicate.**

8. What has been deleted from the deep structure of each of the three sentences in question 6? **The subject *NP* and the verb *be* of the embedded sentence.**

9. What part of the embedded sentence is left in the surface structure of each? **The predicate, or the part that follows *be*.**

10. How do the three sentences in question 6 differ from sentences like *The Mary that scrubs floors knows my cousins*? **Parts have been deleted from the embedded sentence in the deep structure of each of the three sentences in question 6. Nothing has been deleted from the embedded sentence underlying the relative clause in *The Mary that scrubs floors knows my cousins* and, in fact, nothing can be deleted.**

248

Chapter **8**

Another Close Relation: The Possessive

PERFORMANCE OBJECTIVES

The student should be able to

1. Recognize possessive nouns and pronouns.

2. Identify the deep structure of sentences with possessive nouns or pronouns, both on a branching diagram or with a sentence string.

3. Indicate and illustrate the transformations that will change the deep structure of a sentence with a possessive noun or pronoun to the surface structure.

4. Explain how the deep structure of a possessive modifier is like the deep structure of an adjective, place adverbial, appositive, or relative clause modifier.

5. Explain how the derivation of a sentence with a possessive modifier is similar to and how it is different from the derivation of a sentence with an adjective, place adverbial, or appositive modifier.

249

SYNOPSIS

The chapter consists of the following sections:

1. The introductory section (pages L153–54) reviews the following concepts that have been emphasized throughout the text:

a) A deep structure in which one basic sentence is embedded in the *DP* of another underlies many different kinds of noun modifiers.

b) The rules for describing basic sentences can also be used in describing more complicated sentences.

c) Sentences with noun modifiers are derived from a deep structure with one basic sentence embedded in the *DP* of another by two very general transformations: $T_{delete\ be}$ and $T_{repos\ S}$.

2. Another Part Derived from an Embedded Sentence (pages L155–56) identifies possessive nouns and suggests the relationship between possessives and sentences with the verb *have* (*e.g., John's hat is* related to *John has the hat*).

3. Changing Basic Sentences to Sentences with Possessives (pages L156–59) identifies the transformations that will change the deep structure of a sentence with the verb *have* to a sentence with a possessive.

4. How Does *NP + Poss* Appear in the Surface Structure? (page L159) is a short section with no exercises that discusses that possessives end with a sound spelled with *s* and are written with an apostrophe.

5. Embedding an *S* Containing a Possessive (pages L160–65) shows that possessive noun modifiers are derived from embedded sentences with the verb *have* by the possessive transformation. Like other noun modifiers, possessive noun modifiers are derived from sentences embedded in the *DP*'s of other sentences, and with the addition of the possessive transformation are derived in the same way as other noun modifiers.

6. Another Kind of Possessive (pages L165–74) shows that possessive pronouns are derived in the same way as possessive nouns. Most of them (*her, my, your, our,* and *their*) have a different form when they occur without a noun in the surface structure (for example, *It is my book / It is mine*). The section concludes by showing how the various transformations that have been identified operate together in deriving sentences and how we are able, through those transformations, to derive many different sentences from a few basic sentence structures.

7. Review (page L174) provides questions to guide the student in pulling together the basic concepts of the chapter.

TEACHING THE CHAPTER

1. In preparation for teaching the chapter, read pages 42–47 in the "Teacher's Introduction" to this guide and review the chapters in the student text dealing with noun modifiers. You will, of course, want to work through the chapter ahead of time with the key to the exercises in hand.

2. The chapter, which completes the study of noun modifiers in this text, can be taught inductively if you like to teach that way. It relies heavily on what the students have learned in earlier chapters, assuming that they will use what they know about the deep structure of other noun modifiers and the transformations that change them to surface structure in describing possessive modifiers.

3. The introductory paragraphs should be useful in helping students review what they have learned about noun modifiers in preparation for learning about a new modifier. You might want to ask members of the class to identify the deep structure of the three sentences on page L154 and to indicate what transformations are needed to produce the various surface structures. For your information, the derivation of these sentences from the deep structure follows:

$$\overset{\displaystyle S}{\overbrace{\text{the} + \text{the man came to dinner}}} + \text{man ate soup} \Rightarrow$$

$$T_{\text{repos S}}:\ \text{the man} + \overset{\displaystyle S}{\overbrace{\text{the man came to dinner}}} + \text{ate soup} \Rightarrow$$

$$T_{\text{Wh-word}}:\ \text{the man} + \overset{\displaystyle S}{\overbrace{\textbf{that}\ \text{came to dinner}}} + \text{ate soup}$$

$$\overset{\displaystyle S}{\overbrace{\text{the} + \text{the man is in the convertible}}} + \text{man is a doctor} \Rightarrow$$

$$T_{\text{delete be}}:\ \text{the} + \overset{\displaystyle S}{\overbrace{\text{in the convertible}}} + \text{man is a doctor} \Rightarrow$$

$$T_{\text{repos S}}:\ \text{the man} + \overset{\displaystyle S}{\overbrace{\text{in the convertible}}} + \text{is a doctor}$$

$$\emptyset + \emptyset\ \overset{\displaystyle S}{\overbrace{\text{John Smith is the ballplayer}}} + \text{John Smith advertises}$$
$$\text{razor blades} \Rightarrow \qquad 251$$

$$\overset{\overset{\displaystyle S}{\frown}}{\text{T}_{\text{delete be}}: \quad \emptyset + \text{the ballplayer} + \text{John Smith advertises}}$$

razor blades $\Rightarrow$

$$\text{T}_{\text{repos S}}: \quad \emptyset + \text{John Smith} \overset{\overset{\displaystyle S}{\frown}}{+ \text{ the ballplayer }} + \text{advertises}$$

razor blades

4. Throughout, adapt the chapter to your students. Provide additional review for those who need it. Some students may be able to work through the chapter largely on their own. The one thing they should understand is that, with the addition of the possessive transformation, sentences with possessives can be described by the same transformations used to account for other kinds of sentences discussed this year. Such sentences represent another example that the rules of language are economical. In the process of learning to describe a variety of different sentence parts, students should have discovered a very important principle of language. This chapter re-emphasizes this point.

KEY TO THE EXERCISES

EXERCISE 1 — *page L155 (the basis of discussion)*

> **PURPOSE: To focus attention on the possessive and to motivate the exercises that follow.**

A. What relationship does a determiner have to the noun that follows it? **It tells *which* or *how much* or *how many* about the noun.**

B. What parts that you have not yet described do you find in the following sentences?

Note: **The parts are boldfaced.**

1. **Ralph's** gloves disappeared.
2. The **dog's** feet were caked with mud.
3. **Webster's** mother went to the door.
4. The **horse's** mane had been tightly braided.
5. **Amy's** brother was furious.
6. **Frank's** shop is around the corner.
7. The **doll's** hair is made of nylon.
8. **Marcia's** fish swam in circles.

C. Describe the relationship of these parts to the nouns that follow. **They answer the question *which?* or *whose?* about the nouns that follow.**

D. How do you think these parts might be explained?

Answers will vary. The question should be used only to motivate discussion. It is hoped that students may have good suggestions because of their prior experience in describing other kinds of modifiers that occur in the determiner phrase.

EXERCISE 2 — *pages L155–56 (a class exercise)*

> **PURPOSE: To establish a relationship between a possessive and a sentence with the verb *have.***

A. Look at the following pair of sentences.

> John's hat is on the table.
> The hat is on the table.

How is the subject noun phrase in the first sentence different from the subject noun phrase in the second one? **The subject noun phrase in the first sentence includes a possessive.**

B. Which one of the following sentences is most closely related to the first sentence in section A?

1. The hat is on the table that John has.
2. The hat that John likes is on the table.
3. **The hat that John has is on the table.**

C. Construct the diagram that represents the deep structure of *The hat that John has is on the table.*

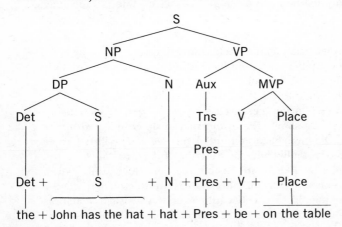

the + John has the hat + hat + Pres + be + on the table

D. What diagram would represent the deep structure of *John's hat is on the table* if we assume it means the same thing as *The hat that John has is on the table*?   **The same diagram that represents the deep structure of *The hat that John has is on the table*.**

Students should read and understand the paragraph following this exercise.

EXERCISE 3 — *pages L156–57 (a class exercise)*

PURPOSE: To establish the relationship between sentences like *John has the hat* and *The hat is John's*.

A. Which one of the following sentences is most closely related to *John has the hat*?

1. The hat is handsome.
2. **The hat is John's.**
3. The hat is here.

B. For many sentences like *John has the hat*, there is a related sentence like *The hat is John's*. Copy the following sentences and then see if you can write a related sentence of this kind for each one. Keep the two sentences side by side so that you can compare them later.

1. Richard has the coat.   **The coat is Richard's.**
2. Martin has the turtle.   **The turtle is Martin's.**
3. The dog has the bone.   **The bone is the dog's.**
4. Gloria has the apron.   **The apron is Gloria's.**
5. The man has the truck.   **The truck is the man's.**
6. The baby has the blanket.   **The blanket is the baby's.**
7. Florence has the plate.   **The plate is Florence's.**
8. Andrew has the key.   **The key is Andrew's.**

The exercise should help students realize that the relationship between *John has the hat* and *The hat is John's* is not unique. In other words, a great many sentences like *John has the hat* have related sentences like *The hat is John's*. Encourage discussion of how the relationship might be shown. Point out that in describing a structure that has not been accounted for, we start with what we already know how to describe. *John has the hat*, and sentences like it, are basic sentences which students can account for with the phrase structure rules. Therefore the problem is to identify the regular way such sentences can be changed to the related sentences with possessives.

Supplementary Information

A word should be said about the kind of possessive that is being discussed in the chapter. Possessives are somewhat ambiguous in English. *The men's shop has a new shipment of ties* might mean "the shop which the men have" or "the shop for men." *She goes to the girls' school* can mean "the school which the girls have" or "the school for girls." We are considering only possessives related to *have* in this chapter.

It is a common misconception that a possessive form in a sentence implies possession in the sense of ownership. Possession or ownership may or may not be implied in the use of the possessive. Possessive forms may merely imply *holding at the moment* or some other close relationship. There is no real ownership implied in any of the following:

I held John's place in line.

Their block was deserted.

I peeked at John's hand in the poker game.

The reason *have* is considered the verb in the deep structure of sentences with possessives is not because of any semantic relationship to ownership or possession but rather because of the sharing of parts and grammatical relationships between sentences like

The boy has the book.

and

The book is the boy's.

However, *have* is a verb very broad in its meaning. In a sentence like *The last hand that I had was a bad one to bid on,* had merely indicates temporary holding, not possession in the sense of ownership. Compare a similar sentence with a possessive: *My hand was no good.* The following sentences should convince any of us that neither the possessive nor *have* necessarily implies ownership: *We rent our apartment, We borrowed the chairs that we have.*

EXERCISE 4—*page L157 (a class exercise)*

PURPOSE: To help students identify the changes they automatically make in transforming sentences like *John has the hat* to sentences like *The hat is John's.*

In two or three sentences, describe the changes you made in the sentences in Exercise 3 in order to write the related sentences. Use the following questions as a guide.

1. What verb do you find in each of the sentences given in Exercise 3? *Have.* What verb occurs in each of the related sentences you wrote? *Be.*
2. What word or words are found before the verb in each of the original sentences in Exercise 3? **Subject NP's.** Is this part found in the rewritten sentences? **Yes.** If so, where? **After the verb.**
3. What part follows the verb in each of the original sentences? **The *NP.*** Is this part found in the rewritten sentence? **Yes.** If so, where? **Before the verb.**
4. Has anything else been changed in the rewritten sentences? **Yes.** If so, what? **The subject *NP* adds a sound spelled with *s*, and when it is written, it is written with an apostrophe.**

Note: **Answers, of course, will vary as far as wording is concerned, but they should include the information found in the answers given above.**

> Before assigning the exercise, have students discuss the questions that precede it. If possible, have them do the exercise individually. If they do the questions one by one, they will have all the information needed to describe the changes made. You may want to go over the questions themselves before assigning the exercise.
>
> *Note:* The paragraph following the exercise explains the use of the symbol *Poss.*

EXERCISE 5 – *page L158 (a class exercise)*

> **PURPOSE: To symbolize the transformation described in Exercise 4 and to emphasize its generality.**

If we use the symbol string $NP^1 + Tns + have + NP^2$ to represent a sentence like *John has the hat,* what symbol string would represent the sentence after it has been transformed into a sentence like *The hat is John's*? (Use the name of the verb that occurs in all sentences of this kind and use the symbol $NP + Poss$ to represent the noun that becomes possessive. The *NP*'s are labeled NP^1 and NP^2 to make it easy to keep track of them after they are moved.) $NP^2 + Tns + be + NP^1 + Poss$

> This exercise should be done at the same time as Exercise 4, probably right in class, since it is a follow-up. You might put the two strings together on the board with a double arrow to show that one kind of structure can be changed (transformed) to another kind of structure by a regular change:

> $NP^1 + Tns + have + NP^2 \Rightarrow NP^2 + Tns + be + NP^1 + Poss$

Note: Tns is used in describing this transformation because it occurs with either past-tense or present-tense verbs.

EXERCISE 6 — *pages L158–59 (a written assignment)*

PURPOSE: To provide practice in identifying the relationship between the deep structure and the surface structure of a possessive.

A. For each of the following sentences, write the sentence that is related to it by the *T*_{Poss} rule.

1.	The car is Mr. White's.	transformed
	Mr. White has the car.	deep structure
2.	Joel has the hamster.	deep structure
	The hamster is Joel's.	transformed
3.	Cynthia has the diamonds.	deep structure
	The diamonds are Cynthia's.	transformed
4.	The toboggan is the boy's.	transformed
	The boy has the toboggan.	deep structure
5.	The catnip is the cat's.	transformed
	The cat has the catnip.	deep structure
6.	George has the papers.	deep structure
	The papers are George's.	transformed
7.	The trains are Robert's.	transformed
	Robert has the trains.	deep structure
8.	The child has the umbrella.	deep structure
	The umbrella is the child's.	transformed
9.	Kate has the notebook.	deep structure
	The notebook is Kate's.	transformed
10.	The lantern is Aunt Emily's.	transformed
	Aunt Emily has the lantern.	deep structure

B. In each pair of related sentences, indicate which sentence is like the deep structure sentence and which is the transformed sentence.

Note: **See section A for answers.**

Note: **Students must decide whether they are transforming a basic sentence (as in 2, 3, 6, 8, and 9) or identifying a basic sentence from which the transformed sentence has been derived (as in 1, 4, 5, 7, and 10).**

257

EXERCISE 7 — *page L160 (a class exercise)*

> PURPOSE: To identify the deep structure of a sentence
> in which a possessive noun is a noun modifier.

A.   What are the two basic sentences found in the deep structure of
The hat that John has is on the table?   **The hat is on the table /
John has the hat.**

B.   Write the sentence string that represents the deep structure of
The hat that John has is on the table, showing how one basic
sentence is embedded in the determiner phrase of the other.
the + John has the hat + hat is on the table

C.   What sentence string will represent the deep structure of *John's
hat is on the table* if it means the same thing as *The hat that John
has is on the table?*   ***the + John has the hat + hat is on the table***

> This exercise returns to an analysis of the sentence *John's
> hat is on the table* that students looked at at the beginning
> of the chapter. It should be used right in class and
> followed immediately with Exercise 8.

EXERCISE 8 — *pages L160–61 (a class exercise)*

> PURPOSE: To help students think through and identify
> the steps in transforming the deep structure of a sentence
> with a possessive noun modifier to surface structure.

Look again at the deep structure string you wrote in Exercise 7. Using
the following questions as a guide, show what steps are necessary
to change this string to *John's hat is on the table.*

1.   What transformation will change the embedded sentence into a
sentence containing a possessive? **The possessive transformation, which moves the subject NP (NP^1) beyond the verb and
makes it possessive, changes the verb to *is*, moves the NP
following the verb (NP^2) to the subject NP position.**   Rewrite
the deep structure string, making this change.   ***the + the hat is
John + Poss + hat is on the table***

2.   What parts occur in the embedded part of your rewritten string
that don't appear in *John's hat is on the table?* **the hat is** What
kind of transformation could remove them?   **A deletion transformation.**   Rewrite the string, making this change.   **the + John
+ Poss + hat is on the table**

3. What other change must be made to the string before it will represent *John's hat is on the table*?   **The determiner *the* before John must be deleted.**   Rewrite the string, making this change.   *John + Poss + hat is on the table*

> **Start with the string students wrote for Exercise 7. You can have students do the exercise individually and discuss it, or you may want simply to put the string on the board and then have students explain the changes that must be made while you make them.**

EXERCISE 9 —*page L161 (a written assignment)*

> **PURPOSE: To provide practice in identifying the deep structure of sentences with possessive noun modifiers and in showing how their deep structure can be transformed to surface structure.**

A. List the possessive noun in each of the following sentences; then write the deep structure sentence from which it derives. For example:

> The man's wife was with him.
> man's: The man had the wife.

1. The girls' packages fell to the ground.
   girls' / The girls had the packages.
2. Marjorie's hair was curly.
   Marjorie's / Marjorie had the hair.
3. Sam's sister keeps a diary.
   Sam's / Sam has the sister.
4. The neighbors' dog guards them faithfully.
   neighbors / The neighbors have the dog.
5. Mrs. Pemberton's coat was hanging on a hook.
   Mrs. Pemberton's / Mrs. Pemberton had the coat.
6. George's car zoomed down the street.
   George's / George had the car.
7. The children's teacher arrived late.
   children's / The children had the teacher.
8. Harry's parrot can say ten words.
   Harry's / Harry has the parrot.

B. Write the deep structure sentence string for four of the sentences in section A and then show, step by step, how the deep structure becomes surface structure. For example:

259

$$\overbrace{\text{the } + \text{ the man had the wife } + \text{ wife was with him}}^{\text{S}} \Rightarrow$$

$$\overbrace{\begin{array}{c}\text{the } + \text{ the wife was the man } + \text{ Poss } + \\ \text{wife was with him}\end{array}}^{\text{S}} \Rightarrow$$

$$\overbrace{\text{the } + \text{ the man } + \text{ Poss } + \text{ wife was with him}}^{\text{S}} \Rightarrow$$

$$\overbrace{\text{the } + \underset{\displaystyle \text{man's}}{\underbrace{\text{man } + \text{ Poss}}} + \text{ wife was with him}}^{\text{S}}$$

1. The girls' packages fell to the ground.

$$\overbrace{\begin{array}{c}\text{the } + \text{ the girls had the packages } + \text{ packages fell to the}\\ \text{ground}\end{array}}^{\text{S}} \Rightarrow$$

$$\overbrace{\begin{array}{c}\text{the } + \text{ the packages were the girls } + \text{ Poss } +\\ \text{packages fell to the ground}\end{array}}^{\text{S}} \Rightarrow$$

$$\overbrace{\begin{array}{c}\text{the } + \text{ the girls } + \text{ Poss } + \text{ packages fell to the}\\ \text{ground}\end{array}}^{\text{S}} \Rightarrow$$

$$\overbrace{\text{the } + \underset{\displaystyle \text{girls'}}{\underbrace{\text{girls } + \text{ Poss}}} + \text{ packages fell to the}}^{\text{S}}\text{ground}$$

2. Marjorie's hair was curly.

$$\overbrace{\text{the } + \text{ Marjorie had the hair } + \text{ hair was curly}}^{\text{S}} \Rightarrow$$

260

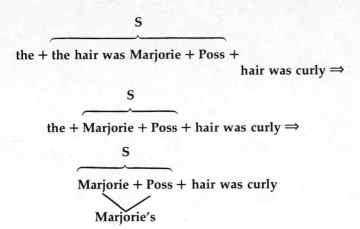

S

the + the hair was Marjorie + Poss +
                              hair was curly ⟹

S

the + Marjorie + Poss + hair was curly ⟹

S

Marjorie + Poss + hair was curly

Marjorie's

3. Sam's sister keeps a diary.

S

the + Sam has the sister + sister keeps a diary ⟹

S

the + the sister is Sam + Poss + sister keeps a diary ⟹

S

the + Sam + Poss + sister keeps a diary ⟹

S

Sam + Poss + sister keeps a diary

Sam's

4. The neighbors' dog guards them faithfully.

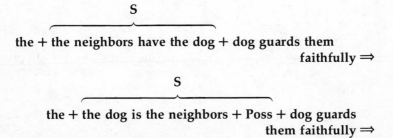

S

the + the neighbors have the dog + dog guards them
                                        faithfully ⟹

S

the + the dog is the neighbors + Poss + dog guards
                                    them faithfully ⟹   261

S

‾‾‾‾‾‾‾‾‾‾‾‾‾‾‾‾‾‾‾‾‾‾‾‾

the + the neighbors + Poss + dog guards them
                                    faithfully ⟹

S

‾‾‾‾‾‾‾‾‾‾‾‾‾‾‾‾‾‾‾‾‾

the + neighbors + Poss + dog guards them
                              faithfully

neighbors'

5. Mrs. Pemberton's coat was hanging on a hook.

S

‾‾‾‾‾‾‾‾‾‾‾‾‾‾‾‾‾‾‾‾‾‾‾‾‾‾

the + Mrs. Pemberton had the coat +
                    coat was hanging on a hook ⟹

S

‾‾‾‾‾‾‾‾‾‾‾‾‾‾‾‾‾‾‾‾‾‾‾‾‾‾

the + the coat was Mrs. Pemberton + Poss +
                    coat was hanging on a hook ⟹

S

‾‾‾‾‾‾‾‾‾‾‾‾‾‾‾‾‾‾‾‾

the + Mrs. Pemberton + Poss +
                    coat was hanging on a hook ⟹

S

‾‾‾‾‾‾‾‾‾‾‾‾‾‾‾‾‾

Mrs. Pemberton + Poss + coat was
                    hanging on a hook

Mrs. Pemberton's

6. George's car zoomed down the street.

S

‾‾‾‾‾‾‾‾‾‾‾‾‾‾‾‾

the + George had the car + car zoomed down the street ⟹

S

‾‾‾‾‾‾‾‾‾‾‾‾‾‾‾‾

the + the car was George + Poss +
                    car zoomed down the street ⟹

S

‾‾‾‾‾‾‾‾‾‾‾‾‾‾‾‾

the + George + Poss + car zoomed down the
                                        street ⟹

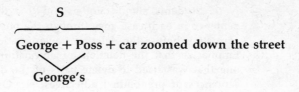

S

George + Poss + car zoomed down the street

George's

7. The children's teacher arrived late.

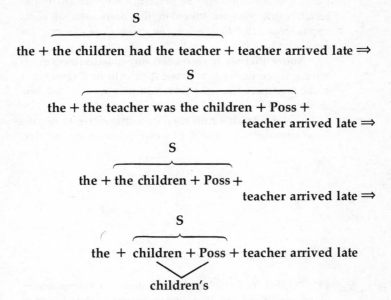

S

the + the children had the teacher + teacher arrived late ⟹

S

the + the teacher was the children + Poss +
                 teacher arrived late ⟹

S

the + the children + Poss +
                 teacher arrived late ⟹

S

the + children + Poss + teacher arrived late

children's

8. Harry's parrot can say ten words.

S

the + Harry has the parrot + parrot can say ten words ⟹

S

the + the parrot is Harry + Poss +
                 parrot can say ten words ⟹

S

the + Harry + Poss + parrot can say ten words ⟹

S

Harry + Poss + parrot can say ten words

Harry's

263

Note: Students should understand that the embedded sentence in each case goes through the possessive transformation before the deletion transformation is applied. Emphasize that the deletion transformation is the same one that was used to delete parts of the deep structure sentences of prenominal adjectives, etc. One additional step, of course, is necessary in deriving sentences with possessive noun modifiers: the determiner of the dominant sentence must also be deleted, a step which, as you recall, must also be taken in the derivation of some appositives *(the George + the barber ⇒ George the barber).*

Notice that we have set the embedded sentences off with a brace under S to make it easy to distinguish the embedded part from the rest. You may want to ask students to do the same.

You might also find this a good exercise to discuss how singular and plural possessive nouns are written.

EXERCISE 10 *— page L162 (a class exercise)*

PURPOSE: To establish how sentences with possessive noun modifiers are like sentences with other kinds of noun modifiers.

A. In what way is the embedded sentence with a possessive like an embedded sentence that becomes an adjective modifier or a place adverbial modifier? **The embedded sentence with a possessive includes the verb** *be.*

B. In what way is the deletion that takes place in a sentence with a possessive like the deletion that takes place in deriving sentences with adjective or place adverbial modifiers? **It is like the deletion that takes place in deriving sentences with adjectives or place adverbial modifiers in that everything up to and including** *be* **is deleted, leaving only what follows** *be.*

C. Write a statement in which you explain the deletions that can take place in a sentence with the verb *be* when that sentence is embedded in a *DP* of another *S.* **When a sentence with the verb** *be* **is embedded in a** *DP* **of another** *S,* **everything up to and including the verb** *be* **can be deleted, leaving only what follows** *be.*

D. Is the position of a possessive in the surface structure like that of an adjective modifier or like that of a place adverbial modifier? **Like that of an adjective modifier.**

> This exercise is primarily a discussion exercise, though item C should probably be written individually. You will want to go right on after the exercise to discuss the material that follows, where the *be*-deletion transformation (formulated in Chapter 7) is modified to include possessive nouns as well as predicates. Before having them look at the material in the text, you might want to ask students how they would revise the transformation to include possessives.

EXERCISE 11 — *page L163 (a written assignment)*

> PURPOSE: To provide practice and to demonstrate that possessive noun modifiers, wherever they occur, can be described by the same set of rules.

A. State what the possessive is in each of the following sentences; then write the deep structure sentence from which it derives.

1. Joel found Ralph's gloves.
   Ralph's / Ralph had the gloves.
2. Miss Sharp washed the child's clothes.
   child's / The child had the clothes.
3. We painted Mr. Sampson's garage.
   Mr. Sampson's / Mr. Sampson had the garage.
4. I rescued George's goldfish.
   George's / George had the goldfish.
5. Some friends bought the girl's cookies.
   girl's / The girl had the cookies.

B. Can a sentence containing a possessive be embedded in any *NP* no matter where the *NP* occurs? **Yes, if the sentence containing the possessive includes an *NP* like the *NP* in which it is embedded.** In Exercise 9, where were all the *S*'s with possessives embedded? **In the subject *NP*'s.** Where are the *S*'s embedded in the sentences in section A above? **In the *VP*.**

C. Write the deep structure sentence string for each of the sentences in section A, showing where the embedding occurs. Then rewrite each string to show how it is changed to the surface structure.

1. Joel found Ralph's gloves.

S

Joel found the + Ralph had the gloves + gloves ⟹

S

Joel found the + the gloves were Ralph + Poss +
gloves ⟹

S

Joel found the + Ralph + Poss + gloves ⟹

S

Joel found Ralph's gloves

2. Miss Sharp washed the child's clothes.

S

Miss Sharp washed the + the child had the clothes +
clothes ⟹

S

Miss Sharp washed the + the clothes were the child + Poss +
clothes ⟹

S

Miss Sharp washed the + child + Poss +
clothes ⟹

S

Miss Sharp washed the child's clothes

3. We painted Mr. Sampson's garage.

S

we painted the + Mr. Sampson had the garage + garage ⟹

S

we painted the + the garage was Mr. Sampson + Poss +
garage ⟹

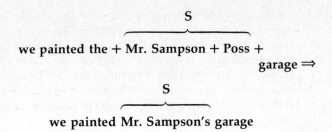

S

we painted the + Mr. Sampson + Poss +
                              garage ⟹

S

we painted Mr. Sampson's garage

4. I rescued George's goldfish.

S

I rescued the + George had the goldfish + goldfish ⟹

S

I rescued the + the goldfish were George + Poss +
                              goldfish ⟹

S

I rescued the + George + Poss + goldfish ⟹

S

I rescued George's goldfish

5. Some friends bought the girl's cookies.

S

some friends bought the + the girl had the cookies +
                              cookies ⟹

S

some friends bought the + the cookies were the girl + Poss +
                              cookies ⟹

S

some friends bought the + the girl + Poss +
                              cookies ⟹

S

some friends bought the girl's cookies   267

Students should understand that what they are to do is essentially the same as what they did in Exercise 9. Take time to discuss the answers in class, perhaps having the transformations put on the board. Reiterate that in all of these sentences the same transformations are being used over and over again and that the same set of phrase structure rules can account for the deep structure of each sentence.

EXERCISE 12 – *page L164 (a written assignment)*

PURPOSE: To extend what is known about possessives in accounting for a relative clause with a possessive.

A. What are the basic sentences in the deep structure of the following?

The bicycle that was the boy's rolled down the hill.

The basic sentence *the boy had the bicycle* is embedded in the basic sentence *the bicycle rolled down the hill.*

B. Write the sentence string that will represent the deep structure of the sentence given in section A and show how the deep structure is changed to surface structure. Use the following questions as a guide.

the + the boy had the bicycle + bicycle rolled down the hill

1. What sentence part is *that was the boy's*? **A relative clause.** To what deep structure sentence is it related? *the boy had the bicycle*

2. What transformation changes a deep structure sentence of this kind to a sentence containing a possessive? **The possessive transformation that reverses the NP's, changes *have* to *be*, and makes the first NP possessive.** Rewrite the string, making this change. *the + the bicycle was the boy + Poss + bicycle rolled down the hill*

3. What two transformations are needed to change this string to *The bicycle that was the boy's rolled down the hill*? $T_{repos\ s}$ and $T_{Wh\text{-}word}$. Rewrite the string showing these steps. **the bicycle + that was the boy + Poss + rolled down the hill**

⌄
boy's

4. The embedded sentences you have been working with in the last few exercises have all consisted of $NP + Tns + have + NP$.

Where have they all been embedded?   **In the *DP* of another sentence.**   How many kinds of surface structure sentences do you think can be made from a deep structure of this kind? Give some examples of each kind.

Answers will probably vary. Three are possible. One, in the following way the embedded sentence can become a relative clause before the possessive transformation is applied:

the + the boy had the bicycle +
                              bicycle rolled down the hill ⟹

T_{repos S}:

    the bicycle + the boy had the bicycle +
                              rolled down the hill ⟹

T_{Wh-word} :

    the bicycle + the boy had that +
                              rolled down the hill ⟹

T_{repos Wh-word}:

    the bicycle + that the boy had +
                              rolled down the hill

Or, two, it can become a relative clause after the possessive transformation is applied, as in the example in section B above. Or, three, the possessive transformation can be applied and *T_{delete be}* can then delete all but the possessive:

the + the boy had the bicycle +
                              bicycle rolled down the hill ⟹

T_{Poss} :

    the + the bicycle was the boy + Poss +
                              bicycle rolled down the hill ⟹

T_{delete be}:

    the + the boy + Poss +
                              bicycle rolled down the hill

T_{delete the}:

    the boy + Poss + bicycle rolled down the hill
                    ∨
              boy's

You may decide to use this as a class exercise rather than as a take-home exercise, depending on your students. You may want to have each step put on the board as the class discusses the questions.

EXERCISE 13 — *pages L164–65 (a written assignment)*

> PURPOSE: **To provide practice in identifying the deep structure of closely related sentences.**

What sentence string represents the deep structure of each of the following groups of sentences?

1. George's bike ran over a nail.
    The bike that George had ran over a nail.
    The bike that was George's ran over a nail.
    the + George had the bike + bike ran over a nail

2. I found Betty's bracelet.
    I found the bracelet that was Betty's.
    I found the bracelet that Betty had.
    I found the + Betty had the bracelet + bracelet

3. The boots that the man has are in the hallway.
    The man's boots are in the hallway.
    The boots that are the man's are in the hallway.
    the + the man has the boots + boots are in the hallway

4. She forgot the cup that is the baby's.
    She forgot the cup that the baby has.
    She forgot the baby's cup.
    she forgot the + the baby has the cup + cup

5. Martin's mail is on the table.
    The mail that is Martin's is on the table.
    The mail that Martin has is on the table.
    the + Martin has the mail + mail is on the table

> If you think students need the practice, you may want to have them indicate the different transformations that change the deep structure they have identified into the three different sentences in each group.

EXERCISE 14 — *pages L165–66 (the basis of discussion)*

> PURPOSE: **To make students aware of the possessive form of pronouns.**

A. In what way are the two sentences in each of the following pairs alike? In what way are they different?

1. The boy's book fell in the mud.
    His book fell in the mud.

2. Mr. Orville's store is having a grand opening.
His store is having a grand opening.

3. The doctor peered at the girl's tonsils.
The doctor peered at her tonsils.

4. The neighbors' garden is in bloom.
Their garden is in bloom.

5. I have borrowed Webster's book.
I have borrowed his book.

6. The woman's umbrella turned inside out.
Her umbrella turned inside out.

7. The keeper brought the penguin's dinner.
The keeper brought its dinner.

8. Sam repaired Mr. Peach's car.
Sam repaired his car.

9. Sarah's violin is valuable.
Her violin is valuable.

10. The children's party has ended.
Their party has ended.

The sentences in each pair are alike except for the NP's that include the possessives.

B. In *The boy's book fell in the mud,* what is the deep structure sentence related to *the boy's*? **The boy had the book.**

C. In *His book fell in the mud,* what do you think the deep structure sentence related to *his* might be? **He had the book.**

> This exercise should be used to motivate the exercises that follow. If students have a firm understanding of the deep structure of possessive nouns, they may be able to suggest what the deep structure of possessive pronouns might be.

EXERCISE 15—*page L166 (the basis of discussion)*

> PURPOSE: To consider if possessive pronouns can be derived by the same transformations as possessive nouns.

The T_{Poss} transformation states that $NP^1 + Tns + have + NP^2$ can be changed to a string containing a possessive which can be represented by $NP^2 + Tns + be + NP^1 + Poss$. Does *He has the book* consist of $NP^1 + Tns + have + NP^2$? **Yes.** If so, can T_{Poss} be applied to it? **Yes.** What would the result be? **The book is his.**

One way to discuss this exercise would be to put the symbol string and the sentence string on the board and then to make the changes there, as follows:

$$\text{NP}^1 + \text{Tns} + \text{have} + \text{NP}^2 \Rightarrow \text{NP}^2 + \text{Tns} + \text{be} + \text{NP}^1 + \text{Poss}$$

| he | has | the book | | the book | is | his |

EXERCISE 16—*page L167 (a written assignment)*

PURPOSE: To provide practice in applying the possessive transformation to sentences with pronouns and to help students identify the two forms of possessive pronouns and know when they are used.

A. For every sentence like *He has the book,* there is a sentence like *The book is his.* Write the related sentence of this kind for each of the following sentences. For example:

We have the car.   The car is ours.

1. He has the football.
   The football is his.
2. She has the shawl.
   The shawl is hers.
3. They have the radio.
   The radio is theirs.
4. I have the monkey.
   The monkey is mine.
5. She has the brushes.
   The brushes are hers.
6. You have the paint.
   The paint is yours.
7. We have the jeep.
   The jeep is ours.
8. You have the hammer.
   The hammer is yours.
9. I have the records.
   The records are mine.
10. They have the pearls.
    The pearls are theirs.

B. Write a sentence related to each of your rewritten sentences in the same way that *His book is here* is related to *The book is his.* For example:

The car is ours.   Our car is here.

1. The football is his.
   His football is here.
2. The shawl is hers.
   Her shawl is here.
3. The radio is theirs.
   Their radio is here.
4. The monkey is mine.
   My monkey is here.
5. The brushes are hers.
   Her brushes are here.
6. The paint is yours.
   Your paint is here.
7. The jeep is ours.
   Our jeep is here.
8. The hammer is yours.
   Your hammer is here.
9. The records are mine.
   My records are here.
10. The pearls are theirs.
    Their pearls are here.

C. List all the pronouns in the sentences in section A. After each one, first list the possessive form you used in the rewritten sentences for section A. Then list the possessive form you used in the sentences you wrote for section B. For the example sentence you would write:

we   ours   our

he	his	his
she	hers	her
they	theirs	their
I	mine	my
she	hers	her
you	yours	your
we	ours	our
you	yours	your
I	mine	my
they	theirs	their

D. Do any of the possessive pronouns have a different form when they precede a noun? **Yes.** If so which ones? *hers/her, theirs/their, mine/my, yours/your, ours/our* How are they different?   **Except for *my/mine* and *his/his*, they add an *s* when they don't precede a noun.**

EXERCISE 17 – *page L168 (a written assignment)*

> **PURPOSE: To demonstrate that the possessive transformation accounts for possessive pronouns as well as for possessive nouns.**

A. What are the two sentences found in the deep structure of *His book fell in the mud*? *The book fell in the mud* and *He had the book.*   Construct a diagram showing how they are related.

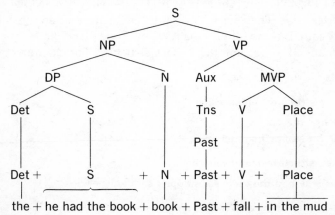

the + he had the book + book + Past + fall + in the mud

273

B. Show, by the following steps, how the string your diagram ends with can be changed to become *His book fell in the mud.*

1. Apply the possessive transformation to the embedded sentence in your string.
2. Apply *T delete be* to the embedded sentence.
3. Remove whatever still appears in the string that isn't part of the surface structure sentence.

S

the + the book was his + book fell in the mud ⟹

S

the + his + book fell in the mud ⟹

S

his + book fell in the mud

> *Note:* We have simplified the description by combining *Tns* with the verb that follows in both the dominant and the embedded sentence. And we have also combined *Poss* with *he* to form *his*.

EXERCISE 18 — *page L169 (a written assignment)*

> PURPOSE: To provide practice and to consolidate student understanding of the derivation of sentences with possessives.

For each of the following sentences, first state what the deep structure sentences are. Then write the sentence string that shows how one is embedded in the other. Finally, show how this deep structure string is changed to become the surface structure. For example:

His car stopped suddenly.

deep structure sentences:

he had the car
the car stopped suddenly

deep structure sentence string:

the + he had the car + car stopped suddenly ⟹

the + the car was he + Poss + car stopped suddenly ⟹

the + **he** + **Poss** + car stopped suddenly ⟹

he + **Poss** + car stopped suddenly

‿

his

1. His shoes are under the bed.

deep structure sentences:
the shoes are under the bed
he has the shoes

deep structure sentence string:

S

the + **he has the shoes** + shoes are under the bed ⟹

S

the + **the shoes are he + Poss** + shoes are under the bed ⟹

S

the + **he + Poss** + shoes are under the bed ⟹

S

he + **Poss** + shoes are under the bed

‿

his

2. I lost her scarf.

deep structure sentences:
I lost the scarf
she had the scarf

deep structure sentence string:

S

I lost the + **she had the scarf** + scarf ⟹

S

I lost the + **the scarf was she + Poss** + scarf ⟹

S

I lost the + **she + Poss** + scarf ⟹

S

I lost + **she** + **Poss** + scarf

‿

her

275

3. Their project has been successful.

   deep structure sentences:
   the project has been successful
   they have the project

   deep structure sentence string:

   S

   the + they have the project + project has been successful ⟹

   S

   the + the project is they + Poss + project has been
   successful ⟹

   S

   the + they + Poss + project has been successful ⟹

   S

   they + Poss + project has been successful

   their

4. My idea will work.

   deep structure sentences:
   the idea will work
   I have the idea

   deep structure sentence string:

   S

   the + I have the idea + idea will work ⟹

   S

   the + the idea is I + Poss + idea will work ⟹

   S

   the + I + Poss + idea will work ⟹

   S

   I + Poss + idea will work

   my

5. They have seen your portrait.

    deep structure sentences:
    they have seen the portrait
    you have the portrait

    deep structure sentence string:

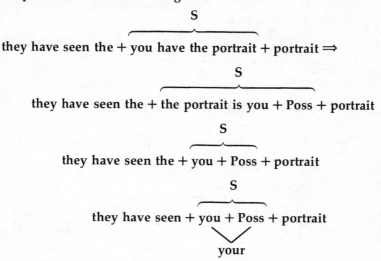

$$S$$

they have seen the + you have the portrait + portrait $\Rightarrow$

$$S$$

they have seen the + the portrait is you + Poss + portrait

$$S$$

they have seen the + you + Poss + portrait

$$S$$

they have seen + you + Poss + portrait

your

> *Note:* It might be useful to ask your students to use a
> different colored ink, or ink and pencil, to set off the
> embedded sentence; or to put the embedded sentence
> under a brace as we have done. If you prefer, you could
> suggest that students combine the pronoun + *Poss* as the
> possessive form at the time they indicate the possessive
> transformation. For example, for sentence 1 you could
> propose the following:

$$S$$

the + he has the shoes + shoes are under the bed $\Rightarrow$

$$S$$

the + the shoes are his + shoes are under the bed

EXERCISE 19 — *page L170 (a written assignment)*

> PURPOSE: To challenge able students to use the pos-
> sessive transformation in deriving a sentence with two
> possessives; and to demonstrate how the possessive trans-
> formation can account for differences in the form of the
> possessive pronoun.

277

A. What are the basic sentences found in the deep structure of the following?

My aunt's dog has fleas.

The dog has fleas. / The aunt has the dog. / I have the aunt. Write the deep structure sentence string showing how the sentences are embedded and then show how this string is changed to become the surface structure.

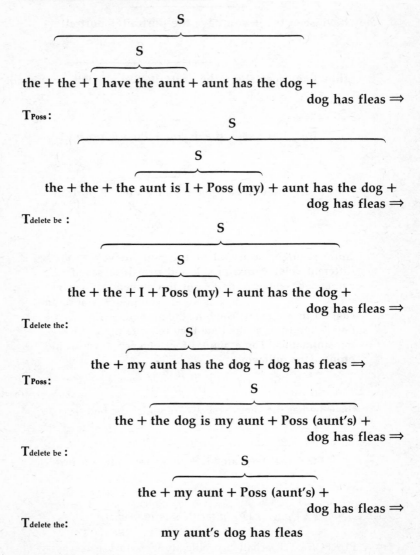

S

the + the + I have the aunt + aunt has the dog +
dog has fleas ⟹

T_{Poss}:

S

the + the + the aunt is I + Poss (my) + aunt has the dog +
dog has fleas ⟹

T_{delete be} :

S

the + the + I + Poss (my) + aunt has the dog +
dog has fleas ⟹

T_{delete the}:

S

the + my aunt has the dog + dog has fleas ⟹

T_{Poss}:

S

the + the dog is my aunt + Poss (aunt's) +
dog has fleas ⟹

T_{delete be} :

S

the + my aunt + Poss (aunt's) +
dog has fleas ⟹

T_{delete the}:

my aunt's dog has fleas

B. Write the sentence strings that represent the deep structure of each of the following and then show the steps by which each becomes surface structure.

The car is hers.
Her car is in the garage.

1. she has the car $\Rightarrow$

   T$_{Poss}$:

   the car is she + Poss
   $\underset{\textstyle hers}{\diagdown\diagup}$

2. the + she has the car + car is in the garage $\Rightarrow$

   T$_{Poss}$:

   S

   the + the car is she + Poss + car is in the garage $\Rightarrow$

   T$_{delete\ be}$:

   S

   the + she + Poss + car is in the garage $\Rightarrow$

   T$_{delete\ the}$:

   S

   she + Poss + car is in the garage
   $\underset{\textstyle her}{\diagdown\diagup}$

C. How do the transformations help explain why one sentence includes *her* and the other *hers*? **In the first, the transformation leaves *she + Poss* with no noun following and it becomes *hers*. In the second, the transformations leave *she + Poss* in front of the noun *car* and it becomes *her*.**

EXERCISE 20 – *page L171 (a written assignment)*

> PURPOSE: **To demonstrate how we use the same rules over and over again to produce new sentences and to provide review of the kinds of sentences that have been accounted for in the text.**

A. For each of the following sentences, list all of the basic deep structure sentences.

1. The green dragon destroyed the castle.
   The dragon destroyed the castle. / The dragon was green.   279

2. The car that he bought is a new Ford.
   The car is a Ford. / He bought the car. / The Ford is new.
3. The plane that lands at noon is a jet.
   The plane is a jet. / The plane lands at noon.
4. Your ideas are preposterous.
   The ideas are preposterous. / You have the ideas.
5. Clouds on the butte mean rain.
   Clouds mean rain. / Clouds are on the butte.
6. Arthur and Henry will fish in the millpond.
   Arthur will fish in the millpond. / Henry will fish in the millpond.
7. Bo's cat swims in the bathtub.
   The cat swims in the bathtub. / Bo has the cat.
8. Sarah ran down the hall and pulled the fire alarm.
   Sarah ran down the hall. / Sarah pulled the fire alarm.
9. Roger the repairman fixed the TV.
   The Roger fixed the TV. / The Roger is the repairman.
10. A girl in the class that meets at noon broke her leg.
    A girl broke the leg. / The girl is in the class. / The class meets at noon. / The girl has the leg.

B. For sentences 3, 5, 7, and 9 make deep structure diagrams. **See below.**

C. For the same sentences in section B, show the transformations by which the deep structure is changed to surface structure.

3. The plane that lands at noon is a jet.

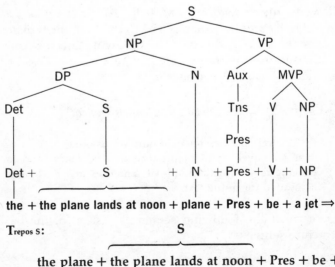

the + the plane lands at noon + plane + Pres + be + a jet ⇒

T$_{repos}$ S: S

the plane + the plane lands at noon + Pres + be +
a jet ⇒

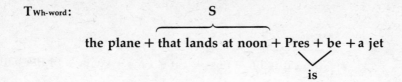

T Wh-word:

the plane + that lands at noon + Pres + be + a jet

is

5. Clouds on the butte mean rain.

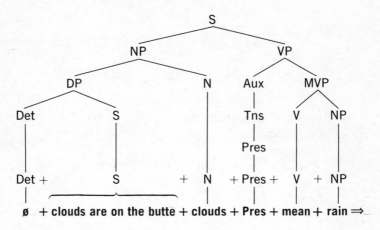

ø + clouds are on the butte + clouds + Pres + mean + rain ⟹

T delete be: S

ø + on the butte + clouds + Pres + mean + rain ⟹

T repos S: S

ø clouds + on the butte + Pres + mean + rain

mean

7. Bo's cat swims in the bathtub.

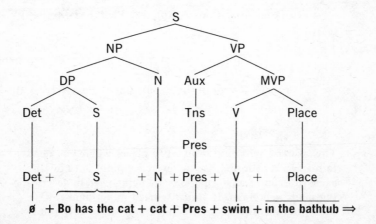

ø + Bo has the cat + cat + Pres + swim + in the bathtub ⟹   281

TPoss:

S

⌢

ø + the cat is Bo + Poss + cat + Pres + swim + in the bathtub ⟹

Tdelete be:

S

⌣

ø + Bo + Poss + cat + Pres + swim + in the bathtub

⌄   ⌄

Bo's   swims

9. Roger the repairman fixed the TV.

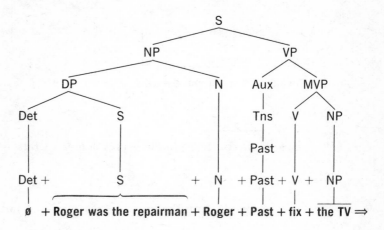

ø + Roger was the repairman + Roger + Past + fix + the TV ⟹

Tdelete be:

S

⌣

ø + the repairman + Roger + Past + fix + the TV ⟹

Trepos S:

S

⌣

ø + Roger + the repairman + Past + fix + the TV

⌄

fixed

This exercise will help to identify places where you need to review. As you discuss the exercise, point out how the same rules and transformations are being used in describing many sentences. If students need more review, have them identify the deep structures and show how trans-

282

formations produce the surface structures of additional sentences. Sentences 1, 4, 5, 7, 9, and 10 all require $T_{delete\ be}$; sentences 2, 3, 5, 9, and 10 require $T_{repos\ s}$; etc.

EXERCISE 21 — *page L172 (a written assignment)*

PURPOSE: To provide practice in identifying the deep structure and in accounting for the surface structure of the various kinds of sentences that have been discussed.

Try to write sentence strings that represent the deep structure of each of the following and then show the steps by which the deep structures become surface structures:

1. Was he flying a small plane?

S

Q + he + Past + be + ing + fly + a + a plane was small + plane ⇒

$T_{delete\ be}$:

S

Q + he + Past + be + ing + fly + a + small + plane ⇒

T_Q:

S

Past + be + he + ing + fly + a + small + plane

⌄ was   ⌄ flying

2. A blue heron was spotted by the hunters.

S

the hunters + Past + spot + a + a heron was blue + heron + by + agent ⇒

$T_{delete\ be}$:

S

the hunters + Past + spot + a + blue + heron + by + agent ⇒   283

T_{passive}:

$$\overset{\displaystyle S}{\overbrace{}}$$

a + blue + heron + Past + be + en + spot + by +
                ⋁   ⋁   the hunters
                was   spotted

3.   George will not eat rare meat.

$$\overset{\displaystyle S}{\overbrace{}}$$

Neg + George + Pres + will eat + ø + meat is rare + meat ⟹

T_{delete be}:

$$\overset{\displaystyle S}{\overbrace{}}$$

Neg + George + Pres + will eat + ø + rare + meat ⟹

T_{Neg}:

$$\overset{\displaystyle S}{\overbrace{}}$$

George + Pres + will not eat + rare + meat
                ⋁
             will

4.   Have you ridden the horse that won the race?

Q + you + Pres + have + en + ride + the +

$$\overset{\displaystyle S}{\overbrace{}}$$

                 the horse won the race + horse ⟹

T_{repos S}:

Q + you + Pres + have + en + ride + the horse +

$$\overset{\displaystyle S}{\overbrace{}}$$

                the horse won the race ⟹

T_{Wh-word}:

Q + you + Pres + have + en + ride + the horse +

$$\overset{\displaystyle S}{\overbrace{}}$$

                that won the race ⟹

T_Q:

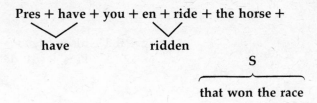

Pres + have + you + en + ride + the horse +

have   ridden

S

that won the race

5. His friend the mailman will not deliver packages.

S

S

Neg + the + he has the + the friend is the mailman + friend +
friend + Pres + will deliver packages ⟹

T_{Poss}:

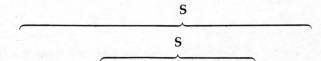

S

S

Neg + the + the friend is + the friend is the mailman + his +
friend + Pres + will deliver packages ⟹

T_{repos S}:

S

Neg + the + the friend is his +
S

the friend is the mailman + friend + Pres +
will deliver packages ⟹

T_{delete be}:

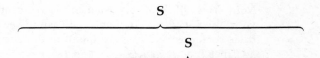

S   S

Neg + the + his + the friend is the mailman +
friend + Pres + will deliver packages ⟹

T_{delete be}:

S   S

Neg + the + his + the mailman + friend +
Pres + will deliver packages ⟹   285

T_{repos S}:

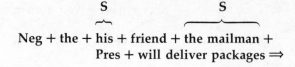

$$\text{Neg} + \text{the} + \text{his} + \text{friend} + \text{the mailman} +$$
$$\text{Pres} + \text{will deliver packages} \Rightarrow$$

T_{Neg}:

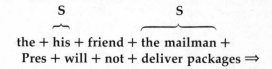

$$\text{the} + \text{his} + \text{friend} + \text{the mailman} +$$
$$\text{Pres} + \text{will} + \text{not} + \text{deliver packages} \Rightarrow$$

T_{delete the}:

his + friend + the mailman +
Pres + will + not deliver packages

will

Note: You will probably want to reserve sentence 5 for your abler students. It should be easy to see that three basic sentences and *Neg* are found in the deep structure and that T_{Poss}, T_{delete be}, T_{repos S}, and T_{Neg} have been used in deriving the surface structure, but actually to go through the steps may be confusing. You may simply decide to put the transformations on the board or on the overhead projector and then to point them out. The advantage of showing the derivation is to emphasize that simple basic S's plus a few general transformations enable us to produce many different kinds of sentences which on the surface appear quite simple.

EXERCISE 22 — *page L174 (a written assignment)*

PURPOSE: To demonstrate how many sentences can be produced by combining basic sentence structures and by using a few general transformations.

Using the structures of the following basic sentences and also *Q*, *Neg*, and *by + agent* in the deep structure, write as many sentences as you can.

The boy has caught the horse.
The horse is wild.
The boy is clever.
The horse is in the pasture.

Answers will vary. The following are possibilities:

The clever boy has caught the horse.
The clever boy has caught the horse in the pasture.
The clever boy has caught the wild horse.
The clever boy has caught the wild horse in the pasture.
The boy that is clever has caught the horse.
The boy has caught the horse that is in the pasture.
Has the boy caught the wild horse?
Hasn't the boy caught the wild horse?
The boy has not caught the horse in the pasture.
The horse in the pasture has been caught by the clever boy.

> *Note:* We have not indicated the deep structures and it is not necessary to do so. If you have able students, however, you might like to ask them to give the deep as well as the surface structures of their sentences along with the transformations involved in deriving the surface structures. Whatever you do, emphasize how many sentences can be produced from a few basic sentence structures and that such production is usually done automatically without conscious thought.

REVIEW *— page L174 (a take-home exercise)*

> PURPOSE: To help students review the important concepts of the chapter.

1. Describe the kind of basic sentence that is embedded in the deep structure of a sentence with a possessive.   **The embedded sentence includes the verb** *have* **as the main verb.**   Where is it embedded?   **In the *DP* preceding the noun that the possessive modifies.**

2. What does the possessive transformation do?   **The possessive transformation reverses the *NP* that follows the verb with the subject *NP* which becomes a possessive noun. In addition, it substitutes the verb** *be* **for the verb** *have.*

3. What basic sentences are found in the deep structure of each of the following sentences?

    > Martin's boat won the race.
    > The boat that Martin has won the race.
    > The boat that is Martin's won the race.

    The boat won the race and *Martin has the boat.*

    Note: **Ask students to delete** *has* **from the second sentence**   287 before they begin, so that all three sentences will have the same deep structure.

4. Describe how the deep structure of the three sentences in question 3 is changed into the three different surface structures. The first sentence is changed to surface structure by the application of T_{Poss} and $T_{delete\ be}$:

Martin's boat won the race.

$$S$$

the + Martin has the boat + boat won the race $\Rightarrow$

$$S$$

the + the boat was Martin + Poss + boat won the race $\Rightarrow$

$$S$$

the + Martin + Poss + boat won the race $\Rightarrow$

$$S$$

Martin's boat won the race

The second sentence is changed to surface structure by the application of $T_{repos\ S}$, $T_{Wh\text{-}word}$, and $T_{repos\ Wh\text{-}word}$:

The boat that Martin has won the race.

$$S$$

the + Martin has the boat + boat won the race $\Rightarrow$

$$S$$

the boat + Martin has the boat + won the race $\Rightarrow$

$$S$$

the boat + Martin has that + won the race $\Rightarrow$

$$S$$

the boat + that Martin has + won the race

The third sentence becomes surface structure by the application of T_{Poss}, $T_{repos\ S}$, and $T_{Wh\text{-}word}$:

288   The boat that is Martin's won the race.

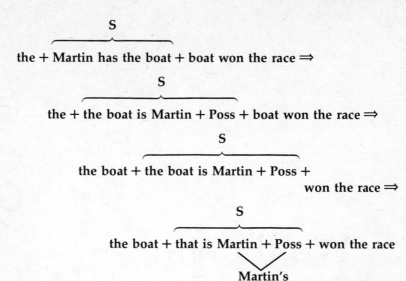

S

the + Martin has the boat + boat won the race ⟹

S

the + the boat is Martin + Poss + boat won the race ⟹

S

the boat + the boat is Martin + Poss +

won the race ⟹

S

the boat + that is Martin + Poss + won the race

Martin's

5. Can *Sylvia's room is upstairs* and *His house burned down* be described by the same set of rules?   **Yes.**   What do these two sentences have in common in their deep structure?   **They both have a basic sentence with the verb *have* that is embedded in the subject *NP*.**

6. In what way is the deep structure of a sentence with a possessive like the deep structure of a sentence with an adjective modifier? **Both have a sentence embedded in the *DP* that precedes the noun that is modified by the possessive and the adjective.** What transformation is used in deriving both?   ***T**delete be* .

Chapter 9

Word Census: English Dictionaries Through the Years

PERFORMANCE OBJECTIVES

The student should be able to

1. Define the following: *loanword, hard-word book, lexicographer, citation slip, OED.*

2. Briefly explain why the first English dictionaries were written, when they appeared, and what they consisted of.

3. Discuss the significance of each of the following in the history of English dictionaries: Robert Cawdrey, Samuel Johnson, Noah Webster.

4. Explain what Samuel Johnson felt was the purpose of a dictionary, how he went about writing his dictionary, and how his dictionary differed from earlier ones.

5. Make clear how Noah Webster's dictionary differed from Samuel Johnson's dictionary.

6. Describe the Oxford English Dictionary and explain its purpose.

7. Discuss how modern dictionaries differ from early dictionaries.

SYNOPSIS

The chapter consists of the following sections:

1. **The introductory paragraph** (page L177) simply mentions that dictionaries as we know them are a fairly recent invention and goes on to suggest what we can learn by studying their history.

2. **Early English Wordbooks** (pages L179–84) describes the beginnings of English dictionaries in the hard-word books written during the Renaissance to define words of foreign origin, and discusses how such books developed into dictionaries in the modern sense. The section includes passages from the first hard-word book, written by Robert Cawdrey, and from a later dictionary written by Nathan Bailey in 1724. Students are asked to examine and compare the two.

3. **Dr. Johnson's Dictionary** (pages L184–92) describes how Samuel Johnson wrote his landmark *Dictionary of the English Language* (published in 1755) in an attempt to pass judgment on the words and expressions of English and thus to set permanent standards for the language. Students are asked to examine a passage from his dictionary and to compare it with passages from earlier dictionaries and with their own.

4. **According to Webster** (pages L192–98) describes the first American dictionary, published by Noah Webster, and how it differed from that of Johnson. Webster understood that change in language is natural and inevitable and that it is futile to try to impose arbitrary standards. He also recognized regional and social differences in the use of English. Again students are asked to look at a passage from Webster's dictionary and to compare it with earlier dictionaries and with their own.

5. **Dictionaries Become Big Business** (pages L199–200) describes the development of dictionaries as a commercial enterprise.

6. **Recording the English Word-Hoard** (pages L200–03) describes the development of *The Oxford English Dictionary*, the purpose of which was to record the origin and use of the entire English vocabulary. The project, which took seventy years to complete, brought together more knowledge about words than has ever been collected anywhere before or since.

7. **Lexicography as a Science** (pages L203–07) describes how modern dictionaries are put together, scientifically and systematically, by the use of citation slips and computers. Unlike the makers of earlier dictionaries, most dictionary makers now simply attempt to describe current usage as precisely as possible, rather than to prescribe what usage should be.

8. Review (pages L207–08) provides questions for reviewing and evaluating the information in the chapter.

TEACHING THE CHAPTER

1. To prepare for teaching the material, simply work through the chapter in the student text, with the key to the exercises in hand. You should also be familiar with the dictionaries that are available to the students so that you will know how to adapt the exercises to what the class has to work with.

2. The chapter consists primarily of expository material describing how dictionaries developed, and its six exercises are designed to help students compare the various dictionaries discussed. Why purists attempted to preserve the language intact, and what the outcome of such attempts was, are emphasized in this material. You should stress, one, that attempts to keep the language from changing or to restore it to an earlier and supposedly purer form are not likely to be effective, and, two, that language change is not something to be deplored; rather, it is natural and inevitable.

3. We suggest that the expository material be assigned for individual reading. Because the exercises, however, are likely to be time consuming, students may weary of them if asked to do them by themselves. Most of such exercises, therefore, can be used as the basis for class discussion after the students have read the text. You might, for instance, assign the material on pages 177–84 — up to "Dr. Johnson's Dictionary" — excluding the exercises, and then use Exercises 1 and 2 for class discussion. The students could be asked to make the required comparisons right in class. You might do the same thing for the sections "Dr. Johnson's Dictionary" and "According to Webster," pages 184–98, and then for the remainder of the chapter, pages 199–207. When the students are requested to look up a great many words or to make numerous comparisons, you could divide the class into groups, assigning the various sections or various groups of words to different groups of students.

4. Some background notes are included below. The key to the exercises also contains not only suggestions for using the exercises but also additional information for the teacher. You should, of course, adapt the chapter to your class and to the abilities of your students.

5. Most of the exercises assume that students are familiar with dictionaries and able to use them with some ease. You may, however, want to begin by reviewing basic dictionary skills, or you may build this review right into your teaching of the chapter. A class trip to the library to examine the various dictionaries found there should be part of your introduction.

Background Information for the Teacher

Long ago it was believed that change in a language represented degeneration; consequently, dictionaries tried to prevent change. That such attempts failed should not surprise present-day students of language; even in the eighteenth century the more perceptive of the purists came to realize that change in language is inevitable. One of those who arrived at this understanding was Dr. Samuel Johnson himself, whose authoritative dictionary was based on the usage of the previous two centuries. Still, Dr. Johnson continued to deplore language change, attempting to slow it down and to prevent words and usages he disapproved of from gaining greater currency. He did this by using pejorative labels and sometimes by simply omitting words and expressions he didn't like. He tried to standardize both usage and spelling, and to a great extent his spelling reforms were successful.

The American pioneer in dictionary making was Noah Webster. He not only accepted the fact of language change, but approved of it. Feeling that a dictionary reflecting current usage, especially American usage, was badly needed, he set himself the task of creating one. He included in his dictionary words which had not previously been recorded in any dictionary—old words, American words, and words in current use in the early nineteenth century. Webster, like Johnson, was very interested in the standardization of spelling and in spelling reform; he is responsible for many of the current differences between British and American spelling. Since Webster's time, most dictionary makers have accepted a more realistic appraisal of the nature of language and of language change and do not view language change with the negative feelings of Johnson and his contemporaries. Yet, surprisingly, that outmoded point of view still finds many supporters.

Even today many people believe, like the purists of Johnson's time, that change in a language leads necessarily to degeneracy and that the English language needs guardians. A little serious thought, however, might provide them with reassurance. Few people, for example, would seriously maintain that the modern Romance languages, such as French, Spanish, Italian, and Portuguese, are in any way less perfect than the Vulgar Latin dialect from which they descended. Similarly, who would say that present-day English is in any way inferior to the language of the Anglo-Saxons?

KEY TO THE EXERCISES

EXERCISE 1 — *pages L179–80 (a class exercise)*

> **PURPOSE:** To examine the first hard-word book, comparing it with modern dictionaries, and to consider why dictionary entries are listed in alphabetical order.

A. If you were reading a Latin or French text (assuming that you could read these languages) and you came across an unfamiliar word, where would you look for information about it? **In a Latin-English or French-English dictionary.** How do you suppose your source might compare with the early bilingual glossaries? **Today's bilingual dictionaries would no doubt be much more complete.**

B. Compare the page from Cawdrey's *Table Alphabeticall* with the dictionary you use at school or at home. How many pages are there between *partition* and *pension* in your dictionary? **Depending, of course, on the particular dictionary the students are using, this will probably vary between eight and twelve pages.** What are some of the entry words in your dictionary that Cawdrey does not include? **Probable answers are *partner*, *partook*, *party*, *pass*, etc.** Can you think of some reasons why they are not in Cawdrey's book? **Possible answers include the following: (1) some of the words were probably not in use in Cawdrey's time; (2) some were probably left out by oversight or because Cawdrey didn't know them; and (3) Cawdrey's purpose was to include only "hard words."** Are there any words in Cawdrey's list that are not in your dictionary? If so, what are they? **Again, this will depend on the particular dictionary being used. However, some students may suggest words that are simply listed in a different order because they are spelled differently, and you should watch for these and have the words rechecked if necessary.** Why do you suppose your dictionary omits them? **Some of these words no longer exist in the language. However, some that do exist may not be listed in an abridged dictionary because they seldom occur and are therefore not useful entries. Cawdrey's list was precisely a list of "hard words" and our abridged dictionaries are not.**

C. Is Cawdrey's definition for *penitentiary* listed in your dictionary? (Note that he spells it *penitentiarie*.) If not, look the word up in *Webster's Third New International Dictionary*, which you will find in most libraries. Is the word used much today in the way that Cawdrey defines it? How do you know? **The students should discover that in their dictionaries the word is not defined** as Cawdrey defines it, as it is no longer commonly used with that meaning. They will find in *Webster's Third* that where this meaning is given, it is labeled *obsolete.*   What is now the most common meaning of this term?   **A place of imprisonment.**   Can you see any connection between this meaning and the one given by Cawdrey?

The students may describe the connection in various ways. In summary, the word *penitentiarie* **was also used at an earlier time to refer to a place for penitents, as the students may have noticed when they consulted** *Webster's Third.* **Probably that was an extended meaning, that is, the term was used at first to designate a kind of person, a religious person who is penitent. Then the place where such people gathered together to atone for their sins was called by the same name. Later on, people saw an analogy between such places of atonement and the places where prisoners were sent as a punishment. Thus,** *penitentiary* **came to be used to mean the latter kind of place as well. This is an interesting example of how meaning changes when words come to be used in new ways. Even though we still have the word** *penitent*, **most of us do not associate it with the word** *penitentiary,* **despite the historical relationship, because we do not think of the prisoners as being penitent, and because the other kind of penitentiary does not exist in our society.**

D. Does Cawdrey's definition of *patronize* (he spells it *patronise*) give a very clear idea of its meaning?   **Most students will feel that it doesn't.**   How does your dictionary define this term?   **It will probably give only current definitions, which will vary somewhat according to the dictionary used.**   What new meanings of the word have developed that are not suggested by Cawdrey's definition?   **The meanings cited should more or less correspond to these: (1) "to trade with a shop or restaurant," (2) "to treat in a condescending manner," and (3) "to support."**

E. Although we now take it for granted that dictionaries list words in alphabetical order, this arrangement was not universal in Cawdrey's day. For this reason, he felt obliged to explain it in his Preface. What are some other ways in which a word list might be organized?   **By subject matter, pronunciation, and word class.**   What are the advantages of these methods of organization?   **A subject-matter grouping would enable a person to find a word dealing with a specific subject, even if he could not remember the word at all; grouping by pronunciation would enable a person to find a word when he was uncertain of the spelling; grouping by word class would probably be helpful to a foreigner who needed to check grammatical points, such as the**   295 forms of irregular verbs and irregular plurals of nouns.   The disadvantages?   To find a word listed according to subject matter, a person would have to know something about the meaning of any word he wished to look up. If words were listed by pronunciation, it would often be difficult for a person to find a word he had read but never heard. If words were arranged by word class, a person would have to know something about the grammatical category of a word before he could look it up. Are there any drawbacks to listing words in an English dictionary alphabetically?   If a person didn't know the correct spelling, or at least the first few letters, he would have a difficult time finding a word in the dictionary. For example, unless he already knew that *pneumonia* began with a *p*, he would not look for it in the right place.

> Before assigning Exercise 1, you should point out that, except when in final position, the letter which corresponds to *s* very much resembles the letter which corresponds to *f* (although, of course, it lacks the crossbar that the *f* has). As a preliminary exercise, you might ask students to pick out all the words containing nonfinal *s*'s. Some of the students may also notice that *u*'s are used in place of *y*'s and that there are two forms of *r*. In answer to the question preceding Exercise 1, students may point out the spellings of *Jewes* and *yearely*, both of which contain an extra *e*; *sheapheards*, which includes extra *a*'s; *patronise*, which is spelled with an *s*; *pearsed* (for *pierced*); and *smale* (for *small*). Many other possibilities also exist.
>
> *Note:* If *Webster's Third New International Dictionary* is not available in your school, you may choose to omit section C of Exercise 1 or else to assign it to students who have access to the public library.

EXERCISE 2—*pages L181–84 (a class exercise)*

PURPOSE: To compare Bailey's dictionary with Cawdrey's hard-word book and with a modern dictionary.

A. How many entries are there between the words *patrimony* and *paucity* in Bailey's dictionary? **30** In Cawdrey's? **2** What might account for the difference? **Bailey's dictionary tried to include all words, not just difficult ones; in addition, he was able to build on the works of previous authors; finally, some new words may have entered the language.** How are Bailey's entries different from Cawdrey's? **A different type face is used.**

Bailey's entry words are all in caps, and he uses italics in labels, etymologies, and definitions. Bailey uses more modern spelling than Cawdrey. However, he capitalizes all nouns, which Cawdrey does not. Bailey uses *to* before all verbs. He gives the derivations of many words. He uses phrases to define words rather than using synonyms, as Cawdrey does. Bailey also includes some usage labels, such as "*Sea Term*," "among the *Papists*," "*in Guinea*."

Give the students time to explore all the differences they find. They may wish to locate several examples of each innovation.

What information do they (that is, Bailey's entries) contain that is not given in Cawdrey's dictionary? **Bailey gives the origin of many words, tells where some words are used or who uses them, identifies verbs clearly as verbs by using *to*, and gives a clearer idea of the meaning of many words by using definitions rather than just synonyms.** Compare the entries of Cawdrey and Bailey for the word *patronage* with the entry in your dictionary. What kind of information about this word is given in your dictionary but not in theirs? **Modern dictionaries will include phonetic spelling, part-of-speech labels, and several additional definitions not found in Cawdrey and Bailey.** Compare Bailey's entry for *patronize* with Cawdrey's. How do they differ? **The two definitions are much the same, but Bailey gives one additional meaning.** Which one is closer to the definition in your dictionary? **Bailey's.**

B. Are there any words in the sample from Bailey's dictionary that are not in your dictionary? **The students will find that there are, and that these are words they don't know.** What might be the reason? **They are words that were used in Bailey's time but are not used now.** What words between *patrimonial* and *paunch* are in your dictionary but not in Bailey's? **This again will vary according to the dictionaries being used by the students; they should find words like *patriotic, patristic, patrolman, patroon, patsy, pattern, patulous, paulownia*.** Can you suggest why this might be so? **Some of these words came into common use after Bailey's time; in some cases, historical information in the definition confirms this. Probably Bailey's dictionary was more selective and less systematic than a modern unabridged dictionary.**

C. Are the words in the sample from Bailey's dictionary listed in the same order as they are in modern dictionaries? **They are not always. The words beginning with *pau-* and *pav-* are not arranged as they would be today. There are also a few simple errors. For example, *patripassians* and *to patrissate* are out of**

297

order.   If not, can you explain why? (If you need help in answering this question, look up *alphabet* in an encyclopedia and see if you find any clues.)   **As our alphabet evolved to its present form, letters were changed to different positions. Another reason is that variants of the same word are given at the same place in Bailey, even if one of them is out of alphabetical order; see, for example,** *patten* **and** *pattin.*

D.   Compare Bailey's definitions of *patrol* and *pavement* with those in your dictionary. Do the meanings of these words seem to have changed since Bailey's time?   **Yes.**   If so, how?   **Today's meanings of** *patrol* **are more general and more diverse. Also, Bailey's definition of noun and verb are relatively independent of each other, but the modern dictionary probably uses the noun** *patrol* **in its definition of the verb;** *pavement* **has wider application than it had then.**

EXERCISE 3 — *pages L191–92 (a class exercise)*

PURPOSE: To compare Johnson's dictionary with earlier dictionaries and with modern dictionaries, and to consider whether or not it is possible to stop a language from changing.

A.   Compare the sample entries from Johnson's dictionary with those from Bailey's dictionary. Which words between *patrimony* and *pattern* are listed by Johnson but not by Bailey?   *Patrocinate, pattenmaker, pattern.*   Which are given by Bailey but not by Johnson?   *Patrinus, patrocination, patrociny, patripassians, patrissate, pattacoon, patte.*   Can you explain these differences?   **They may have been accidental omissions, or Johnson may not have fully approved of some words cited by Bailey. Some of the words cited by Johnson but not by Bailey may have come into use later, but it is more likely that they were simply overlooked by Bailey.**   Try to explain why Bailey gives four entries for *patron* and Johnson only one.   **Bailey gives a separate entry for each meaning; Johnson puts all the different meanings under one entry and numbers them.**

Note that Bailey also has an entry for *patron paramount,* **which students may think is another entry for** *patron.* **You might ask them whether modern practice in this regard is like Bailey's or like Johnson's.**

B.   How are Johnson's entries for *patrimony* and *patronage* different from Bailey's?   **Johnson gives examples from literature to demonstrate the use of these words and provides a more concise**

298

definition of *patrimony* and a slightly more detailed definition of *patronage*, to which he adds a meaning not found in Bailey. He also uses a word-class label, "*n.s.*" Does Johnson's treatment of these terms seem better to you than Bailey's? Why or why not? **Since this question asks for a personal opinion, answers may vary. Some students may like the examples from actual usage; some may not. Elicit reasons for student preferences.**

C. Compare Johnson's first definition of *patron* with the equivalent definitions in Bailey and in a modern dictionary. How does Johnson's definition reflect a personal feeling that is not present in the other definitions? **Johnson shows, by the use of the words *wretch*, *insolence*, and *flattery*, that he has a low opinion of a patron. He does not give an objective definition.**

D. Compare Johnson's etymology for *patter* with that in a modern dictionary. Do they agree? **No.** If not, which one do you think is correct? **Be sure the students understand that although the modern version reflects later scholarship, Johnson's version does appear plausible. You might want to have them check Bailey, who lists *to patter and pray* and provides etymological explanation.** How do you suppose Johnson arrived at his etymology for this word? **The French word *patte*, "*foot*," sounds like the English word *patter*. Johnson assumed that they were related in meaning.**

E. Compare Johnson's entry for *pattern* with the entry in your dictionary. How many separate meanings are given in each? **Johnson gives four for the noun and at least two for the verb; the dictionary the students use will determine the number of definitions, but it will probably be a total of about fifteen.** What does this comparison suggest about the history of the word? **It suggests that the word has accumulated many new meanings over a long period of time.** Does your dictionary give information about the word that Johnson's does not? If so, what? **Modern dictionaries give additional meanings and most modern dictionaries also give a more complete etymology and the pronunciation. They may, in addition, include a synonym and the adjective form *patterned*.**

F. Which words used by Johnson in the excerpts from his Preface on page 186 were unfamiliar to you? **Most students will cite *suffered* and *suffrages*, but there are other difficult words here, also.** What effect does Johnson's choice of these words have on the style of his writing? **The students may feel that his writing seems stilted, dated, and difficult because of these words.**

299

G. Johnson wrote in his Preface that the English of his day was "copious without order, and energetick without rules." In view of what you have learned about the structure of English, would you agree? If not, why do you suppose the language seemed confused and irregular to Johnson?   **The students may suggest a variety of answers. The best answer probably is that Johnson had not examined the basic structure of the language, as they have. One very good observation would be that there were then, as now, many differences between dialects. Also, Johnson was concerned mainly with words, and they are especially susceptible to change and to variations in usage.**

H. In the passages from Johnson's Preface quoted on page 186 the words *suffered* and *suffrages* occur. Does Johnson use these words in the same way that you would expect to see them used today? **It is obvious that he doesn't.**   What definitions does your dictionary give for these words?   **Again, the answers will vary according to the dictionaries used by the students. You could have the definitions read aloud.**   Does your dictionary define the words as Johnson used them?   **Most dictionaries still include definitions for the words as Johnson used them.**

> *Note:* **Some students may need help in reading the passage from the Preface to Dr. Johnson's dictionary (page 186). It contains many of the "hard words" discussed earlier in the chapter. You may want to read that passage with the students, having the class provide clarification for those who do not understand what the passage means. This will prepare them for sections F, G, and H of this exercise.**

EXERCISE 4 — *page L198 (a class exercise)*

> **PURPOSE: To compare Webster's dictionary with Johnson's dictionary and with modern dictionaries and Webster's attitude toward language with Johnson's attitude.**

A. Compare the passages from Webster's Preface quoted on page 192 with those from Johnson's Preface quoted on page 186. In what ways did Webster's attitude toward the language differ from Johnson's?   **The main difference is that Webster regarded change and variety in the language as natural and good, while Johnson deplored it, wishing to slow the changes and to make the language more regular.**   Do Webster's views seem more realistic to you than Johnson's, or less realistic?   **We hope that** the students will have learned enough about the fact that language changes to say "more realistic." Explain why. **Our study of the English language has demonstrated that it is constantly changing without degenerating. Most people consider American English to be as "good" as British English, and regard it as natural that there should be some differences between them.**

B. Compare Webster's entries for the words from *patrimony* through *pattern* with Johnson's. Which entries are in one dictionary but not in the other? **The entries that are in Webster but not in Johnson are** *patriotic, patristic, patristical, patrocination, patrolling, patronized, patronizer, patronizing, patronless, pattering.* In what ways did Webster provide more information about his entry words than Johnson? **His etymologies are more complete and his definitions are broader. He uses the labels "not used" and "little used."** In what ways did Johnson provide more information than Webster? **He usually provided two quotations to illustrate each meaning of a word, whereas Webster used one or more, or just the name of an author who used the word with that meaning.**

C. Compare Webster's spelling of *patronymic* with Johnson's. Which spelling of this word is now used? **Webster's.** See if you can find other words in the excerpts from Johnson's Preface on page 186 whose spelling has changed in a similar way. *Energetick.*

D. Compare Webster's etymology for the word *patrol* with Johnson's. Which seems more complete? **It is clear that Webster's is more complete.** How is Webster's etymology for *patter* different from Johnson's? **Webster suggests a possible alternate etymology.** Does Webster's version seem to be an improvement? **It is hoped that the students will feel that Webster's is an improvement because it shows at least that the etymology was not a settled, known fact.** What etymology does your dictionary give for this word? (If possible, use the unabridged dictionary in your classroom or in the library.) **This may vary according to the dictionaries used by the students, but it may be the etymology mentioned above as Webster's addition. Webster's *Third* indicates that it derives from** *paternoster.*

E. How is Webster's definition of *patriotism* different from the one in your dictionary? **The definition in Webster will seem longer and much more enthusiastic.** Does Webster seem to be editorializing in this definition? (If you are not sure what *editorializing* means, look it up in a dictionary.) **Where Webster talks about the character of a good citizen and says patriotism is the**

301

"noblest passion," he does editorialize. In other words, he sets forth his own personal attitude toward the referent of the word rather than just defining the word.

F. How is Webster's treatment of *patronage* as a verb different from Johnson's? **Johnson calls it "a bad word," which is a value judgment, and doesn't give much information. The reader doesn't know in what sense it is "bad." Webster says "not used," which supplies useful information. He simply states a fact and does not pass judgment.** Whose way of labeling this word seems to you more useful? **It is hoped that the students will find Webster's more useful.**

G. To which words (besides *patronage* as a verb) does Webster give restrictive labels such as "not used" or "little used"? *patrocinate, patrocination, patronal, pauciloquy.* Can you find any of these terms in a current dictionary? (If they are not in the dictionaries you use at school and at home, look them up in an unabridged dictionary in a library.) **These words are all listed at least in** *Webster's Third.* If so, do they carry restrictive labels of any kind? Which ones do? *Patrocinate, patrocination,* **and** *pauciloquy* **are marked** *archaic* **in** *Webster's Third.* **Other labels may be used in other dictionaries.** If there are no restrictive labels, what reasons can you give? **In** *Webster's Third,* *patronal* **is unmarked. Maybe it is still being used. In any case, it would be easy to understand or even coin.**

EXERCISE 5 — *page L203 (a class exercise)*

PURPOSE: To become somewhat familiar with the OED and to compare it with other dictionaries.

A. Compare the OED entries for *patronage* as a noun and verb with the entries for this word in Johnson's (page 189) and Webster's dictionaries (page 195). What kind of information does the OED provide that they do not? **The OED provides an etymological history of the word, including dates, and more complete definitions, as well as several additional definitions. It provides numerous dated citations in chronological order. It also gives the pronunciation. The students may wonder about the label** *"sb."* **It is an abbreviation for** *substantive,* **which is another word for** *noun.*

Next, examine the entries for this word in a modern dictionary. How are they different from those in the OED? **They are much more concise; less detailed.** In light of these differences, would the OED be a good dictionary for classroom, home, or office use? **Probably not.** Explain your answer. **Usually at home or in a classroom or office, one wants only the spelling and a short explanation of a word's modern meaning.** If not, when should it be consulted? **When detailed information about the etymology or meaning of a word is needed, or when information is wanted about a word that appears in a text of an earlier period.**

B. How does the OED label the entry for *patronage* as a verb? **"*Obs.*," an abbreviation for *obsolete*.** How does this compare with Johnson's and Webster's labels? **It is similar to Webster's, but different from Johnson's.** How is the OED's label justified by the quotations illustrating this entry? **The dates given for the quotations are all in the sixteenth, seventeenth, or eighteenth centuries. There are no quotations from later centuries.**

> **This exercise should probably be broken up and assigned to different students or groups of students, who could then report back to the entire class.**

EXERCISE 6 — *pages 206–07 (an outside assignment)*

> PURPOSE: To examine some modern dictionaries and to learn how they are made.

A. Read the introductory pages in several modern dictionaries to find out what their editors have to say about the purposes and uses of their books. How do their statements compare with those of earlier lexicographers as quoted and described in this chapter? **The students will probably find that, because language changes, most introductions will mention the need for the continual updating of dictionaries. Students may give examples of words that had been considered substandard in the past but that are now considered standard. They may also be impressed because modern dictionaries are written by large numbers of people.**

B. People sometimes say that "a word isn't really a word unless it appears in the dictionary." Comment on this view in light of what you have learned about the principles of modern lexicography. **Answers will vary, but the students should realize that a word is coined and used and accepted before it is placed in a dictionary — a dictionary therefore must follow a bit behind current usage.** Comment also on the fact that some words appear in some dictionaries but not in others. **The students should realize that a dictionary, particularly an abridged dictionary, will reflect the prejudices and judgments of its editors**   303 and publishers. Also, the dictionaries may differ in purpose and in date of publication, and there may be some differences in the citations available to the lexicographers.

C. Find a slang term that is now being used by the students in your school, a term that is not listed in any dictionary. Collect a number of citation slips—the more the better—by making note of actual uses of the word in context. (Note, that is, the part of the sentence in which the word occurred or write a description of the situation in which the word was used.) Note any variants in spelling and pronunciation, and any restrictions that seem to limit the use of the word. Try to figure out, if you can, the origin of the term. Finally, write a dictionary entry for the word, following the form and style of the dictionary used in your classroom and basing it on the evidence you have collected. Be as concise as possible; distinguish carefully between the different meanings of the word if there are more than one, and include any derived forms that are closely related to your entry word in origin and meaning.

It may be difficult for some students to find an appropriate word or expression to work on. If so, you could suggest one, or have them find one by listening to a disc jockey on the radio or to the moderator of a television "talk show." Alternatively, you could have the class discuss several suitable words or expressions before the assignment is given. If citation material is scarce, its collection could be handled as a group project, but each student should prepare his own dictionary entry. You could have different students prepare entries to match the styles of different dictionaries.

Sections A and B examine attitudes that prevailed at different times toward language and how these attitudes affected dictionaries. Students should learn that languages change without necessarily degenerating, and that dictionary makers now look upon their task as describing, rather than as shaping, the language. Sections A and B can be done as a class exercise, but section C should be assigned for outside of class.

REVIEW —*pages 207–08 (an outside assignment)*

PURPOSE: To draw together the information about the development of dictionaries and to reinforce the important concepts to be drawn from such an examination.

1. How would you describe the first books about English words?
    **The first ones were in two languages, one being English and
    the other Latin or French. The words of one language were
    listed, followed by their equivalents in the foreign language.
    These books could be called bilingual dictionaries.** What
    kinds of information did they contain? **They only gave the
    most common foreign-language equivalent or equivalents of
    an English word or the most common English equivalent or
    equivalents for any foreign-language word.**

2. How did wordbooks change during the Renaissance? **They
    became lists of difficult English words with easier English
    words as equivalents.** Why? **The main reason for this was
    that many foreign terms were being used by scholars and
    travelers and, in order to understand what such people wrote,
    ordinary readers needed a means of finding out what these
    difficult words meant.**

3. What kind of information does Robert Cawdrey's *Table Alpha-
    beticall* contain? **It gives the meanings of difficult words.**
    How does Cawdrey's dictionary differ from the one you use? **It
    does not contain etymological information, part-of-speech
    labels, pronunciation aids, or usage labels. It does not include
    common words. The spelling is different, and some of the
    letters have different forms. And it uses synonyms or rough
    equivalents rather than actual definitions.**

4. In what ways does Bailey's dictionary differ from Cawdrey's?
    **Bailey's dictionary includes definitions consisting of several
    words instead of listing one or two close synonyms; it gives
    more information about usage and word origins.**

5. How did Samuel Johnson view the role of the lexicographer?
    **He felt that the lexicographer should make judgments about
    the words and expressions of the language, should set up
    standards for others to follow, and should try to prevent the
    language from changing.** How are his attitudes reflected in
    his dictionary? **He quoted examples of usage from writings
    published one or two centuries earlier; he omitted usages he
    found objectionable or, if he included them, labeled them
    "low" or "vulgar."**

6. What were some of the innovations in Johnson's dictionary,
    that is, how did his dictionary differ from previous ones?
    **Johnson's dictionary gave examples drawn from actual usage;
    it also attempted exhaustive coverage.**

7. How did Noah Webster's attitudes about language change differ
    from Dr. Johnson's? **Webster held that language change is**

natural and unpreventable, that you cannot impose arbitrary standards on language usage, and that the American dialects of English are not inferior to the dialects of England.   How did Webster incorporate these attitudes in his dictionary?   **He based his dictionary on current usage, thereby including many new scientific, technical, and commercial terms, as well as many older words which, although they were in general use, had not previously been recorded in dictionaries. Also, he excluded fewer words on the ground that they were "improper" or "vulgar," and included many words used in America but not in the British Isles.**

8.   How is Webster's 1828 dictionary similar to the dictionary you use today?   **It includes part-of-speech labels, etymological information, and usage labels, and it numbers the meanings.**   How might the information contained in the 1828 edition differ from that in the current edition of the Merriam–Webster dictionary?   **The information contained in the 1828 edition would be less complete, less accurate, and less up-to-date than that in the current edition. Certain kinds of information appearing in the current edition might not occur in the 1828 edition.**   Why might you expect these two editions to differ?   **The 1828 edition was compiled, researched, and written almost entirely by one person, and the art of lexicography was less developed than it is today. The later edition benefits from the contributions of a large staff of highly trained lexicographers, from later research in etymology, and from an improved system for presenting information; also, it reflects the usage of a later time.**

9.   What did the compilers of the *Oxford English Dictionary* attempt to do?   **They attempted to record the origin and use of the entire vocabulary of the English language.**   What makes this dictionary the most exhaustive English dictionary produced so far?   **It contains more information about more words than any other English dictionary that has ever been published.**

10.   How do lexicographers go about preparing a dictionary entry?   **A lexicographer prepares "citation slips" that give actual uses of a word in context, together with the source and the date. After a good many slips have been accumulated, he studies and classifies the usages represented and compares the data he has compiled with the entries for the word in various dictionaries. He next organizes his material according to the style used in the dictionary for which the entry is intended and finally writes the entry.**   What does this process tell you about the ways in which the meanings of words are determined?   **In a modern**

dictionary, the meanings of words are determined by a cumulative record of instances of usage. A word has those meanings that it had in the contexts and on the occasions cited by the lexicographers. This suggests that when a word is no longer used with a given meaning, it no longer has that meaning, and when it comes to be used with a new meaning, it gains that meaning. The usage determines the meaning, rather than the other way around.

Though you will, of course, want to discuss the questions in class, students should profit from thinking through the answers on their own outside of class.

TEACHER'S NOTES

TEACHER'S NOTES

TEACHER'S NOTES

TEACHER'S NOTES

TEACHER'S NOTES